DIGGING DEEPER
into
THE REVELATION
of
JESUS CHRIST

The fear of the LORD is the beginning of wisdom.

Psalm 111:10a; Proverbs 9:10a

A Study Guide

Compiled by Michael Copple

Copyright © 2025 by Michael Copple

All rights reserved. No part of this book may be reproduced in any manner whatsoever without written permission except in the case of brief quotations embodied in critical articles and reviews.

This book is a work of non-fiction.

Because of the dynamic nature of the Internet, any web addresses or links contained in this book may have changed since publication and may no longer be valid.

All Scripture quotations are from the New King James Version, New International Version and the King James Version of the Bible..

Cover Design: Ben Bredeweg

Editing and Interior Book Layout/ Design: Elfriede Copple

ISBN 978-1-7389-735-4-5

Printed: June 2025

Unless otherwise noted all Scriptures taken from the New King James Version®.
Copyright © 1982 by Thomas Nelson. Used by permission. All rights reserved.

Scripture quotations marked (KJV) are taken from the King James Version of the Bible.

Scripture quotations marked (NIV) are taken from the Holy Bible, New International Version® NIV® Copyright© 1973, 1978, 1984, 2011, by Biblica, Inc.™ Used with permission of Zondervan. All rights reserved worldwide. www.zondervan.com

Quotations and paraphrased quotations marked *.quoted text * taken from *The Believer's Bible Commentary* by William MacDonald, Art Farstad. Copyright © 1989, 1990, 1992, 1995 by William MacDonald. Used by permission of HarperCollins Christian Publishing. www.harpercollinschristian.com

Quotations and paraphrased quotations marked **.. quoted text ** Bible supplementary information taken from *The King James Study Bible*. Copyright © 1993 by Thomas Nelson. Used by permission of HarperCollins Christian Publishing. www.harpercollinschristian.com

Ed Anthony's *The Revelation—Unveiling Christ & His Glory*
And Dr. Anthony's six messages Columbia Valley Bible Fellowship
Sunday July 30th and Monday 31st, 2017. Used by permission.

Warren Henderson's teaching in six sessions of *The Book of Daniel*
Columbia Valley Bible Fellowship - June 10th - 12th, 2016;
Infidelity and LOYALTY, A DEVOTINAL STUDY OF EZEKIEL AND DANIEL by WARREN HENDERSON, Copyright 2017, BIBLE PROPHECY OVERVIEW graph page 393.
Used by permission.

Vine's Expository Dictionary of Old & New Testament Words by W.E. Vine
Published in 1997 by Thomas Nelson Publishers
Copyright 1996 restored by the GATT Treaty to W. E. Vine Copyright, Ltd., Bath, England
[(1) pg. 177 – (2) pg. 525/526 (both paraphrased)]

Holman Illustrated Bible Dictionary
Copyright 2003 by Holman Bible Publishers Nashville, Tennessee
All Rights Reserved
[(3) pg. 1190]

"The Book of Revelation Simplified" by Dr. Sunny Ezhumattoor
Published by Thekkel Publications (A Division of Narrow Path Ministries, Inc.)
Copyright April 2016. Used by permission.

Acknowledgments

First and foremost, I give thanks to our Triune God for saving many of my loved ones from the Great Tribulation and the Lake of Fire, and giving me eternal life with the Savior and with them. This new life and hope have motivated me to gather the truth of Scripture and consolidate it with explanations from gifted, solid brothers in Christ who have been commended by local assemblies, written commentaries, spoken at conferences, and have always been prepared to exercise their Spiritual gifts.

Our dear brother Randy Amos, went home to be with the Lord Jesus on 3 November 2020. He was gracious to accept my request to edit the first edition of the original study guide. (That was a challenge!) He is credited with suggesting the appropriate title of the first edition, and this has led to the present title. Two of Randy's books have left a profound, positive impact on my growth and walk with the Lord: *The Counterfeit Jesus* and "*The Church*, a Discipleship Manual for the Body of Christ".

Brother Warren Henderson's Old Testament commentary, a project that took 18 years until completion, consisting of 14 volumes was of tremendous value. I am especially grateful for inspiring me with his "Bible Prophecy Overview" in his *Infidelity and Loyalty* commentary on the Books of Ezekiel and Daniel. Warren's way of teaching is comparable to a picture being worth a thousand words.

I stand corrected on some sections in the previous study guide, and I sincerely appreciate the Morning Star Bible Camp Director, Josh Caplan, for having the spirit and moral fiber to approach me. In particular he reproved my commentary on 2 Thessalonians 2:1-3, I am genuinely grateful and edified. Josh gave our brother, Mercer Armstrong, credit for his sound doctrine on that passage.

Ralph Kirchhofer, who went home to be with the Lord on 29 January 2024, had been my mentor for continuing my growth in faith. For 20 years Ralph encouraged me moment by moment to take on more responsibilities, especially to spread the Gospel. Nothing could take away the joy from Ralph. His joy is now even more fulfilled, face-to-face with the Lord Jesus Christ.

My dear friend and solid brother in Christ, Larry Page, ever so kindly and gently, corrected my previous commentary on the Matthew 13 parable of the wheat and tares. He humbly honored God and also gave credit to T. Ernest Wilson's book: *God's Sacred Secrets*. We needed that!

A brother-in-Christ, Ben Bredeweg, created the new cover for this updated version of the previous Study Guide titled "Digging Deep into the Revelation of Jesus Christ – A Study Guide". We thank him for his skill and for being so learned in the Word and for his meticulousness.

My loving wife Elfriede Copple formatted the layout so it would ease comparison of Scripture to commentary and be more appealing and acceptable to you, the reader. Elfriede's gift of service, attention to detail in the publishing process, her devotion, advice and support for me is immeasurable.

I am grateful for my dad and mom (after much prayer and decades of patience) for instilling a foundation of moral values and faith; and for the way they raised my brother and sisters and myself with unfailing love and energy. I only wish I would have listened sooner. I would not be the person I am today without what they have done for me. God has called both of them home. No doubt, I will see them again.

Introduction

An invitation of immense motivation to read and understand this Book is given in **Revelation 1:3**: *Blessed is he who reads and those who hear the words of this prophecy, and keep those things which are written in it; for the time is near.*

The Book of Revelation reveals that the Lord Jesus Christ is Almighty Jehovah God at least seven times: Revelation 1:8; 4:8; 11:17; 15:3; 16:7, 14; 19:15; {21:22}. See also Exodus 3:14; 6:3; John 8:58; and that the Lord Jesus Christ is the King of kings and Lord of lords (Revelation 19:16).

CHAPTER

1. The Lord Jesus gives to John what to write and: John's vision picturing the Lord is strikingly similar to that of Ezekiel Chapter 1.

2. The Lord Jesus is quoted speaking to the seven churches of today's age.

3. The Lord Jesus is quoted speaking to the seven churches of today's age.

4. The redeemed and raptured Church believers worship and praise the Lord, and the 24 elders are described in their new bodies receiving rewards: (Revelation 4:1, 4, 10-11)

5. The Lord Jesus receives the scroll with seven seals, and the saints praise Him.

6. The Antichrist man is revealed as a *beast* who comes in on a white horse to begin the Seven-year Tribulation Period; but his pictured future is marred by next a red, then black, then pale horse representing death. The first six seals are opened (Revelation 6:12).

7. explains the salvation of 144,000 Israelites, and gives prophecy of some who will become believers during the Tribulation Period.

8. Seven trumpets are to sound giving more severe warnings. The first four trumpets are sounded.

9. The 5th and 6th trumpets are sounded; a third of all mankind is killed.

10. Seven thunders utter their voices, but John is told to delay writing.

11. The two witnesses who've been prophesying for the first half of the Tribulation are killed and three-and-a-half days later are taken up to heaven (11:2-12). The seventh trumpet is sounded (11:15).

12. Describes the protection of the sealed Israelites from the woes of the Great Tribulation—that is, the last three-and-a-half years.

13. The Antichrist commits the *abomination of desolation* (Matthew 24:15) by taking over as God in the temple (2 Thessalonians 2:4). This begins the Great Tribulation. The False Prophet requires all to worship the Antichrist and/or his image and to take the mark of 666. Anyone who refuses will be denied the freedom to buy or sell (13:16-18), and those who take the mark will not be able to change their destination of eternal suffering in the lake of fire (Revelation 19:20).

14	Confirms that anyone who takes the mark of the beast will suffer eternally (14:9-11).
15	The seven vials (bowls) containing the seven plagues of God's furious wrath are prepared to be poured out onto the earth.
16	Revelation 16-17: Seventh Bowl (vial) poured out and the Lord Jesus Second Coming ends war of Armageddon and the Seven-year Tribulation Period.
17	details War effects on the fall of Babylon's religious system
18	details War effects on the fall of Babylon's commercial system
19	details Church saints returning from heaven with the Lord that ended the Chapter 16 war and see the Antichrist and False Prophet cast alive into the eternal lake of fire
20	details Satan being locked in the pit for one-thousand years, then Christ's Millennial Reign, then Satan released and joining with Gog and Māgog for war against the Lord cast into the lake of fire. Then all unbelievers will bow the knee at the Great White Throne and be cast into the eternal lake of fire.
21	moves to the eternal state of a new heaven and new earth, describing the beauty
22	continues picturing the splendor of heaven and warns against adding to or taking away anything from this Book.

The invitation to read and hear this Book was given in 1:3. The final invitation to anyone reading this is given in 22:17, the fifth to last verse in the Holy Bible, by the Spirit and the bride:

Revelation 22:17 *And the Spirit and the bride say, "Come!" And let him who hears say, "Come!" And let him who thirsts come. Whoever desires, let him take the water of life freely.*

Of the 404 verses in Revelation, 265 contain verses alluding to 550 Old Testament references. Certain numbers like seven, and twelve have special significances in Revelation:

The number 7 is found 54 times in the Book of Revelation alone!

7 churches (1:11), 7 lampstands (1:13), 7 stars (1:16), 7 messages (2:1-3:22), 7 Spirits (3:1; 4:5) – refers to the Holy Spirit in His fullness,

7 seals (5:1), 7 trumpets (8:2), 7 bowls or vials (15:7), 7 mountains (17:9), and 7 blessings (1-22).

The number 12, even 12 x 12=144 (144.000; 7:4-8; 14:1), 12 gates, 12 angels at the gates, 12 tribe names, 12 foundations, names of the twelve apostles of the Lamb (21:12-14), and 12 fruits (22:2).

HELPFUL NOTES

Christ's Words "in Red" Changed to "Tekton Pro Font"

Scripture has been taken from *The Holy Bible, New King James Version*, published by Thomas Nelson, Inc., Copyright 1994 unless otherwise noted. In the original, the words of Christ were in red. For this study guide the color has been eliminated and replaced with Tekton Pro font.

The following charts can be found at the back of this Study Guide:

Daniel's Prophecy Timeline,

Bible Prophecy Timeline,

End Times Major Events Timeline, and

The Beginning of Babylonian Religion

God gave the visions to John the Apostle which he wrote in this Book.

Though written mostly with envisioned chronological time of events, the order often jumps from "real time" toward the later events to take place; then returns to the sequence of occurrences.

How to Use This Study Guide

This Study Guide contains Scriptures from the New King James Version, New International Version and King James Version Bibles. The guide has been prepared with four columns - Scripture verses and commentary are conveniently printed across both facing pages. When each page is turned Scripture of the Book of *The Revelation of Jesus Christ* will be in the left-most column #1. In column #2, next to the Scripture will be commentary on the printed verses with references to other verses and passages within the Bible. To save the reader from searching and turning to those other Books, the reference verses and passages have been printed in column #3 on the side-facing page. Then column #4 consists of the commentary for those reference verses. Without turning any pages these four columns are side by side to use time more effectively and promote and enhance ease of understanding. Being difficult to fit all explanation into 4 columns, *the purpose of this study is to promote learning, discussion, and blessing.*

In the 2nd column, reference verses mentioned in the commentary are underlined. These verses are printed out in the 3rd column (on the side facing page). Bible study participants who have used this Study Guide have suggested that it is good to pause at theses column 2 underlined verses, then go to the column 3 printed verses and to its commentary in column 4. Then return to where you paused in column 2 to continue reading the Revelation Scripture commentary. This keeps one's mind on the train of thought.

In the 4th column, commentary of "Reference Verses", these verses have been underlined to lessen the need for "guessing" what is being referred to. There are some other reference verses that are not underlined because their sentences or phrases have not been printed nor commented on in this compilation. It is left up to each person's motivation to look up these verses and to keep them in proper context.

Some Scripture words/phrases have been printed in **bold** for *emphasis only* since the original Scripture does not include this sort of highlighting. These are pointed out merely for enhancement of understanding the context correlation in the commentary columns.

When a comment of explanation is added to a quoted commentary (in the second and fourth columns on the right side of each page), [brackets] are made use of indicating that it is merely for clarification and differentiation written by Michael Copple.

This guide has been prepared and edited with careful and prayerful study comparing Scripture to Scripture to maintain our God's original intention on how to understand what is written. As Randy Amos says on page "iv" of *The Church—A Discipleship Manual for the Body of Christ*:

> the *"goal is to simply look at the Bible and with the Spirit's power, communicate what He says. If it cuts across man's interpretation, so be it."*

See next page for visual "How to Use This Study Guide"

Visual of "How to Use This Study Guide"

- We chose this 4 Column Format across both facing pages for ease of studying.

- At the top of each Column are the Book of Revelation **Chapter** and **Verse Numbers** that are being discussed on the particular page.

- **Column 1** contains the Scripture of the Book of Revelation.
- **Column 2** states Commentary on the Bible Verses, printed in **Column 1**.
  Reference Verses which are mentioned in the Commentary are underlined to make you aware that these verses are printed out in **Column 3** for ease of studying.
- **Column 3** (on the side-facing page) – here you will find any **Reference Verses** printed out that were mentioned and underlined in the Commentary from **Column 2**. Only Reference Verses which are underlined will be quoted in Column 3.
- **Column 4** consists of the Commentary for the Reference Verses from **Column 3**.

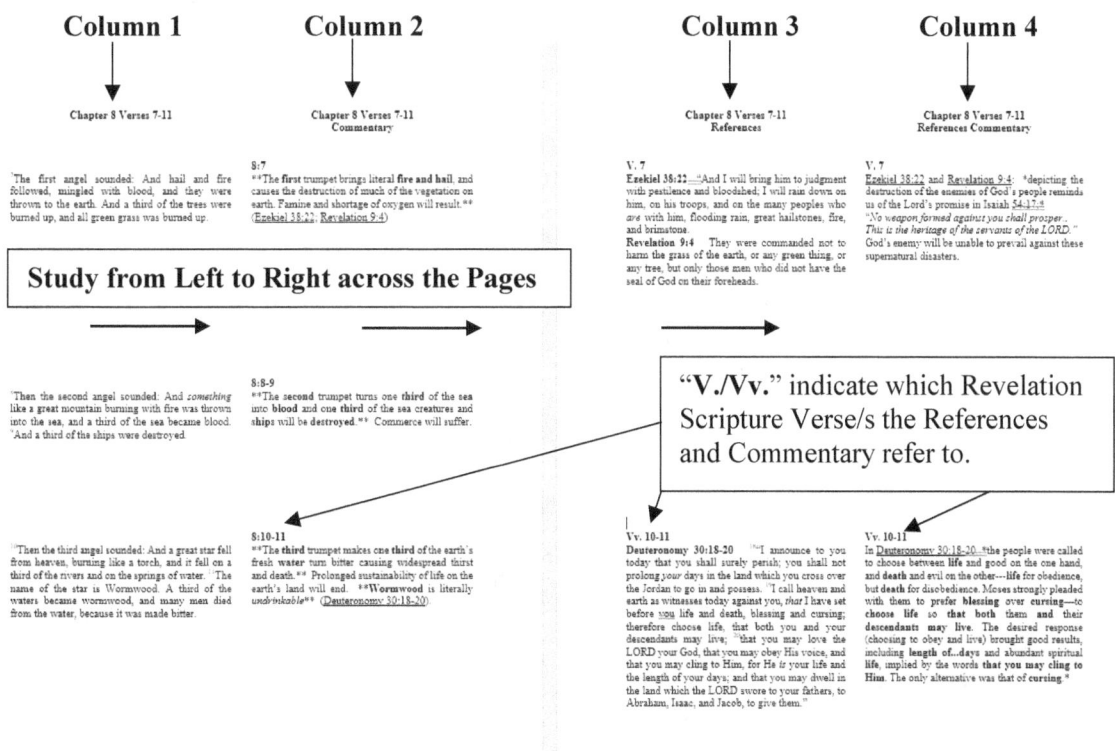

- **Jesus' Words** which are usually in "**RED**" are printed in a different **Font** to distinguish them from the rest of the Scripture.
- "**Continued on Next Set of Pages Under References/Commentary**" (a note at the bottom of **Column 3** and **4**) indicates a continuation on the following set of pages due to lack of space. And in those instances, **Column 1 Scripture** and **part of Column 2 Commentary** are repeated—partly or completely—on the next left facing page for context.

The Revelation of Jesus Christ
Chapter 1 Verses 1-6

Revealing the Revelation
Chapter 1 Verses 1-6
Commentary

The Revelation of Christ and What Must Happen

¹The Revelation of Jesus Christ, which God gave Him to show His servants —things which must shortly take place. And He sent and signified *it* by His angel to His servant John, ²who bore witness to the word of God, and to the testimony of Jesus Christ, to all things that he saw. ³Blessed *is* he who reads and those who hear the words of this prophecy, and keep those things which are written in it; for the time *is* near.

1:1-3
Christ's testimony reveals that He is God Himself. The Revelation of Jesus Christ is both *from* Christ and about Christ. We see this also in Revelation 22:6, 16, and 20. **Things which must shortly take place** refers to the Rapture of the Church, and next, to "the Day of the Lord"—*Day of the Lord* refers to the end of the Seven-year Tribulation (Revelation 19:20-21) followed by the Millennial Reign and Great White Throne Judgment (20:11-15). Although no one has seen God in all His essence, people have seen God in Jesus Christ (John 1:18; 14:9).

Verse 3 gives the reasons the Spirit motivates us to seek more deeply. We need to let others know.

⁴John, to the seven churches which are in Asia: Grace to you and peace from Him who is and who was and who is to come, and from the seven Spirits who are before His throne,

1:4
The greetings are from John, the Savior, and the seven Spirits, to the seven churches. Although the churches are named, the very words of the Head of the Church—the Lord Jesus Christ—should be heeded with all somberness by all local churches today: **"hear what the Spirit says to the churches."** [NIV] (Revelation 2:7b)

⁵and from Jesus Christ, the faithful witness, the firstborn from the dead, and the ruler over the kings of the earth. To Him who loved us and washed us from our sins in His own blood,

1:5
Jesus Christ is the witness of John's Book of *The Revelation* prophecy.

⁶and has made us kings and priests to His God and Father, to Him *be* glory and dominion forever and ever. Amen.

1:6
Jesus Christ has made believers to be kings and priests (1 Peter 2:5, 9a) while reminding us that all glory is given to our God—not ourselves.

Chapter 1 Verses 1-6
References

Vv. 1-3

John 1:18 No one has seen God at any time. The only begotten Son, who is in the bosom of the Father, He has declared *Him*.

John 14:9 Jesus said to him, "Have I been with you so long, and yet you have not known Me, Philip? He who has seen Me has seen the Father; so how can you say, 'Show us the Father'?"

Chapter 1 Verses 1-6
References Commentary

Vv. 1-3

John 1:18 combined with John 14:9 tells us that [God] the Father is seen and heard *in* His only begotten Son because the Father sent Him to be alive in us. The Lord Jesus Christ said to the Jews who sought to kill Him:

John 5:37-38 ³⁷"And the Father Himself, who sent Me, has testified of Me. You have neither heard His voice at any time, nor seen His form. ³⁸But *you do not have His word abiding in you*, because whom He sent, Him you do not believe."

Christ Jesus is equally God with His Father who is God (Philippians 2:5b-6).

V. 6

1 Peter 2:5 you also, like living stones, are being built into a spiritual house to be a holy priesthood, offering spiritual sacrifices acceptable to God through Jesus Christ. [NIV]

1 Peter 2:9a But you are a chosen people, a royal priesthood,... [NIV]

V. 6

1 Peter 2:5, 9a: *The **spiritual house** is built of all believers in Christ, and is therefore the same as the Church.* All believers are saints and priests—representatives of the Head of the Church, the Lord Jesus.

Chapter 1 Verses 7-11	Chapter 1 Verses 7-11 Commentary
	1:7-8 He will be seen by all at His Second Coming, whether then or during His Millennial Reign or at the Great White Throne of judgment (Zechariah 12:10).
⁷Behold, He is coming with clouds, and every eye will see Him, even they who pierced Him. And all the tribes of the earth will mourn because of Him. Even so, Amen. ⁸"I am the Alpha and the Omega, the Beginning and the End," says the Lord, "who is and who was and who is to come, the Almighty."	Jesus Christ is the equal Almighty God with the Father (Revelation 15:3; 16:7; 19:15, 19:11). The Lord Jesus Christ is referred to as the great I AM when mentioned in John 8:58 with Exodus 3:14, and YHWH, (Jehovah in NKJ Bible reference of Exodus 6:3). Isaiah 41:4; 48:12.
	1:9-20 Introduction: These verses give John's vision of the **Son of Man** (Revelation 1:13)—a title the Savior gave for Himself especially in the Gospel of Luke.
⁹I, John, both your brother and companion in the tribulation and kingdom and patience of Jesus Christ, was on the island that is called Patmos for the word of God and for the testimony of Jesus Christ.	**1:9** John writes of his tribulation on the Island of Patmos off the SW coast of today's Turkey.
¹⁰I was in the Spirit on the Lord's Day, and I heard behind me a loud voice, as of a trumpet,	
¹¹saying, "I am the Alpha and the Omega, the First and the Last," and, "What you see, write in a book and send it to the seven churches which are in Asia; to Ephesus, to Smyrna, to Pergamos, to Thyatīra, to Sardis, to Philadelphia, and to Lāodicēa."	**1:11** *Jesus tells John to **write** the vision he had seen.* What John wrote, we are reading today: In Chapter 1, "**which are**" were the churches of the early part of the Church Age addressed in Chapters 2 and 3. The seven churches in Chapters 2 and 3 are typified in today's different churches. Christ's accolades and rebukes are still relevant today.

Chapter 1 Verses 7-11
References

Vv. 7-8

Zechariah 12:10 "And I will pour on the house of David and on the inhabitants of Jerusalem the Spirit of grace and supplication; then they will look on Me whom they pierced. Yes, they will mourn for Him as one mourns for *his* only son, and grieve for Him as one grieves for a firstborn."

Isaiah 41:4 "Who has performed and done *it*, calling the generations from the beginning? 'I, the LORD, am the first; and with the last I *am* He.'"

Chapter 1 Verses 7-11
References Commentary

Vv. 7-8

Zechariah 12:10: *The people **will mourn** bitterly when they **look on** the Messiah **whom they pierced**. The One **whom they pierced** was the Lord Jesus Christ, Jehovah. Mourning for an **only son** was the deepest form of sorrow for an Israelite.*

Isaiah 41:4: The passage (Isaiah 41:2-4) which contains this verse 4 *is about Jehovah raising up Cyrus to decree that the Jews be released from captivity. The Lord raised up Cyrus to have one generation succeed another, but even with the last generation, the Jehovah Lord Jesus is still the same.* Jeremiah 52:27-30 gives the prophesy of the Jews being taken into captivity. 2 Chronicles 36:22-23, Ezra 1:1-4 and Isaiah 44:28-45:1 provide further confirmation of the biblical prophesies and the historical fulfillments of these prophesies.

The fact that hundreds of past prophesies have come to fruition, lends incredible proof for knowing the prophesies in this *Revelation of Jesus Christ* will also surely be fulfilled.

Chapter 1 Verses 12-16

¹²Then I turned to see the voice that spoke with me. And having turned I saw seven golden lampstands, ¹³and in the midst of the seven lampstands *One* like the Son of Man, clothed with a garment down to the feet and girded about the chest with a golden band. ¹⁴His head and hair *were* white like wool, as white as snow, and His eyes like a flame of fire; ¹⁵His feet *were* like fine brass, as if refined in a furnace, and His voice as the sound of many waters; ¹⁶He had in His right hand seven stars, out of His mouth went a sharp two-edged sword, and His countenance *was like* the sun shining in its strength.

**Chapter 1 Verses 12-16
Commentary**

1:12-16
John describes God in his vision. John's vision resembles Ezekiel's more detailed vision, with angels as well, in Ezekiel 1:4-28. (Ezekiel 1:4, 7, 10, 13, 24, 26-28)

Chapter 1 Verses 12-16
References

Vv. 12-16
Ezekiel 1:4   I looked, and I saw a windstorm coming out of the north — an immense cloud with flashing lightning and surrounded by brilliant light. The center of the fire looked like glowing metal, ... [NIV]

Ezekiel 1:7   Their legs were straight; their feet were like those of a calf and gleamed like burnished bronze. [NIV]
Ezekiel 1:10   Their faces looked like this: Each of the four had the face of a human being, and on the right side each had the face of a lion, and on the left side of an ox; each also had the face of an eagle. [NIV]

Ezekiel 1:13   The appearance of the living creatures was like burning coals of fire or like torches. Fire moved back and forth among the creatures; it was bright, and lightning flashed out of it. [NIV]

Ezekiel 1:24   When they went, I heard the noise of their wings, like the noise of many waters, like the voice of the Almighty, a tumult like the noise of an army; and when they stood still, they let down their wings. ...

Ezekiel 1:26-28

-CONTINUED ON NEXT SET OF PAGES UNDER REFERENCES!-

Chapter 1 Verses 12-16
References Commentary

Vv. 12-16
Ezekiel 1:4:   *The first Chapter of Ezekiel is taken up with a vision of the glory of God among the Jewish captives.* The **windstorm** coming out of the north represents the Babylonians whom God used as agents of His judgment: **fire** (Divine judgment)—to punish the Jews by having them exiled.

Ezekiel 1:7, 10:   The four living creatures: probably cherubim angels—represent God's majesty: **lion**; power: **ox**; swiftness: **eagle**; and wisdom: **face of a** man. The **straight legs** show strength, **feet like a calf** point to stability and firm stance.

Ezekiel 1:13: The **burning coals of fire, torches** and **bright fire** convey God's glory and pure, burning justice.

Ezekiel 1:24:   The **noise of many waters** in Ezekiel's time may be symbolic of many living creatures moving rapidly in reaction to Almighty God's sovereign authority. But, more specifically here in John's vision, the noise (or **tumult** in Ezekiel 1:24) may be the sound of an army, possibly the Christian warriors (Revelation 14:1-2). Isaiah 17:12-13 is also comparable with God's rebuking of the nations that exiled Israel in Isaiah's time.

-CONTINUED ON NEXT SET OF PAGES UNDER REFERENCES COMMENTARY!-

Chapter 1 Verses 12-16

-VERSES 12-16 REPEATED FROM PREVIOUS PAGE-

¹²Then I turned to see the voice that spoke with me. And having turned I saw seven golden lampstands, ¹³and in the midst of the seven lampstands *One* like the Son of Man, clothed with a garment down to the feet and girded about the chest with a golden band. ¹⁴His head and hair *were* white like wool, as white as snow, and His eyes like a flame of fire; ¹⁵His feet *were* like fine brass, as if refined in a furnace, and His voice as the sound of many waters; ¹⁶He had in His right hand seven stars, out of His mouth went a sharp two-edged sword, and His countenance *was like* the sun shining in its strength.

**Chapter 1 Verses 12-16
Commentary**

-VERSES 12-16 COMMENTARY REPEATED FROM PREVIOUS PAGE-

1:12-16
John describes Jesus in his vision. John's vision resembles Ezekiel's more detailed vision, with angels as well, in Ezekiel 1:4-28. (Ezekiel 1:4, 7, 10, 13, 24, 26-28)

Chapter 1 Verses 12-16 References	Chapter 1 Verses 12-16 References Commentary
-CONTINUED FROM PREVIOUS PAGE-	-CONTINUED FROM PREVIOUS PAGE-

Vv. 12-16

Ezekiel 1:26-28 ²⁶And above the firmament over their heads *was* the likeness of a throne, in appearance like a sapphire stone; on the likeness of the throne *was* a likeness with the appearance of a man high above it. ²⁷Also from the appearance of His waist and upward I saw, as it were, the color of amber with the appearance of fire all around within it; and from the appearance of His waist and downward I saw, as it were, the appearance of fire with brightness all around. ²⁸Like the appearance of a rainbow in a cloud on a rainy day, so *was* the appearance of the brightness all around it. This *was* the appearance of the likeness of the glory of the LORD. So when I saw *it*, I fell on my face, and I heard a voice of One speaking.

Vv. 12-16

Ezekiel 1:26-28: The Godhead appears in the likeness of humanity, though *God is Spirit* (John 4:24) **the likeness of the throne *was* a likeness with the appearance of a man high above it.** The Messiah, God incarnate—God in the flesh, Jesus, is the representative of the "fullness of the Godhead (Colossians 2:9), so this can be a prelude to the incarnation ("became flesh and dwelt among us" John 1:14) of Messiah in His character as Savior and Judge.

Chapter 1 Verses 17-20

¹⁷And when I saw Him, I fell at His feet as dead. But He laid His right hand on me, saying to me, "Do not be afraid; I am the First and the Last. ¹⁸I *am* He who lives, and was dead, and behold, I am alive forevermore. Amen. And I have the keys of Hādēs and of Death.

¹⁹Write the things which you have seen, and the things which are, and the things which will take place after this.

²⁰The mystery of the seven stars which you saw in My right hand, and the seven golden lampstands: The seven stars are the angels of the seven churches, and the seven lampstands which you saw are the seven churches.

Chapter 1 Verses 17-20 Commentary

1:17-18
James 2:26 explains that the dead body in the grave has been separated from the soul and spirit. When the body of an unbelieving soul dies It is in the grave called Hādēs.

1:19
*Jesus tells John to write of the past things he has seen, the things that are presently happening (the present church age), and **things which will take place after this** (after the Church is raptured; Chapters 4 to 22)*. John saw the **things** soon coming: the Rapture, Judgment Seat of Christ (for rewards) in heaven, the Seven-year Tribulation, Christ's Second Coming, Armageddon. Millennial Reign, Great White Throne Judgment (judging unbelievers), New Heaven, New Earth, etc.

The Seven-year Tribulation is thoroughly described in Chapters 6 to 19. Chapter 16:16 begins the gathering for the Battle of Armageddon and ends in 16:19. Effects of the battle are detailed in Chaps 17-19. Also things to come: the marriage of the Lamb and His bride the Church in heaven (19:7 calls the Church His *wife*). The marriage supper takes place on earth.

1:20
Jesus tells the mystery of **seven stars** and **seven golden lampstands**.
"The seven stars are the angels of the seven churches" in Chapters 2 and 3; (1 Corinthians 11:10)
"The seven lampstands...are the seven churches."

Chapter 1 Verses 17-20
References

Vv. 17-18
James 2:26 As the body without the spirit is dead, so faith without deeds is dead. [NIV]

V. 20
1 Corinthians 11:10 For this reason the woman ought to have a symbol of authority on her head, because of the angels.

Chapter 1 Verses 17-20
References Commentary

Vv. 17-18
James 2:26: In the Scriptures, *death* never denotes nonexistence. When a believer dies, the soul and spirit are in heaven (2 Corinthians 5:8). However, when a person who dies without being in Christ, his soul and spirit are in the grave until brought to the Great White Throne Judgment (Revelation 20:13-15).

V. 20
1 Corinthians 11:10 Transitioning to Revelation Chapters 2 and 3 we read that the Lord Jesus is addressing the angels of each church indicating admonitions to 5 churches. May we today share this warning to local churches which are falling away.

Chapter 2 Verses 1-5

**Chapter 2 Verses 1-5
Commentary**

Jesus Speaks to the First Two of Seven Churches

"The Things Which are," is the Present Church Age

The number *seven* is God's number representing perfection and completion. The seven Churches here in Chapters 2 and 3 could be representing all the churches of today's Church Age.

¹To the angel of the church of Ephesus write, 'These things says He who holds the seven stars in His right hand, who walks in the midst of the seven golden lampstands; ²I know your works, your labor, your patience, and that you cannot bear those who are evil. And you have tested those who say they are apostles and are not, and have found them liars; ³and you have persevered and have patience, and have labored for My name's sake and have not become weary. ⁴Nevertheless I have *this* against you, that you have left your first love. ⁵Remember therefore from where you have fallen; repent and do the first works, or else I will come to you quickly and remove your lampstand from its place—unless you repent.

2:1-5
Here in verse 1 the Lord Jesus emphasizes the description of Himself as John described Him in Chapter 1 (Revelation 1:13, 16).

The message to **the church** at **Ephesus** who labored, were patient, could not stand those who **are evil**, **tested** spirits and **found** some to be **liars**, *******but* they **left** (*not necessarily lost nor have come back to*) their **first love**** and must **repent**. *The Lord introduces Himself as the One **who holds the seven stars in His right hand, who walks in the midst of the seven lampstands.** Most of the descriptions of the Lord in these letters are similar to that which is found in Chapter 1*. After complementing the Ephesians for their **works**, **labor**, intolerance of **evil**, and ability to discern false **apostles** and deal with them accordingly, the Lord confronted them with their tragedy— *that they had **left** their **first love**. The fire of their affection had died down. They were still *mostly* sound in doctrine and active in service, but the true motive of all worship and service was missing* because, apparently, they were not in the whole counsel of God (Acts 20:27; Ephesians 6:13-14a).

*If they would fail to **remember** and to **repent**, the Lord would **remove** the **lampstand** at Ephesus; that is, the assembly would cease to exist. Its testimony would die out.*

Chapter 2 Verses 1-5
References

Chapter 2 Verses 1-5
References Commentary

V. 1-5

Revelation 1:13   and in the midst of the seven lampstands *One* like the Son of Man, clothed with a garment down to the feet and girded about the chest with a golden band. ...
Revelation 1:16   He had in His right hand seven stars, out of His mouth went a sharp two-edged sword, and His countenance *was* like the sun shining in its strength.

V. 1-5

Revelation 1:13, 16:   *There was nothing between Christ the Lord and the individual lampstands; no agency, hierarchy, or organization. Each church was independent.* Local churches need no earthly head office with man to make inapt decisions and interfere with God's design. Satan can easily attack an earthly headquarters and that can affect many local churches, but it is more difficult for Satan to go after each self-sufficient local church which recognizes the only Head of the assembly to be the Lord Jesus Christ.

Acts 20:27   "For I have not hesitated to proclaim to you the whole will of God." [NIV]

Acts 20:27:   God does not hide any of His Scripture and neither should we.

Ephesians 6:13-14a   ¹³Therefore put on the full armor of God, so that when the day of evil comes, you may be able to stand your ground, and after you have done everything, to stand. ¹⁴Stand firm then with the belt of truth around your waist, [NIV]

Ephesians 6:13-14a: *It isn't surprising that God's Word tells us the first piece of armor is **truth**. We must take the responsibility to seriously uphold His truth. But it is also necessary for the **truth** to hold us—accountable.*

Chapter 2 Verse 6	**Chapter 2 Verse 6** **Commentary**
⁶But you have this in your favor: You hate the practices of the Nicōlāitans, which I also hate. [NIV]	**2:6** In verse 6 *we cannot be sure who the Nicōlāitans were.* However, they are mentioned again in Revelation 2:15 immediately following *the doctrine of Bālaam* in Revelation 2:14, and the Lord repeats His hatred of their deeds and their doctrine. Their teaching, it seems, is that of the false prophet Bālaam—the wicked apostate who loved the wages of unrighteousness (Numbers 22:7; Numbers 25:1-2[3]; 2 Peter 2:15[3]).*

Chapter 2 Verse 6 References	Chapter 2 Verse 6 References Commentary
V. 6 **Revelation 2:14-15** ¹⁴"But I have a few things against you, because you have there those who hold the doctrine of Bālaam, who taught Bālak to put a stumbling block before the children of Israel, to eat things sacrificed to idols, and to commit sexual immorality. ¹⁵Thus you also have those who hold the doctrine of the Nicōlāitans, which thing I hate."	**V. 6** <u>Revelation 2 14-15</u>: **The doctrine of Bālaam** and **of the Nicōlāitans** are doctrines the Lord hates. This **doctrine** includes *things sacrificed to idols **and** sexual immorality and the practice of false teaching by prosperity preaching (Numbers Chapters 22-25).*
Numbers 22:7 And the elders of Mōab and the elders of Midian departed with the rewards of divination in their hand; and they came unto Bālaam and spake unto him the words of Bālak. [KJV] **Numbers 25:1-2** ¹And Israel abode in Shittim, and the people began to commit whoredom with the daughters of Mōab. ²And they called the people unto the sacrifices of their gods, and the people did eat, and bowed down to their gods. [KJV]	
2 Peter 2:15 They have left the straight way and wondered off to follow the way of Bālaam son of Bēor, who loved the wages of wickedness. [NIV]	In <u>2 Peter 2:15</u> the main reason the false teachers claim to teach the truth of God's Word is because they use their so-called ministry for financial gain. 1 Timothy 6:5b: *supposing that gain is godliness:*...[KJV] 1 Peter 5:2: *Feed the flock of God which is among you, taking the oversight thereof, not by constraint, but willingly; not for filthy lucre, but of a ready mind;* [KJV]

Chapter 2 Verses 7-8

⁷Whoever has ears, let him hear what the Spirit says to the churches. To the one who is victorious, I will give the right to eat from the tree of life, which is in the Paradise of God. [NIV]

⁸To the angel of the church in Smyrna write: These are the words of him who is the First and the Last, who died and came to life again. [NIV]

Chapter 2 Verses 7-8
Commentary

2:7
The Ephesians' overcoming would prove the reality of their conversion experience. In general, however, an overcomer is one who believes that Jesus Christ is the Son of God (1 John 5:4-5).

2:8
This message is to the church at Smyrna who will be tested in tribulation by the devil for ten days in prison, but he who overcomes will not be hurt by the second death (the lake of fire) and will receive the crown of life.

Chapter 2 Verses 7-8
References

V. 7

1 John 5:4-5 ⁴for everyone born of God overcomes the world. This is the victory that has overcome the world, even our faith. ⁵Who is it that overcomes the world? Only he who believes that Jesus is the Son of God. [NIV]

Chapter 2 Verses 7-8
References Commentary

V. 7

*The world's methods are a monstrous scheme of temptations, always trying to get us to lose our focus on God and from what is eternal, and seeking to occupy us with what is temporary and sensual. People of the world have become the victims of temporary, passing things. Only the believer who is **born of God** can actually **overcome the world**, because by **faith** (1 John 5:4-5) he is able to rise above the *temporary*, perishing things of this world and to see things in their true, *eternal* perspective. It is not the great scientist or philosopher or psychologist, but the simple believer who realizes the difference between things which are temporary and things which are eternal.* The scientist might know a lot of information, but the difference between knowledge and wisdom is this:

A knowledgeable man can know a lot of information from many books he has read, but with wisdom from God a man can tell what is true or what is false about the things he knows.

Chapter 2 Verses 9-11

⁹I know your afflictions and your poverty—yet you are rich! I know about the slander of those who say they are Jews and are not, but are a synagogue of Satan. [NIV]

¹⁰Do not be afraid of what you are about to suffer. I tell you, the devil will put some of you in prison to test you, and you will suffer persecution for ten days. Be faithful, even to the point of death, and I will give you life as your victor's crown. [NIV]

¹¹Whoever has ears, let him hear what the Spirit says to the churches. The one who is victorious will not be hurt at all by the second death. [NIV]

Chapter 2 Verses 9-11
Commentary

2:9
The saints of Smyrna had a lack of money and temporary material things, but they were rich in spiritual blessings. The Lord encourages us *to be willing to die rather than deny our faith in* Him (Matthew 10:22b).

2:10
The crown of life is for human testing even to martyrdom. The Lord Jesus commends the church in Smyrna and lets them know they will be persecuted (John 15:20), but He holds nothing against them.

2:11
Again the willing hearer is encouraged to listen to the Spirit's advice (Psalm 27:14).

*Here an overcomer is one who proves the reality of his faith by choosing to go to heaven with a good conscience rather than to stay on earth with a bad one. He will not be affected by **the second death,** the doom of all unbelievers (Revelation 20:6, 14).*

Chapter 2 Verses 9-11 References	Chapter 2 Verses 9-11 References Commentary
V. 9 **Matthew 10:22b** "but he who stands firm to the end will be saved." [NIV]	**V. 9** **"He that endures to the end will be saved"**. This is a promise of perseverance not a teaching that salvation may be lost. Rather, it indicates that those who are truly saved will indeed endure to the end.** John 10:28-29 confirms the believer's life is eternal. Nothing can change this fact. (Romans 8:38-39)
V. 10 **John 15:20** "Remember the word that I said to you, 'A servant is not greater than his master.' If they persecuted Me, they will also persecute you. If they kept My word, they will keep yours also."	**V. 10** We can expect to be persecuted (John 15:20), no matter how slight or how severe. *But we cannot expect better treatment than our Lord Jesus received. Our word will be refused just as was the Savior's* —and still is rejected by many to this day.
V. 11 **Psalm 27:14** Wait on the LORD: be of good courage, and he shall strengthen thine heart: wait; I say, on the LORD. [KJV]	**V. 11** A wise man listens to advice. (Proverbs 12:15) [NIV]
Revelation 20:6 Blessed and holy are those who have part in the first resurrection. The second death has no power over them, but they will be priests of God and of Christ and will reign with him for a thousand years. [NIV]	**The First Resurrection** (Revelation 20:6) has three principal phases: 1. The resurrection of Christ; 2. The Rapture of and resurrection of His Church; 3. The Old Testament believers and Tribulation martyred saints on earth.
Revelation 20:14 Then Death and Hādēs were cast into the lake of fire. This is the second death.	Revelation 20:14: **The second death** is preceded by a resurrection of the unsaved to face the Lord at the Great White Throne. In this **second death** the unbeliever just keeps dying; it is **eternal punishment in the lake of fire** which will never be quenched (Isaiah 66:24; Jeremiah 7:20; Ezekiel. 20:47-48; Mark 9:44, 46, 48; Jude 7).

Chapter 2 Verses 12-13

Chapter 2 Verses 12-13
Commentary

Jesus Speaks to the Third and Fourth of Seven Churches

¹²"And to the angel of the church in Pergamos write, 'These things says He who has the sharp two-edged sword:

2:12
The message to the **church** at **Pergamos** who held fast to the name of Jesus *but* ate things sacrificed to idols and committed sexual immorality must repent.
***The sharp two-edged sword** is the word of God (Hebrews 4:12-13) and represents Jesus Christ as Judge* (John 5:22, 27).

¹³I know your works, and where you dwell, where Satan's throne *is*. And you hold fast to My name, and did not deny My faith even in the days in which Antipas *was* My faithful martyr, who was killed among you, where Satan dwells.

2:13
The reason **Pergamos** was called the place of **Satan's throne** in verse 13 was because ***Pergamos** was the Asia Minor headquarters for the cult of emperor-worship. **Antipas** was of this assembly, and he was martyred for his confession of the Lord Jesus. He was the first known Asian to die for refusing to worship the Roman emperor.*

Chapter 2 Verses 12-13
References

V. 12

Hebrews 4:12-13 ¹²For the word of God is living and active. Sharper than any double-edged sword, it penetrates even to dividing soul and spirit, joints and marrow; it judges the thoughts and attitudes of the heart. ¹³Nothing in all creation is hidden from God's sight. Everything is uncovered and laid bare before the eyes of him to whom we must give account. [NIV]

John 5:22 "For the Father judges no one, but has committed all judgment to the Son."...
John 5:27 "and has given Him authority to execute judgment also, because He is the Son of Man."

Chapter 2 Verses 12-13
References Commentary

V. 12

Hebrews 4:12-13: *The Greek here for *word is logos*. This refers, not to the living Word Jesus, but to the living written word, the Bible.* It is the Word that judges us, not we who judge the word. Nothing escapes our Creator's notice; He, *being omniscient, is constantly aware of all that is going on in the universe.* Unbelief is detected by the living Lord.

John 5:22, 27: All things now *and* at the final judgment are committed to the Son, as we honor the Father. And every one who does not thus honor the Son, does not honor the Father who sent Him (1 John 2:23).

Chapter 2 Verses 14-17

¹⁴But I have a few things against you, because you have there those who hold the doctrine of Bālaam, who taught Bālak to put a stumbling block before the children of Israel, to eat things sacrificed to idols, and to commit sexual immorality. ¹⁵Thus you also have those who hold the doctrine of the Nicōlāitans, which thing I hate. ¹⁶Repent, or else I will come to you quickly and will fight against them with the sword of My mouth. ¹⁷He who has an ear, let him hear what the Spirit says to the churches. To him who overcomes I *will give some of the hidden manna to eat. And I will give him a white stone, and on the stone a new name written which no one knows except him who receives it.'*

Chapter 2 Verses 14-17
Commentary

2:14-17
***But** the Lord reprimanded them in verses 14-15 for permitting men with evil *doctrine* to attempt to continue in Christian fellowship.* Some have said that **The** *doctrine of* Bālaam written in 1400 BC (Numbers Chapters 22-25; 31) indoctrinates flocks of the churches still today (2 Peter 2:15; Jude 11b).

Additional to the false preaching problems mentioned, this refers to the practice of false prosperity preaching (John 10:11-13).

Also, **the doctrine of the Nicōlāitans** could possibly be pointing to those who serve for monetary gain as well as eating things sacrificed to idols and to committing sexual immorality (1 Timothy 6:3-5, 1 Timothy 6:10).

Many commended, solid brothers in Christ, along with their families, have proven to have sincere trust and faith for the Lord to provide. They serve eagerly and willingly and do not serve for monetary gain (1 Peter 5:2).
Therefore, this monetary gain does not apply to those who are in full time service to the Lord and have no other means of income. They are working not only for a living but also to serve our living God (2 Thessalonians 3:7-10).

Chapter 2 Verses 14-17
References

Vv. 14-17
2 Peter 2:15 They have left the straight way and wondered off to follow the way of Bālaam son of Bēor, who loved the wages of wickedness. [NIV]
Jude 11b …they have rushed for profit into Bālaam's error; … [NIV]

John 10:11-13 ¹¹"I am the good shepherd. The good shepherd lays down his life for the sheep. ¹²The hired hand is not the shepherd who owns the sheep. So when he sees the wolf coming, he abandons the sheep and runs away. Then the wolf attacks the flock and scatters it. ¹³The man runs away because he is a hired hand and cares nothing for the sheep." [NIV]

1 Timothy 6:10 For the love of money is a root of all kinds of evil. Some people, eager for money, have wandered from the faith and pierced themselves with many griefs. [NIV]

Chapter 2 Verses 14-17
References Commentary

Vv. 14-17
2 Peter 2:15: Bālaam's name is in the Bible over 60 times, yet he is remembered for his **wages of wickedness**. When we leave this life on earth what do we want to be remembered for?

1 Timothy 6:10: In Revelation 2:15 **the doctrine of the Nicōlāitans, which thing I hate** — it is interesting to note that hate is the antonym of love. **The love of money is a root of all kinds of evil.**

Chapter 2 Verses 18-20

¹⁸And to the angel of the church in Thyatīra write, 'These things says the Son of God, who has eyes like a flame of fire, and His feet like fine brass: ¹⁹I know your works, love, service, faith, and your patience; and *as* for your works, the last *are* more important than the first. ²⁰Nevertheless I have a few things against you, because you allow that woman Jezebel, who calls herself a prophetess, to teach and seduce My servants to commit sexual immorality and eat things sacrificed to idols.

Chapter 2 Verses 18-20
Commentary

2:18-20
*The **eyes** speak of piercing vision, and the **feet** of **brass** threaten judgment.* The message **to the church** at **Thyatīra** who had works of love, faith, and patience *but* had a woman called Jezebel *teaching* (Numbers 16:3, 31-32a; Isaiah 3:12b; Genesis 3:6; Romans 15:4; 1 Corinthians 10:6, 11) and seducing Christ's servants to commit sexual and spiritual immorality (Revelation 2:20) and eat things sacrificed to idols.

Chapter 2 Verses 18-20 References	Chapter 2 Verses 18-20 References Commentary
Vv. 18-20 **Numbers 16:3** And they gathered themselves together against Moses and against Aaron, and said unto them, Ye take too much upon you, seeing all the congregation are holy, every one of them, and the LORD is among them: wherefore then lift ye up yourselves above the congregation of the LORD? [KJV] **Numbers 16:31-32a** ³¹And it came to pass, as he had made an end of speaking all these words, that the ground clave asunder that was under them: ³²ᵃAnd the earth opened her mouth, and swallowed them up,... [KJV]	Vv. 18-20 Numbers 16:3, 31-32a: The first verse in Numbers 16:3, (**They**) refers to 250 Israelites of the congregation. Our Lord and Savior is tremendously serious about His prescription for how to conduct the Church meeting. God's Word warns us that only men are to speak in the churches (1 Corinthians 14:34; 1 Timothy 2:11-12). Jesus also warns that a **hireling** is one who serves for monetary gain (John 10:11-13). There are many trustworthy hirelings today who've answered a Spiritual calling. However, there are also *men who choose the ministry as a comfortable occupation, without true love for God's sheep.* A **hireling** who is a *prosperity preacher* serves for pay. When danger approaches, the heart of the preacher will show who sincerely cares about the flock. Further, hiring women in religious leadership positions then doubly contradicts the Scriptures which prescribe separate essential roles for women than for men (1 Corinthians 14:34-35; 1 Timothy 2:11-14; 3:1-13; Titus 1:5-9; 2:1-5).
Isaiah 3:12b "And women rule over them. O My people! Those who lead you cause you to err, and destroy the way of your paths."	Isaiah 3:12b: **indicates the utter failure of male responsibility and spiritual leadership in their society as **women rule over them**...and **cause you to err**. Sadly, we see the same happening today which happened in Isaiah's time 2,700 years ago.
Genesis 3:6 And when the woman saw that the tree was good for food, that it was pleasant to the eyes, and a tree to be desired to make one wise, she took of the fruit thereof, and did eat, and gave also gave unto her husband with her; and he did eat. [KJV]	Genesis 3:6: The first time man was irresponsible to his wife was when Adam did not protect Eve when she took of the fruit and ate. Of course, Adam should have reminded her of when God commanded not to *eat of* that fruit or they would *surely die*. (Genesis 3:17) But he did not take on the responsibility; rather he listened to her instead of listening to God.
Romans 15:4; **1 Corinthians 10:6, 11**	
-CONTINUED ON NEXT SET OF PAGES UNDER REFERENCES!-	-CONTINUED ON NEXT SET OF PAGES UNDER REFERENCES COMMENTARY!-

Chapter 2 Verses 18-27

-VERSES 18-20 REPEATED FROM PREVIOUS PAGE-

¹⁸And to the angel of the church in Thyatīra write, 'These things says the Son of God, who has eyes like a flame of fire, and His feet like fine brass: ¹⁹I know your works, love, service, faith, and your patience; and as for your works, the last are more important than the first. ²⁰Nevertheless I have a few things against you, because you allow that woman Jezebel, who calls herself a prophetess, to teach and seduce My servants to commit sexual immorality and eat things sacrificed to idols.

Chapter 2 Verses 18-27 Commentary

-VERSES 18-20 COMMENTARY REPEATED FROM PREVIOUS PAGE-

2:18-20
*The **eyes** speak of piercing vision, and the **feet of brass** threaten judgment.* The message to **the church at Thyatīra** who had works of love, faith, and patience *but* had a woman called Jezebel *teaching* (Numbers 16:3, 31-32a; Isaiah 3:12b; Genesis 3:6; Romans 15:4; 1 Corinthians 10:6, 11) and seducing Christ's servants to commit sexual and spiritual immorality (Revelation 2:20) and eat things sacrificed to idols.

Chapter 2 Verses 21-27

²¹And I gave her time to repent of her sexual immorality, and she did not repent. ²²Indeed I will cast her into a sickbed, and those who commit adultery with her into great tribulation, unless they repent of their deeds. ²³I will kill her children with death, and all the churches shall know that I am He who searches the minds and hearts. And I will give to each one of you according to your works. ²⁴Now to you I say, and to the rest in Thyatīra, as many as do not have this doctrine, who have not known the depths of Satan, as they say, I will put on you no other burden. ²⁵But hold fast what you have till I come. ²⁶And he who overcomes, and keeps My works until the end, to him I will give power over the nations— ²⁷'He shall rule them with a rod of iron; they shall be dashed to pieces like the potter's vessels' —as I also have received from My Father;

Chapter 2 Verses 21-27 Commentary

2:21-27
Christ gave her time to repent, but she did not repent. Therefore Jesus says, "Indeed I will cast her into a sickbed (in place of her bed of lust), and those who commit adultery with her into great tribulation (they will not be raptured), unless they repent of their deeds. I will kill her children with death"...*Those who have not known the depths of Satan will receive no other burden, and to he who overcomes, and keeps Christ's works until the end will receive power over the nations. Then all the churches would know that the Lord is watching and that He rewards according to man's deeds.*

Chapter 2 Verses 18-27 References	Chapter 2 Verses 18-27 References Commentary
-CONTINUED FROM PREVIOUS PAGE-	**-CONTINUED FROM PREVIOUS PAGE-**
Vv. 18-20	**Vv. 18-20**
Romans 15:4 For everything that was written in the past was written to teach us, so that through endurance and the encouragement of the Scriptures we might have hope. [NIV] **1 Corinthians 10:6** Now these things occurred as examples to keep us from setting our hearts on evil things as they did. [NIV] **1 Corinthians 10:11** These things happened to them as examples and were written down as warnings for us, on whom the fulfillment of the ages has come. [NIV]	Romans 15:4; 1 Corinthians 10:6, 11: The Church, Christ's body, should learn from the Old Testament examples and follow God's New Testament principles' prescription.

Chapter 2 Verse 28	Chapter 2 Verse 28 Commentary
²⁸I will also give that one the morning star. [NIV]	**2:28** *The Lord Jesus is the Bright and Morning Star (Revelation 22:16; 2 Timothy 1:10b). Just as the morning star appears in the heavens before the sun rises, so Christ will appear as the Morning Star to rapture His Church to heaven seven years prior to His Second Coming when He will appear as the Sun of Righteousness to reign over the earth (1 Thessalonians 4:13-18; 5:1-4, 9; Malachi 4:2a).*

Chapter 2 Verse 28	Chapter 2 Verse 28
References	References Commentary

V. 28

Revelation 22:16 *"I, Jesus, have sent My angel to testify to you these things in the churches. I am the Root and the Offspring of David, the Bright and Morning Star."*

2 Timothy 1:10b our Savior, Jesus Christ, who has destroyed death and brought life and immortality to light through the gospel. [NIV]

1 Thessalonians 4:13-18 ¹³But I do not want you to be ignorant, brethren, concerning those who have fallen asleep, lest you sorrow as others who have no hope. ¹⁴For if we believe that Jesus died and rose again, even so God will bring with Him those who sleep in Jesus. ¹⁵For this we say to you by the word of the Lord, that we who are alive *and* remain until the coming of the Lord will by no means precede those who are asleep. ¹⁶For the Lord Himself will descend from heaven with a shout, with the voice of an archangel, and with the trumpet of God. And the dead in Christ will rise first. ¹⁷Then we who are alive *and* remain shall be caught up together with them in the clouds to meet the Lord in the air. And thus we shall always be with the Lord. ¹⁸Therefore comfort one another with these words.

1 Thessalonians 5:1-4 ¹But concerning the times and the seasons, brethren, you have no need that I should write you. ²For you yourselves know perfectly that the day of the Lord so comes as a thief in the night. ³For when they say, "Peace and safety!" then sudden destruction comes upon them, as labor pains upon a pregnant woman. And they shall not escape. ⁴But you, brethren, are not in darkness, so that this Day should overtake you as a thief.

1 Thessalonians 5:9 For God did not appoint us to suffer but to receive salvation through our Lord Jesus Christ. [NIV]

Malachi 4:2a

-CONTINUED ON NEXT SET OF PAGES UNDER REFERENCES!-

V. 28

Revelation 22:16; 2 Timothy 1:10b
The original Greek for **you in the Revelation 22:16 is plural—the revelation is for all believers** *The Bright and Morning Star*, Jesus, will soon rapture His bride. The Lord Jesus made known the surety of life and immortality: (2 Timothy 1:10b)

We know from the New Testament that all Church Age believers will be raptured before the Tribulation begins (1 Thessalonians 4:13-18; 2 Thessalonians 1:6-7; 2:1-8; Romans 11:25-26; Revelation 4:1). When reflecting on the "Rapture Passage" in 1 Thessalonians 4:13-18 the reader needs to realize that in the original scroll there were no numbered chapters or verses.

1 Thessalonians 5:1-4 Unbelievers who might realize they have missed the Rapture, and may have heard of the Great Tribulation, would then have reason to presume the time or season that *only* the Father establishes. (Matthew. 24:36). **The day of the Lord so comes as a thief in the night.**

1 Thessalonians 5:9 It is unlikely the Groom would allow *part of His bride* to be subjected to the wrath of God in any part of the Tribulation, and verse 9 confirms we are saved from wrath and saved for eternal life. John 3:36, Romans 5:9, 1 Thessalonians 1:10, and Revelation 3:10 further confirm this truth.

-CONTINUED ON NEXT SET OF PAGES UNDER REFERENCES COMMENTARY!-

Chapter 2 Verses 28-29

**Chapter 2 Verses 28-29
Commentary**

**-VERSE 28 REPEATED
FROM PREVIOUS PAGE-**

**-VERSE 28 COMMENTARY
REPEATED FROM PREVIOUS PAGE-**

²⁸*I will also give that one the morning star.* [NIV]

2:28
*The Lord Jesus is the Bright and Morning Star (Revelation 22:16; 2 Timothy 1:10b).

Just as the morning star appears in the heavens before the sun rises, so Christ will appear as the Morning Star to rapture His Church to heaven*. Then, at His Second Coming, He will appear as the Sun of Righteousness to reign over the earth (1 Thessalonians 4:13-18; 5:1-4, 9; Malachi 4:2a).

Chapter 2 Verse 29

**Chapter 2 Verse 29
Commentary**

²⁹*Who has ears, let him hear what the Spirit says to the churches.* [NIV]

2:29
*Thus the overcomer is promised a part in the Rapture. From this point on, only those who overcome are expected to have *an ear* to *hear what the Spirit says to the churches.**

Chapter 2 Verses 28-29 References	Chapter 2 Verses 28-29 References Commentary
-CONTINUED FROM PREVIOUS PAGE-	**-CONTINUED FROM PREVIOUS PAGE-**
V. 28	**V. 28**
Malachi 4:2a But to you who fear My name The Sun of Righteousness shall arise with healing in His wings...	Malachi 4:2a: ****The Sun of Righteousness** is a figurative representation of the Messiah** Those who are born-again believers will overcome the world having been healed of their sin condition and *will triumph over their foes like ashes under their feet* (Malachi 4:3).

Chapter 3 Verses 1-4

¹"And to the angel of the church in Sardis write, 'These things says He who has the seven Spirits of God and the seven stars: "I know your works, that you have a name that you are alive, but you are dead. ²Be watchful, and strengthen the things which remain, that are ready to die, for I have not found your works perfect before God. ³Remember therefore how you have received and heard; hold fast and repent. Therefore if you will not watch, I will come upon you as a thief, and you will not know what hour I will come upon you. ⁴You have a few names even in Sardis who have not defiled their garments; and they shall walk with Me in white, for they are worthy.

Chapter 3 Verses 1-4
Commentary

The Lord Jesus Christ Speaks to Two of the Last Three of Seven Churches

3:1-4
The message is to **the church** at **Sardis** who has a name indicating they are **alive** (*Sardis means *those escaping* or *renovation**), **but they are **dead**.** Perhaps they *simply went through a formal, dull routine and were not overflowing with spiritual life.* Obviously, their **works** are not perfect before God. They must have been so **dead** in spirit and **works** that some of them had no soundness of faith. Their belief in the genuine doctrines taught in the Scriptures must have become unrecognizable. The local church leaders are urged by the Spirit to shepherd the flock of God. If they do not serve in a worthy manner, they will be held accountable (Acts 20:28; 1 Peter 5:2-3). So they—the elders and the flock—must **repent** and watch for Christ's return or He **will come upon** them like **a thief**. Apparently, only a **few** of them were walking with the Lord and were worthy.

We must remember, these prescriptions given by the Lord Jesus apply at this present time in this Church Age before the Rapture. In the chronological order of the Book of Revelation, the Rapture does not happen until the next chapter (Chapter 4:1).

Chapter 3 Verses 1-4
References

Chapter 3 Verses 1-4
References Commentary

Chapter 3 Verses 5-6

⁵*He who overcomes shall be clothed in white garments, and I will not blot out his name from the Book of Life; but I will confess his name before My Father and before His angels.* ⁶*He who has an ear, let him hear what the Spirit says to the churches.*"

Chapter 3 Verses 5-6
Commentary

3:5-6
Those who have sincerely repented, and believe the Father sent His Son to shed His blood to forgive them, to die so that they can have life, and resurrected Him back to life will have their names written in **the Book of Life**. We all need to be constantly aware that authors of Bible commentaries, Bible dictionaries, and even this study guide, and churches that use the name of Jesus and Christianity can be controlled by Satan's tricks. We all need to arm ourselves with the whole counsel of God—that is, the entire Word of God—the Bible—and we need to pray without ceasing (Acts 20:27; Ephesians 6:10-20).

The Lord Jesus Christ who is the Judge will confess the name only of genuine believers (Revelation 6:9; 7:14b; Philippians 4:3d; Revelation 19:20b, 15; Matthew 10:32-33).

The Son of God is our Advocate who will plead for our names before the Father. With the magnificent title of Mediator, the Spirit in God's Word instructs us to pray to the Father in the name of the Lord Jesus Christ (Ephesians 5:20; Colossians 3:17).

Chapter 3 Verses 5-6
References

Vv. 5-6
Ephesians 6:10-20 [10]Finally, be strong in the Lord and in his mighty power. [11]Put on the full armor of God so that you can take your stand against the devil's schemes. [12]For our struggle is not against flesh and blood, but against the rulers, against the authorities, against the powers of this dark world and against the spiritual forces of evil in the heavenly realms. [13]Therefore put on the full armor of God, so that when the day of evil comes, you may be able to stand your ground, and after you have done everything, to stand. [14]Stand firm then, with the belt of truth buckled around your waist, with the breastplate of righteousness in place, [15]and with your feet fitted with the readiness that comes from the gospel of peace. [16]In addition to all this, take up the shield of faith, with which you can extinguish all the flaming arrows of the evil one. [17]Take the helmet of salvation and the sword of the Spirit, which is the word of God. [18]And pray in the Spirit on all occasions with all kinds of prayers and requests. With this in mind, be alert and always keep on praying for all the saints. [19]Pray also for me, that whenever I open my mouth, words may be given me so that I will fearlessly make known the mystery of the gospel, [20]for which I am an ambassador in chains. Pray that I may declare it fearlessly, as I should. [NIV]

Revelation 6:9; 7:14b;
Philippians 4:3d;
Revelation 19:20b, 15;
Matthew 10:32-33);
Ephesians 5:20.

-CONTINUED ON NEXT SET OF PAGES UNDER REFERENCES!-

Chapter 3 Verses 5-6
References Commentary

Vv. 5-6
Christ lives in each and every believer. The life we now live in the flesh we live by faith in the Son of God. (Galatians 2:20). A church which follows Christ is a church that is alive. We are the living body of the living Head—the Lord Jesus Christ. Each living believer is a member of the living Body—the universal Church. An "*organization*" is *not* a "living thing". A church which is *controlled by* an organizational headquarters is a **dead** church (Revelation 3:1). A church that is "alive"—a living body—responds to the directions, the prescription and the commands, given by the living Head. Satan attacks the Body to kill Christianity, so each member of the Body is exhorted to put on the **full armor of God** (Ephesians 6:10-20).

When we are exhorted to speak **fearlessly** in Ephesians 6:19-20 we need not speak only to others **to make known...the gospel**, but we need also to speak **fearlessly** to our God. The indwelling Spirit of God within us helps us to remember to give Him **thanks always for all things...in the name of our Lord Jesus Christ**; because **all things** are made through Him (John 1:3).

-CONTINUED ON NEXT SET OF PAGES UNDER REFERENCES COMMENTARY!-

Chapter 3 Verses 5-6

-VERSES 5-6 REPEATED FROM PREVIOUS PAGE-

⁵He who overcomes shall be clothed in white garments, and I will not blot out his name from the Book of Life; but I will confess his name before My Father and before His angels. ⁶He who has an ear, let him hear what the Spirit says to the churches.'"

Chapter 3 Verses 5-6 Commentary

-PART OF COMMENTARY VERSES 5-6 REPEATED FROM PREVIOUS PAGE-

3:5-6

The Lord Jesus Christ who is the Judge will confess the name only of genuine believers (Revelation 6:9; 7:14b; Philippians 4:3d; Revelation 19:20b; 20:15; Matthew 10:32-33).

The Son of God is our Advocate who will plead for our names before the Father. With the magnificent title of Mediator, the Spirit in God's Word instructs us to pray to the Father in the name of the Lord Jesus Christ (Ephesians 5:20; Colossians 3:17).

Chapter 3 Verses 5-6 References	Chapter 3 Verses 5-6 References Commentary
-CONTINUED FROM PREVIOUS PAGE-	-CONTINUED FROM PREVIOUS PAGE-
Vv. 5-6	Vv. 5-6
Revelation 6:9 When He opened the fifth seal, I saw under the altar the souls of those who had been slain for the word of God and for the testimony which they held. **Revelation 7:14b** "These are the ones who come out of the great tribulation, and washed their robes and made them white in the blood of the Lamb."	Revelation 6:9; 7:14b: The unbelievers *prior* to the Rapture who will become believers and be slain for maintaining their testimony during the Great Tribulation, will come out of this horrific time wearing white robes which have been washed in the blood of the Savior. The 144,000 Jews will also have become believers at this time.
Philippians 4:3d …whose names *are* in the Book of Life.	Philippians 4:3d: Their names will be in the **Book of Life** and they will live everlasting lives with the previously raptured saints.
Revelation 19:20b These two were cast alive into the lake of fire burning with brimstone **Revelation 20:15** And anyone not found written in the Book of Life was cast into the lake of fire. **Matthew 10:32-33** *32"Therefore whoever confesses Me before men, him I will also confess before My Father who is in heaven. 33But whoever denies Me before men, him I will also deny before My Father who is in heaven."*	Revelation 19:20b; 20:15; Matthew 10:32-33: The individuals who take the mark of the beast and deny Jesus will also be resurrected—but resurrected to judgment at the Great White Throne and will be thrown into the eternal lake of fire (Daniel 12:2). The importance of listening—that is, absorbing and believing with a sincere heart—cannot be more emphasized than the Lord Jesus Christ has already done in Revelation 3:6.
Ephesians 5:20 always giving thanks to God the Father for everything, in the name of our Lord Jesus Christ. [NIV]	Ephesians 5:20: We overcome and win the battle by staying focused in the Word of God, spreading the Gospel message, and continuing endlessly in prayer **to the Father in the name of the Lord Jesus Christ.**

Chapter 3 Verses 7-13

⁷And to the angel of the church of Philadelphia write, 'These things says He who is holy, He who is true, He who has the key of David, He who opens and no one shuts, and shuts and no one opens". ⁸I know your works. See, I have set before you an open door, and no one can shut it; for you have a little strength, have kept My word, and have not denied My name. ⁹Indeed I will make *those* of the synagogue of Satan, who say they are Jews and are not, but lie—indeed I will make them come and worship before your feet, and to know that I have loved you. ¹⁰Because you have kept My command to persevere, I also will keep you from the hour of trial which shall come upon the whole world, to test those who dwell on the earth. ¹¹Behold, I am coming quickly! Hold fast what you have, that no one may take your crown. ¹²He who overcomes, I will make him a pillar in the temple of My God, and he shall go out no more. I will write on him the name of My God and the name of the city of My God, the New Jerusalem, which comes down out of heaven from My God. And *I will write on him* My new name. ¹³He who has an ear, let him hear what the Spirit says to the churches.'"

Chapter 3 Verses 7-13
Commentary

3:7-13
The message is to **the church** at ****Philadelphia** (its name means "Brotherly Love")** who have faithfully **kept** God's Word and have been righteous and faithful in all the counsel of God. *By having been true believers they will be raptured, and they will be kept out of the Seven-year Tribulation Period.* This is the church which goes by the principles and prescriptions of the New Testament. This is the church we desire to emulate. Verse 7 repeats and fulfills the prophecy of Isaiah 22:22. We, like the church at **Philadelphia** want to be ever pleasing to our God (Philippians 2:13; Colossians 1:10a;

1 Thessalonians 4:1b; Hebrews 13:21) and see every soul in His flock receive blessings referred to in the Book of Revelation (1:3; 19:9; 20:6; 22:7, 22:14).

There are two more blessings in Revelation, but these refer to the saints who will come to believe during the Tribulation Period (Revelation 14:13b; 16:15b), and it is our prayer that all in our midst will be raptured while still alive and will not have to go through the horrific, dreadful Tribulation Period.

Chapter 3 Verses 7-13
References

Vv. 7-13
Philippians 2:13 for it is God who works in you both to will and to do for *His* good pleasure.
Colossians 1:10a that you may walk worthy of the Lord, fully pleasing *Him*,

1 Thessalonians 4:1b we instructed you how to live in order to please God, [NIV]
Hebrews 13:21 complete in every good work to do His will, working in you what is well pleasing in His sight, through Jesus Christ, to whom *be* glory forever and ever. Amen.

Revelation 14:13b "Blessed are the dead who die in the Lord from now on." [NIV]
Revelation 16:15b "Blessed is he who stays awake and keeps his clothes with him, so that he may not go naked and be shamefully exposed." [NIV]

Chapter 3 Verses 7-13
References Commentary

Vv. 7-13
Philippians 2:13, Colossians 1:10a:
The primary goal of each and every local church leader should be to keep the traditions and adhere to the principles of the New Testament early church. God's Word clearly tells us to do so (1 Corinthians 11:2; 1 Timothy 1:10; 2 Timothy 1:13; Titus 1:9) . Sincere confession of Jesus Christ involves commitment to Him as Lord and the One and Only Savior. The indwelling Holy Spirit guides each believer to walk worthy of the calling and to be pleasing to Him and our Father.

1 Thessalonians 4:1b; Hebrews 13:21:
We need to stay focused and listen to and apply God's Word to be pleasing to Him.
We also need to remember the price He paid for our souls.

Revelation 14:13b; 16:15b: And we need to stay motivated by the hope we have of His soon coming appearing to take us up alive forevermore.

Chapter 3 Verses 14-17

**Chapter 3 Verses 14-17
Commentary**

**Jesus Speaks to the Seventh of
Seven Churches**

¹⁴"And to the angel of the church of the Lāodicēans write, 'These things says the Amen, the Faithful and True Witness, the Beginning of creation of God: ¹⁵I know your works, that you are neither cold nor hot. I could wish you were cold or hot. ¹⁶So then, because you are lukewarm, and neither cold nor hot, I will vomit you out of My mouth. ¹⁷Because you say, 'I am rich, have become wealthy, and have need of nothing'—and do not know that you are wretched, miserable, poor, blind, and naked—

3:14-17
The message to **the church** at **Lāodicēa** who were only **lukewarm** will experience the Lord Jesus vomiting them out of His mouth...unless they **repent** (Revelation 3:19).

The very name *Lāodicēa means either *the people ruling* or *the judgment of the people.** They did not credit the Lord Jesus Christ with being the Head of the Church, the Almighty Creator, nor being the worthy Sovereign Righteous Judge.

The expression, "**the Beginning of the creation of God**" means, at the very least, that Jesus began all **creation** (Isaiah 44:24; Colossians 1:16-17; John 1:1-3, Hebrews 1:8-10).

He is the Head of the new creation: the Church. He was never created; He is *eternal*. He is pre-eminent over all creation.

2 Corinthians 5:17a: *Therefore, if anyone is in Christ, he is a new creation;* [NIV]

In Revelation 5:11 the raptured Church believers are referred to as *living creatures. And the number of them was* [will be] *ten thousand times ten thousand, and thousands of thousands.*

The **Lāodicēans** are **rich**, have need of nothing, and do not even realize they **are wretched, miserable, poor, blind, and naked**. Those who listen and heed and overcome will be saved.

| Chapter 3 Verses 14-17 References | Chapter 3 Verses 14-17 References Commentary |

Vv. 14-17

Isaiah 44:24 Thus says the LORD, your Redeemer, and He who formed you from the womb: I *am* the LORD, who makes all *things*, who stretches out the heavens all alone, who spreads abroad the earth by Myself;

Colossians 1:16-17 ¹⁶For by Him all things were created that are in heaven and that are on earth, visible and invisible, whether thrones or dominions or principalities or powers. All things were created through Him and for Him. ¹⁷And He is before all things, and in Him all things consist.

John 1:1-3 ¹In the beginning was the Word, and the Word was with God, and the Word was God. ²He was in the beginning with God. ³All things were made through Him, and without Him nothing was made that was made.

Vv. 14-17

*God presents Himself to the faithful remnant as **Redeemer**, Jehovah (**the LORD**), our Creator* who started our life in the womb (Isaiah 44:24; Colossians 1:16-17; John 1:1-3).

He loves us from eternal time past and expects our life on earth to last *"from the womb to the tomb"* (Alveda King).

Hebrews 1:8-10 ⁸But to the Son *He says:* *"Your throne, O God, is forever and ever; A scepter of righteousness is the scepter of Your kingdom.* ⁹*You have loved righteousness and hated lawlessness; therefore God, Your God, has anointed You with the oil of gladness more than Your companions."* ¹⁰And: *"You, LORD, in the beginning laid the foundation of the earth, and the heavens are the work of Your hands."*

God the Father is quoted in Hebrews 1:8-10 calling His Son "God" and "LORD". The Father even testifies that His Son created ***the earth and the heavens*** with His own ***hands***.

Chapter 3 Verse 18

¹⁸*I counsel you to buy from Me gold refined in the fire, that you may be rich; and white garments, that you may be clothed, that the shame of your nakedness may not be revealed; and anoint your eyes with eye salve, that you may see.*

Chapter 3 Verse 18
Commentary

3:18
The Lord counseled them **to buy from** Him **gold refined in the fire.** *This could mean divine righteousness, which is bought without money or price (Isaiah 55:1).

Or it may mean genuine faith, which when tested **in the fire**, results in praise, honor, and glory at the revelation of Jesus Christ* (1 Corinthians 3:9-14; 1 Peter 1:7; Romans 11:25b).

*****White garments** refer to practical righteousness in everyday life. And they should **anoint** their **eyes with eye salve**, that is, gain true spiritual vision through the enlightenment of the Holy Spirit.* Here the expression is used metaphorically to remind us of Christ applying saliva to the blind man's eyes so that he, physically, could see (Mark 8:23-25).
1 Corinthians 2:14 informs us that, upon believing, we receive the ability to understand God's Word. Furthermore, Ephesians 1:17-18 tells us the Father *may give you the spirit of wisdom and revelation in the knowledge of Him, the eyes of your understanding being enlightened; that you may know what is the hope of His calling.*

We will see the elders with crowns in Revelation 4:4, so it is also possible that some of the raptured believers are rewarded by Christ at this time—right after the Rapture. Revelation 22:12

Chapter 3 Verse 18 References	Chapter 3 Verse 18 References Commentary
V. 18 **Isaiah 55:1** "Come, all you who are thirsty, come to the waters; and you who have no money, come, buy and eat! Come, buy wine and milk without money and without cost. [NIV]	**V. 18** *The Spirit of God sends out the evangelistic message for His mankind creation to return to Himself. He invites **everyone** everywhere to His free (**without money**), saving grace* (Isaiah 55:1). *All that's necessary is a consciousness of need (**thirst**).*
1 Corinthians 3:9-14 ⁹For we are God's fellow workers; you are God's field, *you are* God's building. ¹⁰According to the grace of God which was given to me, as a wise master builder I have laid the foundation, and another builds on it. But let each one take heed how he builds on it. ¹¹For no other foundation can anyone lay than that which is laid, which is Jesus Christ. ¹²Now if anyone builds on this foundation *with* gold, silver, precious stones, wood, hay, straw, ¹³each one's work will become clear; for the Day will declare it, because it will be revealed by fire; and the fire will test each one's work, of what sort it is. ¹⁴If anyone's work which he has built on *it* endures, he will receive a reward. If anyone's work is burned, he will suffer loss; but he himself will be saved, yet so as through fire. **1 Peter 1:7** These have come so that your faith -of greater worth than gold, which perishes even though refined by fire- may be proved genuine and may result in praise, glory and honor when Jesus Christ is revealed. [NIV] **Romans 11:25b** until the fullness of the Gentiles has come in.	1 Corinthians 3:9-14; 1 Peter 1:7; Romans 11:25b; Revelation 22:12: The harvest **field** is the humankind of the world. Quoting Erdman, "We are fellow-workers who belong to God and are working with one another." In the phrase *you are* **God's building**, the word *you* is plural meaning all believers. In 1 Corinthians 3:16 it is also plural. The Holy Spirit indwells each individual believer *and* the body of Christ—the Church. Believers are Christ's representatives, His ambassadors; we carry His aroma and reflect His light to shine on those who might realize their life changing relationship with the Lord Jesus Christ. The ultimate result is the finished "building"—the last Gentile to fill the only remaining vacant slot for the last piece of **gold, silver,** or **precious stone** who will be the one to complete the building of His Church—His Body—the Bride of Christ. When this **fullness of the Gentiles has come in**, then Christ will descend to the clouds, and the voice which John heard say, **"Come up here"** (Revelation 4:1) will be heard like a trumpet by all believers as He calls us up to meet Him in the air (1 Thessalonians 4:13-18)! Upon being with the Lord face-to-face, He will test us at the judgment seat of Christ and we will be rewarded **according to** our **work.**
Revelation 22:12 "And behold, I am coming quickly, and My reward *is* with Me, to give to every one according to his work."	Revelation 22:12: Perhaps this is a second time He is on the judgment seat, this time, near the beginning of His Millennial Reign. These could possibly be rewards for those who will be saved during the Tribulation.

Chapter 3 Verses 19-22

¹⁹As many as I love, I rebuke and chasten. Therefore be zealous and repent. ²⁰Behold, I stand at the door and knock. If anyone hears My voice and opens the door, I will come in to him and dine with him, and he with Me. ²¹To him who overcomes I will grant to sit with Me on my throne, as I also overcame and sat down with My Father on His throne.

²²He who has an ear, let him hear what the Spirit says to the churches.'"

Chapter 3 Verses 19-22 Commentary

3:19-21
The Lord's *love* for the Church is stated in verse 19 verifying the fact that He rebukes and chastens them. He genuinely, truly cares and loves us all. Those who follow the Lord Jesus Christ in humility, rejection, and suffering will also follow Him in glory.

3:22
After the last word in verse, 3:22, **the churches** are not mentioned again until the last Chapter, Revelation 22:16, because the churches that have overcome are about to be **raptured** in the very next verse after 3:22—Chapter 4:1 (matches Romans 11:25, 1 Corinthians 15:51-52 and 1 Thessalonians 4:16-17). Since believers will be taken up to meet Christ in the air, and right on up into heaven, they will not suffer the upcoming Tribulation Period on earth. Chapters 4 and 5 speak about the raptured Church in heaven during the time the unbelievers on earth are experiencing the beginning sorrows of the Tribulation Period. Their Seven-year Tribulation experiences are described in Chapters 6 to 19.

Chapter 3 Verses 19-22 References	Chapter 3 Verses 19-22 References Commentary
V. 22 **Revelation 22:16** "I, Jesus, have sent My angel to testify to you these things in the churches. I am the Root and the Offspring of David, the Bright and Morning Star."	**V. 22** Revelation 22:16: Jesus, as **the Bright and Morning Star**, will rapture His Church. All believers will bow their knee to Him at the judgment seat of Christ. It is probable that at this time many who served Him well will receive rewards. We will see in Revelation 4:4 that the elders are already wearing *crowns of gold on their heads*. Now that the Spirit indwelled Church is taken out of the way, the Antichrist will be revealed (2 Thessalonians 2:7-8), in Revelation 6:2-8. God will bring judgment onto unbelievers by way of the Seven-year Tribulation Period which will be ended in chapters 16-19 by the Battle of Armageddon. Following that will **be the new age: the Messianic Kingdom**. The reason it is called the *new age* is because it is the age which follows the Church Age and the Tribulation Period. At the end of the one-thousand-year Millennial reign, all *unbelievers* will bow their knee to the Lord Jesus Christ at the Great White Throne and receive their due eternal punishment for rejecting Him.

Chapter 4 Verse 1-11

¹After these things I looked, and behold, a door *standing* open in heaven. And the first voice which I heard *was* like a trumpet speaking with me, saying, "Come up here, and I will show you things which must take place after this." ²Immediately I was in the Spirit; and behold, a throne set in heaven, and *One* sat on the throne. ³And He who sat there was like a jasper and a sardius stone in appearance; and *there was* a rainbow around the throne, in appearance like an emerald. ⁴Around the throne *were* twenty-four thrones, and on the thrones I saw twenty-four elders sitting, clothed in white robes; and they had crowns of gold on their heads. ⁵And from the throne proceeded lightnings, thunderings, and voices. Seven lamps of fire *were* burning before the throne, which are the seven Spirits of God. ⁶Before the throne *there was* a sea of glass, like crystal. And in the midst of the throne, and around the throne, *were* four living creatures full of eyes in front and in back. ⁷The first living creature *was* like a lion, the second living creature like a calf, the third living creature had a face like a man, and the fourth living creature *was* like a flying eagle. ⁸*The* four living creatures [seraphim] each having six wings, were full of eyes around and within. And they do not rest day or night, saying: "Holy, holy, holy, Lord God Almighty, Who was and is and is to come!" ⁹Whenever the living creatures give glory and honor and thanks to Him who sits on the throne, who lives forever and ever, ¹⁰the twenty-four elders fall down before Him who sits on the throne and worship Him who lives forever and ever, and cast their crowns before the throne, saying: "¹¹You are worthy, O Lord, to receive glory and honor and power; for You created all things, and by Your will they exist and were created."

**Chapter 4 Verse 1-11
Commentary**

**First Half of the
Seven-Year Tribulation Begins
The Church is Raptured
Rewards of Crowns are Issued**

Chapters 4 and 5 begin "the things that shall be hereafter" (Revelation 1:19)

4:1-11   (-Introduction-)
Chapter 4:1-11 presents a picture of what is happening around God's throne in heaven upon the Church being raptured (Romans 11:25-26a; 1 Thessalonians 4:13a, 16-17; 1 Corinthians 15:52).

In Revelation 4:8 we see the second time in this Book that the Lord Jesus Christ is revealed as being equal to the Father and Holy Spirit as Lord God Almighty.

**-VERSES OF
REVELATION 4:1-11
WITH DETAILED
COMMENTARY, REFERENCES
AND REFERENCES
COMMENTARY
CAN BE FOUND ON THE NEXT
SETS OF PAGES-**

Chapter 4 Verse 1-11 References	Chapter 4 Verse 1-11 References Commentary
4:1-11 (-Introduction-) **Romans 11:25-26a** ²⁵For I do not desire, brethren, that you should be ignorant of this mystery, lest you should be wise in your own opinion, that blindness in part has happened to Israel until the fullness of the Gentiles has come in. ²⁶ªAnd so all Israel will be saved, as it is written: **1 Thessalonians 4:13a** But I do not want you to be ignorant, brethren... **1 Thessalonians 4:16-17** ¹⁶For the Lord Himself will descend from heaven with a shout, with the voice of an archangel, and with the trumpet of God. And the dead in Christ will rise first. ¹⁷Then we who are alive *and* remain shall be caught up together with them in the clouds to meet the Lord in the air. And thus we shall always be with the Lord.	**4:1-11 (-Introduction-)** Jesus said in Matthew 13:11 that the mysteries of the kingdom of heaven have been given now that He has come, but the **mystery** had not been given to those in the Old Testament ages. ****The fullness of the Gentiles** refers to the time when the last Gentile will have been saved and the Church will be removed from the earth by the Rapture** **and so all Israel will be saved** (Zechariah 13:8-9; Romans 11:25-26a; 1 Thessalonians 4:13a, 16-17). 1 Thessalonians 5:9 is noteworthy: *For God did not appoint us to suffer wrath, but to receive salvation through our Lord Jesus Christ.* [NIV] This is in agreement with 1 Thessalonians 1:10 which tells us *Jesus delivers us from the wrath to come.* Also, Romans 5:9 tells us this: *Much more then, being now justified by his blood, we shall be saved from wrath through him.* [KJV] After the Rapture of the Church, and during the Seven-year Tribulation, national salvation will come to ****the Twelve Tribes of Israel (12,000 from each tribe; 144,000**** total of newly converted Christian Jews, Revelation 7:4). God has temporarily blinded—or set Israel aside for the sake of the Gentiles, but He has not forgotten them because of His promise to their fathers. It is interesting to note that Romans Chapters 9, 10 and 11 are respectively the Jews in the past, in the present, and in the future. The chronological order in Romans 11:25-26a is in agreement with what we see here in Revelation. The Rapture is based upon the eye-witnessed fact that Jesus died and rose again. The certainty of every believer's hope to also be resurrected is based on the resurrection of Jesus Christ.
1 Corinthians 15:52 in a flash, in the twinkling of an eye, at the last trumpet. For the trumpet will sound, the dead will be raised imperishable, and the mortal with immortality. [NIV]	The **trumpet** in 1 Corinthians 15:52 is the same as we see in Revelation 4:1 and 1 Thessalonians 4:16. It is called the last trumpet in 1 Corinthians 15:52 signaling the end of the Church age. There will be seven more trumpets sounding through the Tribulation Period (Revelation 8:2 and 8:6). Incidentally, the words "trumpet" and "trumpets" are in the Bible one-hundred-ten times.

Chapter 4 Verse 1

¹After these things I looked, and behold, a door *standing* open in heaven. And the first voice which I heard *was* like a trumpet speaking with me, saying, "Come up here, and I will show you things which must take place after this."

**Chapter 4 Verse 1
Commentary**

4:1
The Church is called **up**, that is, raptured. The words of this verse match directly with the words in other reference verses having to do with the Rapture: 1 Thessalonians 4:16-17; 1 Corinthians 15:52.

In Revelation 11:12a, there is a loud voice telling the two witnesses to "Come up here". **Things** which must be hereafter will be shown throughout this Book; these "**things**" include His Judgment Seat, the Seven-Year wrath of God Tribulation, the Second Coming of Christ, Armageddon and defeat of the Antichrist and his followers, Christ's Millennial Reign, Gog and Magog and Satan's eternal doom, the Great White Throne Judgment; and the New Heaven and New Earth. All these and more will be revealed in the Chapters from here on.

Chapter 4 Verse 1
References

V. 4:1

1 Thessalonians 4:16-17a ¹⁶For the Lord Himself will descend from heaven with a shout, with the voice of an archangel, and with the trumpet of God, and the dead in Christ will rise first. ¹⁷ᵃThen we who are alive *and* remain shall be caught up together with them in the clouds to meet the Lord in the air.

1 Corinthians 15:52 in a flash, in the twinkling of an eye, at the last trumpet. For the trumpet will sound, the dead will be raised imperishable, and the mortal with immortality. [NIV]

Revelation 11:12a Then they heard a loud voice from heaven saying to them, "Come up here." [NIV]

Chapter 4 Verse 1
References Commentary

V. 4:1

We are told the Rapture begins with a voice and the trumpet both in Revelation 4:1 and here in 1 Thessalonians 4:16.

The trumpet is repeated twice in 1 Corinthians 15:52, the first time being referred to as the *last trumpet*. The *last trumpet* is most likely referring to the *last trumpet* of the Church Age, since the Church is being raptured. It is obviously not the last trumpet ever; seven trumpets are referred to in Revelation 8, 9, and 11.

In Revelation 11:12a the two witnesses are seen ascending to heaven after having lain dead in the street three-and-a-half days (Revelation 11:11).

Chapter 4 Verses 2-3

²Immediately I was in the Spirit; and behold, a throne set in heaven, and *One* sat on the throne. ³And He who sat there was like a jasper and a sardius stone in appearance; and *there was* a rainbow around the throne, in appearance like an emerald.

Chapter 4 Verses 2-3
Commentary

4:2-3
John describes God much like Ezekiel does in Ezekiel 1:22-28. This being **in the Spirit** up at the **throne** in heaven is very similar to Paul the Apostle being *caught up to the third heaven* in 2 Corinthians 12:2.

Chapter 4 Verses 2-3
References

Vv. 2-3
Ezekiel 1:22-28 ²²The likeness of the firmament above the heads of the living creatures *was* like the color of an awesome crystal, stretched out over their heads. ²³And under the firmament their wings *spread out* straight, one toward another. Each one had two which covered one side, and each one had two which covered the other side of the body. ²⁴When they went, I heard the noise of their wings, like the noise of many waters, like the voice of the Almighty, a tumult like the noise of an army; and when they stood still, they let down their wings. ²⁵A voice came from above the firmament that *was* over their heads; whenever they stood, they let down their wings. ²⁶And above the firmament over their heads *was* the likeness of a throne, in appearance like a sapphire stone; on the likeness of the throne *was* a likeness with the appearance of a man high above it. ²⁷Also from the appearance of His waist and upward I saw, as it were, the color of amber with the appearance of fire all around within it; and from the appearance of His waist and downward I saw, as it were, the appearance of fire with brightness all around. ²⁸Like the appearance of a rainbow in a cloud on a rainy day, so *was* the appearance of the brightness all around it. This *was* the appearance of the likeness of the glory of the LORD. So when I saw *it*, I fell on my face, and I heard a voice of One speaking.

Chapter 4 Verses 2-3
References Commentary

Vv. 2-3
The firmament here (Ezekiel 1:22-28) comes from the same Hebrew word in Genesis 1:6-7 for the expanse created by God on the second day. The **living creatures are cherubim angels. Its dazzling brilliance was an appropriate reminder of God's holiness and awe-inspiring majesty.** **The noise of many waters** could refer to *the multitude of many people who make a noise like the roar of the seas* and God Almighty's voice rebuking them (Isaiah 17:12-13). But the **voice from above the firmament** was no doubt the **voice of the Almighty** (Ezekiel 1:24). The Godhead appears in the likeness of humanity. The Messiah (Christ Jesus) God incarnate is the representative of the "fullness of the Godhead" (Colossians 2:9). **The glory of the LORD** is that glory which shines fully in the person of Jesus Christ (2 Corinthians 4:6) and is a constant theme in the Book of Ezekiel.

Chapter 4 Verses 4-5

⁴Around the throne *were* twenty-four thrones, and on the thrones I saw twenty-four elders sitting, clothed in white robes; and they had crowns of gold on their heads. ⁵And from the throne proceeded lightnings, thunderings, and voices. Seven lamps of fire *were* burning before the throne, which are the seven Spirits of God.

**Chapter 4 Verses 4-5
Commentary**

4:4-5
****Twenty-four elders** are possibly the twelve sons of Israel (Exodus 28:10-12, 29-30) and the twelve God chosen apostles of the raptured Church in heaven. They are wearing **crowns** of reward from the judgment seat of Christ.** Romans 14:10b tells us we (believers) *shall all stand before the judgment seat of Christ*.
(1 Corinthians 3:12-15; 2 Corinthians 5:10)

The **white robes picture their righteousness which has now been judged and purified,** and they are wearing **crowns** showing they have been judged at the Judgment Seat of Christ. Their sanctification process has been completed.
David divided the Levitical priesthood into 24 sections in 1 Chronicles 24:7-19. Believers here in the Church Age were seen as a kingdom of priests (Revelation 1:6). (1 Peter 2:5, 9).
The **seven lamps and **seven Spirits** symbolize the Holy Spirit of God (1:4;** Isaiah 11:2; Zechariah 3:9; Zechariah 4:10).

Chapter 4 Verses 4-5
References

Vv. 4-5

1 Corinthians 3:12-15 ¹²Now if anyone builds on this foundation *with* gold, silver, precious stones, wood, hay, straw, ¹³each one's work will become clear; for the Day will declare it, because it will be revealed by fire; and the fire will test each one's work, of what sort it is. ¹⁴If anyone's work which he has built on *it* endures, he will receive a reward. ¹⁵If anyone's work is burned, he will suffer loss; but he himself will be saved, yet so as through fire.

2 Corinthians 5:10 For we must all appear before the judgment seat of Christ, that each one may receive what is due him for the things done while in the body, whether good or bad. [NIV]

Chapter 4 Verses 4-5
References Commentary

Vv. 4-5

Each one's work will become clear: Romans 14:11 quotes Isaiah 45:23:
For it is written, As I live, saith the Lord, every knee shall bow to me, and every tongue shall confess to God. [KJV]

Philippians 2:10 also confirms:
That at the name of Jesus every knee should bow, of things in heaven, and things in earth, and things under the earth. [KJV]

Both saints and, eventually, unbelievers will bow the knee: Acts 24:15 quotes Paul the apostle:
And have hope toward God, which they themselves also allow, that there shall be a resurrection of the dead, both of the just and unjust." [KJV]

The justified ones whom God views as righteous to receive eternal life are believers who will bend the knee at the judgment seat of Christ before His Millennial reign (1 Corinthians 3:12-15); the unjustified unbelieving ones who reject Christ will be judged at the Great White Throne at the end of the Millennial Reign.

2 Corinthians 5:10: The just will be eternally with the Lord in heaven, and the unjust will then be eternally suffering in the lake of fire.

Chapter 4 Verse 6

⁶Before the throne *there was* a sea of glass, like crystal. And in the midst of the throne, and around the throne, *were* four living creatures full of eyes in front and in back.

Chapter 4 Verse 6
Commentary

4:6
*The **sea of glass like crystal** tells us that the throne is located in a place undisturbed by the relentless temptations of this world, or by the opposition of the wicked, who are like a troubled sea* (Ephesians 4:14; Hebrews 5:13-14).

Around the throne, were four living creatures: compares with Ezekiel 1:5-6.

These **four living creatures** are obviously the four cherubim, each with four wings, and were delegated the task of preventing anything and everything having to do with sin from coming near the throne. They are fixed in their positions of guarding. Then, in verse 8 we will see the four seraphim, each having six wings, in flight, circling above and looking everywhere all the time.

Chapter 4 Verse 6
References

V. 6
Ephesians 4:14 Then we will no longer be infants, tossed back and forth by the waves, and blown here and there by every wind of teaching and by the cunning and craftiness of men in their deceitful scheming. [NIV]
Hebrews 5:13-14 ¹³Anyone who lives on milk, being still an infant, is not acquainted with the teaching about righteousness. ¹⁴But solid food is for the mature, who by constant use [practice] have trained themselves to distinguish good from evil. [NIV]

Ezekiel 1:5-6 ⁵and in the fire was what looked like four living creatures. In appearance their form was that of a man, ⁶but each of them had four faces four wings. [NIV]

[**Note** on Cherubim⁽¹⁾ and Seraphim**:** They are *created* beings just as we humans are *created* beings. Therefore, angels are not from eternity past nor are they, or we, omniscient as is our God. Cherubim in the Old Testament were all of one piece at the two ends of the golden lid on the Ark of the Covenant inside the Holy of Holies. This signifies that the redeemed and glorified creatures—both angelic and human—were bound up with the sacrifice of Christ. Being in union with Christ then proceeds out of the Mercy Seat. The function of the redeemed cherubim, seraphim, and humans is depicted as being in fellowship with God as well as being there for serving Him.

Chapter 4 Verse 6
References Commentary

V. 6
Believers avoid three dangers when exercising their Spiritual gifts in God's prescribed manner: Immaturity, instability, and gullibility. Most serious of all is the danger of deception (Ephesians. 4:14; Hebrews 5:13-14).
*Saints will inevitably meet some false cultist who impresses them by zeal and apparent sincerity. Because he uses *religious* language, they assume he must be a true Christian. When we study the Bible for ourselves, we are able to see through the deceitful juggling of words* and we are able to discern false teachers and are able to avoid them and to withdraw ourselves from such (Proverbs 4:14-16; Romans 16:17; 2 Thessalonians 3:6; 1 Timothy 6:5).

Ezekiel 1:5-6: Note the resemblances of the visions in the prophecies given by John in Revelation 4 verses 6 and 7 and Ezekiel's **four living creatures** and likeness **of a man**.

The cherubim (cherubim is plural, with the letters *im* at the end, cherub is singular) compared to the seraphim are much the same except for primary duties. The cherubim are primarily guards, or attendants, "attached"—"*united*"—to God's throne (Exodus 25:18-19), whereas the seraphim flew above and around (Isaiah 6:2-7) to attend God's throne and offer praises to Him. God's angelic court serves as an example to each believer: As redeemed created beings who are eternally thankful for being *united* with our Savior—in Him and Him in us—our primary purpose in our life now and eternal is to serve and worship God.]

Chapter 4 Verse 7   **Chapter 4 Verse 7**
                                          Commentary

⁷The first living creature *was* like a lion, the second living creature like a calf, the third living creature had a face like a man, and the fourth living creature *was* like a flying eagle.

4:7
The lion represents strength (Psalm 103:20: *Bless the LORD, you His angels, who excel in strength, who do His word, heeding the voice of His word.*);
**the calf signifies service (Hebrews 1:14);
the **face** of **a man** denotes *intelligence* (God the Son), and **eagle** swiftness (Daniel 9:21** -23, Daniel 9:24, 25-27; Ezekiel 1:10, 14; Revelation 6:1, 3, 5, 7).

Chapter 4 Verse 7
References

V. 7
Hebrews 1:14: Are not all angels ministering spirits sent to serve those who will inherit salvation? [NIV]

Daniel 9:21-23: ²¹while I was still in prayer, Gabriel, the man I had seen in the earlier vision, came to me in swift flight about the time of the evening sacrifice. ²²He instructed me, and said to me, "Daniel, I have now come to give you insight and understanding. ²³As soon as you began to pray, an answer was given, which I have come to tell you, for you are highly esteemed. Therefore, consider the message and understand the vision: [NIV]

Daniel 9:24: Seventy weeks are determined upon thy people and upon thy holy city, to finish the transgression, to make an end of sins, to make reconciliation for iniquity, and to bring in everlasting righteousness, and to seal up the vision and prophecy, and to anoint the most Holy. [KJV]

Daniel 9:25-27;
Ezekiel 1:10, 14;
Revelation 6:1, 3, 5, 7

-CONTINUED ON NEXT SET OF PAGES UNDER REFERENCES!-

Chapter 4 Verse 7
References Commentary

V. 7
Hebrews 1:14: They are angel spirit beings (Hebrews 1:13). *Angels are inferior to the Son of God just as servants are inferior to the Universal Sovereign.*

Daniel 9:21-23: Daniel prayed for help to understand the vision. God sent **Gabriel** who *gave Daniel an outline for Israel's future* (Daniel 9:21-27). God's Word also gives us a prescription for eternal life.

Daniel 9:24: Warren Henderson explains in his book *Infidelity and Loyalty* pg. 391: The Hebrew word *shabua* is translated "week", but literally means "seven", much like our English word dozen means twelve of *something*. The "something" is determined by the context. …
Based on how the final week is described elsewhere in Scripture, we are able to conclude that a week is speaking of seven years". So the first phrase **Seventy Weeks are determined** is actually 7 x 70 which equals 490 years. The first 483 of the 490 years began when Nehemiah started re-building the wall of Jerusalem, and ended at Christ's crucifixion. The rest of verse 24 explains the same thing Romans 3:21-22 reveals: When Christ is believed upon the believers will have the righteousness of God through faith in Jesus Christ. The anointing of the Most Holy means that the Father commissioned the Son to shed His blood and die for the sins of the world.

(Prophecy Timeline in back of this Study Guide)

-CONTINUED ON NEXT SET OF PAGES UNDER REFERENCES COMMENTARY!-

Chapter 4 Verse 7   **Chapter 4 Verse 7**
                                                  Commentary

-VERSE 7 REPEATED   **-VERSE 7 COMMENTARY**
FROM PREVIOUS PAGE -   **REPEATED FROM PREVIOUS PAGE-**

4:7

⁷The first living creature *was* like a lion, the second living creature like a calf, the third living creature had a face like a man, and the fourth living creature *was* like a flying eagle.

The **lion represents strength** (Psalm 103:20: *Bless the LORD, you His angels, who excel in strength, who do His word, heeding the voice of His word*.);

the **calf signifies service (Hebrews 1:14);

the **face** of **a man** denotes *intelligence* (God the Son), and **eagle** swiftness (Daniel 9:21** -23, Daniel 9:24, 25-27; Ezekiel 1:10, 14; Revelation 6:1, 3, 5, 7).

Chapter 4 Verse 7 References	Chapter 4 Verse 7 References Commentary
-CONTINUED FROM PREVIOUS PAGE-	**-CONTINUED FROM PREVIOUS PAGE-**
V. 7	V. 7
Daniel 9:25-26: ^{25}"Know therefore and understand, *that* from the going forth of the command to restore and build Jerusalem Until Messiah the Prince, *there shall be* seven weeks and sixty-two weeks; the street shall be built again, and the wall, even in troublesome times. ^{26}"And after the sixty-two weeks Messiah shall be cut off, but not for Himself; and the people of the prince who is to come shall destroy the city and the sanctuary. The end of it *shall be* with a flood, and till the end of the war desolations are determined.	Daniel 9:25-26: Gabriel explains that Nehemiah's rebuilding of Jerusalem shall be **seven weeks** or 49 years, and then **sixty-two** more **weeks** or 434 more years until the crucifixion of Christ. 49 years plus 434 years totals 483 years. The **prince** [Antichrist] **who is to come** will happen at a time presently unknown to everyone except God. In AD70 Nehemiah's work was destroyed. **And till the end**: means the end of the Church Age—time of the Gentiles-Rapture of the Church—the time that only the Father knows (Matthew 24:36).
Daniel 9:27: Then he shall confirm a covenant with many for one week; but in the middle of the week He shall bring an end to sacrifice and offering. And on the wing of abominations shall be one who makes desolate, even until the consummation, which is determined, is poured out on the desolate."	Daniel 9:27: **Then** means *after* the rapture of the Church, *then* begins the Seven-year Tribulation—he—the antichrist—**shall confirm a covenant**—make a peace treaty—**with many**—all those who are left behind—for **one week**—seven years—signifying the beginning of the Tribulation Period. In the middle of the week—three-and-a-half years—the *Great* Tribulation begins. The *abomination of desolation* in Matthew 24:15 marks this same exact time, as the antichrist takes over the temple and claims he is God (2 Thessalonians 2:4).
Ezekiel 1:10, 14; Revelation 6:1, 3, 5, 7	
-CONTINUED ON NEXT SET OF PAGES UNDER REFERENCES!-	-CONTINUED ON NEXT SET OF PAGES UNDER REFERENCES COMMENTARY!-

Chapter 4 Verse 7	Chapter 4 Verse 7 Commentary

-VERSE 7 REPEATED FROM PREVIOUS PAGE -

-VERSE 7 COMMENTARY REPEATED FROM PREVIOUS PAGE-

⁷The first living creature *was* like a lion, the second living creature like a calf, the third living creature had a face like a man, and the fourth living creature *was* like a flying eagle.

4:7
The **lion represents strength** (Psalm 103:20: *Bless the LORD, you His angels, who excel in strength, who do His word, heeding the voice of His word.*);
the **calf signifies service (Hebrews 1:14);
the **face** of **a man** denotes *intelligence* (God the Son), and **eagle** swiftness (Daniel 9:21** -23, Daniel 9:24, 25-27; Ezekiel 1:10, 14; Revelation 6:1, 3, 5, 7).

Chapter 4 Verse 7 References	Chapter 4 Verse 7 References Commentary
-CONTINUED FROM PREVIOUS PAGE-	-CONTINUED FROM PREVIOUS PAGE-

V. 7

V. 7

Ezekiel 1:10: Their faces looked like this: Each of the four had the face of a man, and on the right side each had the face of a lion, and on the left the face of an ox; each also had the face of an eagle. [NIV]

Ezekiel 10:14: Each of the cherubim had four faces: One face was that of a cherub, the second the face of a man, the third the face of a lion, and the fourth the face of an eagle. [NIV]

Ezekiel 1:10, 14: The four faces represent God's omniscience, omnipresence and omnipotence. To give a more detailed account: The four faces are representative of the four themes of the four Gospels. Matthew: The Lord Jesus is King—like the **lion** is king of beasts. Mark: The Lord Jesus is Servant—like the ox, a beast of burden serving man. Luke: The Lord is called Son of Man—like the face of a man—a human. John: The Son of God—like the Eagle high in the sky above everything.

Revelation 6:1   Now I saw when the Lamb opened one of the seals; and I heard one of the four creatures saying with a voice like thunder, "Come and see."

Revelation 6:1:   **The first seal represents the beginning of Christ's judgment of unbelievers on the earth during the Tribulation Period.**   In verse 2, the Antichrist is coming metaphorically on a white horse to conquer souls of the lost.

Revelation 6:3   When He opened the second seal, I heard the second living creature saying, "Come and see."

Revelation 6:3:   **The second seal represents war and lack of peace.**   In verse 4, the red horse signifies that peace will be taken away by 10 nations and Gog and Magog. (Ezekiel 38)

Revelation 6:5   When He opened the third seal, I heard the third living creature say, "Come and see."

Revelation 6:5-6:   **The third seal** black horse **represents inflation and famine.**   Possible rumors of oil shortage (6:6).

Revelation 6:7   When He opened the fourth seal, I heard the voice of the fourth living creature say, "Come and see."

Revelation 6:7-8:   **The fourth seal pale horse brings death to a fourth of the earth's population through war, famine, and pestilence.**

Chapter 4 Verse 8

⁸*The* four living creatures each having six wings, were full of eyes around and within. And they do not rest day or night, saying: "Holy, holy, holy, Lord God Almighty, Who was and is and is to come!"

Chapter 4 Verse 8 Commentary

4:8
The four living creatures are seraphim angels. **Their **eyes** symbolize wisdom; the **wings** depict movement.** They worship God as did the seraphim in Isaiah's vision (Isaiah 6:1-3).

The angelic vision is much like Ezekiel 10:15-22. Ezekiel 1:4-14 is printed here to provide the incredible similarities to Ezekiel 10:15-22 printed in the *Reference Column*.

Ezekiel 1:4-14 ⁴I looked, and I saw a windstorm coming out of the north –an immense cloud with flashing lightning and surrounded by brilliant light. The center of the fire looked like glowing metal, ⁵and in the fire was what looked like four living creatures. In appearance their form was that of a man, ⁶but each of them had four faces and four wings. ⁷Their legs were straight; their feet were like those of a calf and gleamed like burnished bronze. ⁸Under their wings on their four sides they had the hands of a man. All four of them had faces and wings, ⁹and their wings touched one another. Each one went straight ahead; they did not turn as they moved. ¹⁰Their faces looked like this: Each of the four had the face of a man, and on the right side each had the face of a lion, and on the left the face of an ox; each also had the face of an eagle. ¹¹Such were their faces. Their wings were spread out upward; each had two wings, one touching the wing of another creature on either side, and two wings covering its body. ¹²Each one went straight ahead. Wherever the spirit would go, they would go, without turning as they went. ¹³The appearance of the living creatures was like burning coals of fire or like torches. Fire moved back and forth among the creatures [conveying God's glory and pure, burning justice]; it was bright, and lightning flashed out of it. ¹⁴The creatures sped back and forth like flashes of lightning. [NIV]

Chapter 4 Verse 8
References

V. 8

Isaiah 6:1-3 ¹"In the year that King Uzziah died, I saw the Lord sitting on a throne, high and lifted up, and the train of His *robe* filled the temple. ²Above it stood seraphim; each one had six wings: with two he covered his face, with two he covered his feet, and with two he flew. ³And one cried to another and said: Holy, holy, holy *is* the LORD of hosts; the whole earth *is* full of His glory!"

Ezekiel 10:15-22 ¹⁵Then the cherubim rose upward. These were the living creatures I had seen by the Chēbar River. ¹⁶When the cherubim moved, the wheels beside them moved; and when the cherubim spread their wings to rise from the ground, the wheels did not leave their side. ¹⁷When the cherubim stood still, they stood still; and when the cherubim rose, they rose with them, because the spirit of the living creatures was in them. ¹⁸Then the glory of the LORD departed from over the threshold of the temple and stopped above the cherubim. ¹⁹While I watched, the cherubim spread their wings and rose from the ground, and as they went, the wheels went with them. They stopped at the entrance to the east gate of the LORD'S house, and the glory of the God of Israel was above them. ²⁰These were the living creatures I had seen beneath the God of Israel by the Chēbar River, and I realized that they were cherubim. ²¹Each had four faces and four wings, and under their wings was what looked like the hands of a man. ²²Their faces had the same appearance as those I had seen by the Chēbar River. Each one went straight ahead. [NIV]

Chapter 4 Verse 8
References Commentary

V. 8

In Isaiah 6:1-3 Isaiah's vision was that of the Lord Jesus Christ, **sitting on a throne, high and** exalted. *The **seraphim** had four wings for reverence and two for service. These indicate the holiness of God and require that God's servants (us) be cleansed before serving Him.* We come each first day of the week with a clear conscience and clean heart to remember Christ's work with a dedicated remembrance time.

Ezekiel 10:15 emphasizes that **the cherubim** were the same as **the living creatures** he had seen **by the Chēbar River** [a channel of the Euphrates River SE of Babylon] in Chapter 1.

Following are comments on both Ezekiel 1:4-14 (see opposite page for Scripture) and 10:15-22:

*The **four living creatures**, *attached to God*, **had four faces (lion, ox, eagle, man)**, four **wings**, straight feet, and hands under its wings, all symbolizing those attributes of God which are seen in creation: His majesty (**lion**), power (**ox**), swiftness (**eagle**), and wisdom (**man**). (Many forget about the God above the cloud, who sits on the throne. They worship the creation rather than the Creator Himself.) Beside each living creature there was **a wheel**, or rather **a wheel** within a wheel (perhaps one wheel at right angle to the other like a gyroscope). Thus the vision seems to represent a throne-chariot, with **wheels...on the earth**, four living creatures supporting a platform, and the **throne** of God above it.*

Ezekiel explains what he viewed in 43:3 as "*the vision which I saw when He came to destroy the city.*" *In other words, the vision depicted God in His glory coming out of the north in judgment on Jerusalem, the Babylonians being the agents of His judgment.*

♦In Revelation 4:8 it is the second time that the Lord Jesus Christ is declared to be Almighty God (Revelation 1:8 was the first time).

Chapter 4 Verses 9-11

⁹Whenever the living creatures give glory and honor and thanks to Him who sits on the throne, who lives forever and ever, ¹⁰the twenty-four elders fall down before Him who sits on the throne and worship Him who lives forever and ever, and cast their crowns before the throne, saying: "¹¹You are worthy, O Lord, to receive glory and honor and power; for You created all things, and by Your will they exist and were created."

Chapter 4 Verses 9-11
Commentary

4:9-11
All of heaven worships the Lord Jesus Christ (Revelation 1:18).

The angels praise His character, and the **elders** (and Church—we believers) praise His creative power. God has the right to rule and the sovereign authority to judge the earth, because He is both holy and the Creator of all (Colossians 1:17).

In Revelation 4:4b the twenty-four elders had crowns of gold on their heads. Here in verse 10, they cast the crowns before the throne and worship the Lord. They obviously have new bodies since they have heads and limbs with which to cast the crowns.
(1 Corinthians 15:51-53; Philippians 3:20-21)

Chapter 4 Verses 9-11 References	Chapter 4 Verses 9-11 References Commentary

Vv. 9-11

Revelation 1:18 *I am He who lives, and was dead, and behold, I am alive forevermore. Amen. And I have the keys of Hādēs and of Death.*

Vv. 9-11

Revelation 1:18: Christ is alive, and His body—the Church—is alive, and His Word is alive (Hebrews 4:12)! Since He is alive, His body is also alive—His body of Church believers are alive in Him and worship Him.

Colossians 1:17 And He is before all things, and in Him all things consist.

Colossians 1:17: Jesus Christ is the Creator. (John 1:3; Colossians 1:16; Hebrews 1:10)

1 Corinthians 15:51-53 ⁵¹Listen, I tell you a mystery: We will not all sleep, but we will all be changed— ⁵²in a flash, in the twinkling of an eye, at the last trumpet. For the trumpet will sound, the dead will be raised imperishable, and we will be changed. ⁵³For the perishable must cloth itself with the imperishable, and the mortal with immortality. [NIV]

Philippians 3:20-21 ²⁰For our citizenship is in heaven, from which we also eagerly wait for the Savior, the Lord Jesus Christ, ²¹who will transform our lowly body that it may be conformed to His glorious body, according to the working by which He is able even to subdue all things to Himself.

1 Corinthians 15:51-53; Philippians 3:20-21: Whether a believer is dead or alive, at the time of the Rapture, in the twinkling of an eye, his spirit will be instantaneously gathered with the saints who have died and all will be given a transformed body. Those whom the Lord deems worthy of a reward will have them upon their heads. (Revelation 4:4, 10) Our spirits and souls will be within our new bodies (Philippians 3:20-21). It is the compiler's opinion that our status of *bride* shall also be changed. It is difficult to think that the Bridegroom would have us living with Him unless the marriage takes place. We are no longer called the bride; however, the next two times the Church is given a name, we are called the Lamb's *wife* (Revelation 19:7; 21:9). The term *bride* in Revelation 21:9 is coupled with the term *wife*. In these verses and in 22:17 *bride* can be translated to mean *a son's wife*. In fact, my own wife, of nearly a quarter of a century, is often called my *bride*. Scripture does not specify exactly when the marriage will take place; therefore I will not be dogmatic about a specific time of the Lord's marriage to His Church.

Chapter 5 Verses 1-4

Chapter 5 Verses 1-4
Commentary

Sealed Scroll Tells of God's Tribulation Wrath

¹And I saw in the right *hand* of Him who sat on the throne a scroll written inside and on the back, sealed with seven seals.

5:1
John sees in God the Father's right hand the scroll sealed with seven seals. All the messages have been sealed by the authority of God. We know the Father is the One seated **on the throne**, because we learn in verse 6 that the Lord Jesus is standing **in the midst of the throne**, and He is **in the midst of the elders**. The breaking of the seals will reveal the message inside each part of the ****scroll which contains the Tribulation judgments of God**** (Ezekiel 2:9-10; Daniel 8:26; 12:4; Revelation 6; 8:1).

²Then I saw a strong angel proclaiming with a loud voice, "Who is worthy to open the scroll and to loose its seals?" ³And no one in heaven or on the earth or under the earth was able to open the scroll, or to look at it. ⁴So I wept much, because no one was found worthy to open and read the scroll, or to look at it.

5:2-4
No one among mankind or angels could be found to remove the seals and read the scroll. Only Christ could do so. (Isaiah 29:11)

Chapter 5 Verses 1-4
References

V. 1

Ezekiel 2:9-10 ⁹Now when I looked, there was a hand stretched out to me; and behold, a scroll of a book *was* in it. ¹⁰Then He spread it before me; inside and on the outside, and written on it *were* lamentations and mourning and woe.

Daniel 8:26 "The vision of the evenings and mornings that has been given you is true, but seal up the vision, for it concerns the distant future." [NIV]

Daniel 12:4 "But you, Daniel, close up and seal the words of the scroll until the time of the end. Many will go here and there to increase knowledge." [NIV]

Vv. 2-4

Isaiah 29:11 For you this whole vision is nothing but words sealed in a scroll. And if you give the scroll to someone who can read, and say to him, "Read this, please," he will answer, "I don't know how to read." [NIV]

Chapter 5 Verses 1-4
References Commentary

V. 1

In Ezekiel 2:9-10 the prophet *was forewarned that his ministry would be unpopular. We too are forewarned that a true presentation of the Gospel will be offensive to the unsaved. It is commonly known as "the offenses of the cross." To some people we are the aroma of death* (2 Corinthians 2:15).

Daniel 8:26: In Revelation 5:9 we read that the Lord Jesus is worthy to take the scroll and open the seals because this is the end times. In fact, in Revelation 22:10 John is told not to *seal up the words of the prophecy of this book, because the time is near.* [NIV]

Daniel 12:4 teaches us that *(quoting Tregelles) "many shall scrutinize the book from end to end." Many will study the prophetic Word and **knowledge** of it **will** surely **increase** during the Great Tribulation.* It is so interesting—**until the time of the end**—that we have reached **the time of the end**, and are able right now to see the **words** of Daniel's prophecy being fulfilled.

Vv. 2-4

Isaiah 29:11: This verse can be misconstrued to make one think it agrees with the truly sealed words. The **vision** *here* was of the false seers—false prophets. People's willful blindness brings judicial blindness upon themselves. God's Word is unintelligible — indiscernible— to them (1 Corinthians 2:14). To some it is a **sealed** book, to others it is illegible. Everyone who does not accept it has an excuse. Therefore, *The Revelation of Jesus Christ* is hereby opened.

Chapter 5 Verses 5-7

⁵But one of the elders said to me, "Do not weep. Behold, the Lion of the tribe of Judah, the Root of David, has prevailed to open the scroll and to loose its seven seals." ⁶And I looked, and behold, in the midst of the throne and of the four living creatures, and in the midst of the elders, stood a Lamb as though it had been slain, having seven horns and seven eyes, which are the seven Spirits of God sent out into all the earth. ⁷Then He came and took the scroll out of the right hand of Him who sat on the throne.

Chapter 5 Verses 5-7
Commentary

5:5-7
Christ is presented both as a **Lion (Ruler) from the tribe of Judah (Genesis 49:10)

and as **a Lamb**
(Redeemer: Isaiah 53:7; John 1:29).

The **Root of David** shows a Messianic connection with the Davidic covenant (2 Samuel 7:16; Isaiah 11:1)** and Christ the Lamb—the Messiah.
The seven Spirits depict perfect completeness: the complete fullness of God. The Savior took the scroll from the right hand of the Father who was sitting on the throne (Revelation 5:7).

The following verses should be repeated for emphasizing the One of whom we are reading:

Isaiah 53:7 *He was oppressed and He was afflicted, yet He opened not His mouth; He was led as a lamb to the slaughter, and as a sheep before its shearers is silent, so He opened not His mouth.*

2 Samuel 7:16 *And thine house and thy kingdom shall be established for ever before thee: thy throne shall be established for ever.* [KJV]

Isaiah 11:1 *There shall come forth a Rod from the stem of Jesse, and a Branch shall grow out of his roots* (Romans 11:16-24).

Chapter 5 Verses 5-7 References	Chapter 5 Verses 5-7 References Commentary
Vv. 5-7 **Genesis 49:10** The scepter shall not depart from Judah, nor a lawgiver from between his feet, until Shīlōh comes; and to Him *shall be* the obedience of the people.	**Vv. 5-7** **The scepter**, a rod, is a symbol of kingship. In Genesis 49:10 *Shīlōh represents the Messiah (Christ).* Those who obey Him are those who love Him (John 14:15).
Isaiah 53:7 He was oppressed and He was afflicted, yet He opened not His mouth; He was led as a lamb to the slaughter, and as a sheep before its shearers is silent, so He opened not His mouth. **John 1:29** The next day John saw Jesus coming toward him, and said, "Behold! The Lamb of God who takes away the sin of the world!"	Isaiah 53:7 and John 1:29 take us back to *the blood of the lambs slain during the Old Testament period that did not put away sin. Those lambs were pictures or types, pointing forward to the fact that God would one day provide a **Lamb** who would actually *take away* the sin.* Only those sinners who receive the Lord Jesus as Savior are forgiven of their sins.
2 Samuel 7:16 And thine house and thy kingdom shall be established for ever before thee: thy throne shall be established for ever. [KJV]	*David's dynasty of 2 Samuel 7:16 has been interrupted since the Babylonians exiled the Jews, but it will be restored when Christ, the Seed of David, returns to govern over all the earth* during His Millennial Reign.
Isaiah 11:1 There shall come forth a Rod from the stem of Jesse, and a Branch shall grow out of his roots.	The passage of Isaiah 11 carries us forward to the Second Coming of Christ. Here in verse one we first see the lineage of the Son of David, **a Rod** [Shoot] **from the stem** [stock or trunk] **of Jesse**, who was David's father (1 Samuel 17:12). **A Branch shall grow** means it will be fruitful.

Romans 11:16-24

CONTINUED ON NEXT SET OF PAGES UNDER REFERENCES!	**CONTINUED ON NEXT SET OF PAGES UNDER REFERENCES COMMENTARY!**

Chapter 5 Verses 5-7　　　　**Chapter 5 Verses 5-7**
　　　　　　　　　　　　　　　　　　　　Commentary

**-LAST COMMENTARY REPEATED
FROM PREVIOUS PAGE-**

Isaiah 11:1 *There shall come forth a Rod from the stem of Jesse, and a Branch shall grow out of his roots* (Romans 11:16-24).

Chapter 5 Verses 5-7
References

-CONTINUED FROM PREVIOUS PAGE-

Vv. 5-7

Romans 11:16-24 ¹⁶If the part of the dough offered as firstfruits is holy, then the whole batch is holy; if the root is holy, so are the branches. ¹⁷If some of the branches have been broken off, and you, though a wild olive shoot, have been grafted in among the others and now share in the nourishing sap from the olive root, ¹⁸do not boast over those branches. If you do, consider this: You do not support the root, but the root supports you. ¹⁹You will say then, "Branches were broken off so that I could be grafted in." ²⁰Granted. But they were broken off because of unbelief, and you stand by faith. Do not be arrogant, but be afraid. ²¹For if God did not spare the natural branches, he will not spare you either. ²²Consider therefore the kindness and sternness of God: sternness to those who fell, but kindness to you, provided that you continue in his kindness. Otherwise, you also will be cut off. ²³And if they do not persist in unbelief, they will be grafted in, for God is able to graft them in again. ²⁴After all, if you were cut out of an olive tree that is wild by nature, and contrary to nature were grafted into a cultivated live tree, how much more readily will these, the natural branches, be grafted into their own olive tree?
[NIV]

Chapter 5 Verses 5-7
References Commentary

-CONTINUED FROM PREVIOUS PAGE-

Vv. 5-7

Romans 11:16-24: Two metaphors are used in the Romans 11 passage: the first metaphor is **the firstfruit** and **the batch** (v. 16).

*The **firstfruit** and **the batch** speak of dough, not of fruit. In Numbers 15:19-21 we read that a piece of dough was consecrated to the Lord as a heave offering—meaning that if the piece of dough is set apart to the Lord, so is all the dough that might be made from it. In this passage the **firstfruit** is Abraham. He was **holy** in the sense that he was set apart by God. The second metaphor is **the root** and **its branches** (Vv. 17-18). Again, Abraham is the **root**. The **branches** that **were broken off** picture the unbelieving portion of the twelve tribes of Israel. But only some of the **branches** were removed. A remnant, including Paul himself, had received the Lord. **With them** the Gentiles partook of the root and fatness of **the olive tree**.*

The **olive tree** is not Israel, but rather God's line of privilege down through the centuries. It is also important to know that *the wild olive branch is not the Church but the Gentiles viewed collectively.*

(Interestingly, the next verse—Romans 11:25—reveals the Rapture of the Church by the last believer being brought in, and verse 26 informs us that Israel *will then* be saved—during the Tribulation.)

We will see those 144,000 being saved and sealed in Revelation Chapter seven after the Church is raptured in Chapter four and praises Christ in Chapter five. The Antichrist is revealed in Chapter six.

Chapter 5 Verses 8-14

⁸Now when He had taken the scroll, the four living creatures and the twenty-four elders fell down before the Lamb, each having a harp, and golden bowls full of incense, which are the prayers of the saints. ⁹And they sang a new song, saying: "You are worthy to take the scroll, and to open its seals; for You were slain, and have redeemed us to God by Your blood out of every tribe and tongue and people and nation, ¹⁰And have made us kings and priests to our God; and we shall reign on the earth." ¹¹Then I looked, and I heard the voice of many angels around the throne, the living creatures, and the elders; and the number of them was ten thousand times ten thousand, and thousands of thousands, ¹²saying with a loud voice: "Worthy is the Lamb who was slain to receive power and riches and wisdom, and strength and honor and glory and blessing!" ¹³And every creature which is in heaven and on the earth and under the earth and such as are in the sea, and all that are in them, I heard saying: "Blessing and honor and glory and power *Be* to Him who sits on the throne, and to the Lamb, forever and ever! ¹⁴Then the four living creatures said, "Amen!" And the twenty-four elders fell down and worshiped Him who lives forever and ever.

Chapter 5 Verses 8-14
Commentary

5:8-14
John heard **the voice of many angels around the throne**, he heard the voice of **the living creatures**, and he heard the voice of **the elders.** We human beings are living creatures. The living creatures represent the raptured Church. Some might have difficulty to realize that we are called *creatures*, but in 2 Corinthians 5:17a: *Therefore, if anyone is in Christ, he is a new creation...* [NIV]
and in James 1:18: *Of his own will begat he us with the word of truth, that we should be a kind of firstfruits of his creatures.* [KJV]

The number of them will be ten thousand times ten thousand (10 million) and thousands of thousands. (Daniel 7:10).

The creatures and the elders praise the Lamb for having been the Redeemer through His blood (verse 9) and for giving authority [in the future] to reign on the earth. Myriads of angels also praise the Lamb for His glory and wisdom, and every area of creation worships both the Father and the Lamb. The prayers are probably prayers of thanks for salvation and for the future fulfillment of the Messianic Kingdom.

Chapter 5 Verses 8-14
References

Chapter 5 Verses 8-14
References Commentary

Vv. 8-14

Vv. 8-14

Daniel 7:10 A fiery stream issued and came forth before Him. A thousand thousands ministered to Him; ten thousand times ten thousand stood before Him. The court was seated, and the books were opened.

Daniel 7:10: Daniel prophesied the same prophecy as John envisioned, but in about 550 BC, 1,000 years prior to John's *Revelation*!

Chapter 6 Verse 1

**Chapter 6 Verse 1
Commentary**

**What is to Come in First Half of the
Seven-Year Tribulation**

**The Warnings of Christ's Day of Judgment
Begins with the first 6 Seals being Opened**

¹Now I saw when the Lamb opened one of the seals; and I heard one of the four living creatures saying with a voice like thunder, "Come and see."

6:1
****The seals describe what the beginning of Christ's judgment (a Day of the Lord) will be for unbelievers on earth during the Tribulation period. These judgments nearly mirror those predicted by Christ in Matthew 24:9-28.

The purpose of the Tribulation Period is to punish the unbelievers for their sin and rejection of Christ *and* to bring a remnant to faith in the Lord Jesus Christ. ****

Chapter 6 Verse 1
References

V. 1

Matthew 24:9-28 ⁹"*Then they will deliver you up to tribulation and kill you, and you will be hated by all nations for My name's sake.* ¹⁰*And then many will be offended, will betray one another, and will hate one another.* ¹¹*Then many false prophets will rise up and deceive many.* ¹²*And because lawlessness will abound, the love of many will grow cold.* ¹³*But he who endures to the end shall be saved.* ¹⁴*And this gospel of the kingdom will be preached in all the world as a witness to all the nations, and then the end will come.* ¹⁵*"Therefore when you see the 'abomination of desolation,' spoken of by Daniel the prophet, standing in the holy place"* (whoever reads, let him understand), ¹⁶*"then let those who are in Judea flee to the mountains.* ¹⁷*Let him who is on the housetop not go down to take anything out of his house.* ¹⁸*And let him who is in the field not go back to get his clothes.* ¹⁹*But woe to those who are pregnant and to those who are nursing babies in those days!* ²⁰*And pray that your flight may not be in winter or on the Sabbath.* ²¹*For then there will be great tribulation, such as has not been since the beginning of the world until this time, no, nor ever shall be.* ²²*And unless those days were shortened, no flesh would be saved; but for the elect's sake those days will be shortened.* ²³*"Then if anyone says to you, 'Look, here is the Christ!' or 'There!' do not believe it.* ²⁴*For false christs and false prophets will rise and show great signs and wonders to deceive, if possible, even the elect.* ²⁵*See, I have told you beforehand.* ²⁶*"Therefore if they say to you, 'Look, He is in the desert!' do not go out; or 'Look, He is in the inner rooms!' do not believe it.* ²⁷*For as the lightning comes from the east and flashes to the west, so also will the coming of the Son of Man be.* ²⁸*For wherever the carcass is, there the eagles will be gathered together.*

Chapter 6 Verse 1
References Commentary

**Still in the First Half of Tribulation
Seeing "Things to Come"**

V. 1

Jesus explains the first half of the Tribulation in Matthew 24:9-14 and the second half (the Great Tribulation) in Matthew 24:15-28.

The Tribulation begins with the Antichrist promising peace (Daniel 9:27), but Israel's peace will be broken by an attack by 10 nations including Gog and Māgog. The false teachings, offenses and lawlessness we see today will grow much worse. This battle of Gog is thoroughly explained in Ezekiel 38 and 39. The second half, the Great Tribulation is brought about by the Antichrist bringing an end to sacrifice and offering (Daniel 9:27b) when he takes over the temple claiming he is God (2 Thessalonians 2:4). This is the abomination of desolation. Those caught in the Tribulation who are reading the Scriptures are advised to flee to the mountains and to refuse to take the mark of the beast.

In Matthew 24:29-31 (quoted below) Jesus explains the judgments and His Second Coming to the earth at the end of the Great Tribulation.

Matthew 24:29-31 "²⁹"*Immediately after the tribulation of those days the sun will be darkened, and the moon will not give its light; the stars will fall from heaven, and the powers of the heavens will be shaken.* ³⁰*Then the sign of the Son of Man will appear in heaven, and then all the tribes of the earth will mourn, and they will see the Son of Man coming on the clouds of heaven with power and great glory.* ³¹*And He will send His angels with a great sound of a trumpet, and they will gather together His elect from the four winds, from one end of heaven to the other.*"

Chapter 6 Verse 2

²And I looked, and behold, a white horse. He who sat on it had a bow; and a crown was given to him, and he went out conquering and to conquer.

Chapter 6 Verse 2
Commentary

6:2
Apparently, a man has made a peace treaty for a one-world-government. His probable rationale is based on the idea that if there is only *one nation*, then there could be no war since there would be no other nation with which to have a clash. This man, called a beast, is the Antichrist (Daniel 9:27a).

The Antichrist man is now revealed. His seven-year career is depicted by this white horse representing *peace*, and verses 4, 7, and 8, respectively: the red horse: upheaval and killings; the black horse: enormous inflation and famine; and the pale horse: death—to the Antichrist and his followers. The first seal initiates the conquest by the false savior—the false messiah, the Antichrist. The last phrase of verse 2 tells us that the Antichrist went out to conquer. What is he hoping to conquer? That would be the souls of as many people as possible. The first six of seven seals will be opened here in Chapter 6. The seventh and last will be opened in 8:1.

Matthew 24:5 *"For many will come in My name, saying, 'I am the Christ,' and will deceive many."*

These *many who will come* has been occurring for the past several years. We are in the beginning of sorrows (Matthew 24:8). The *horseman* on the white horse here is not the same as the one described in Revelation 19:11, who is Christ in His Second Coming. In the midpoint of the Tribulation the Antichrist will commit the abomination of desolation, desolating the temple of God.

(2 Thessalonians 2:3c-4; Daniel 11:21b, 36-37)

Chapter 6 Verse 2
References

V. 2
Daniel 9:27a then he shall confirm a covenant with many for one week.

2 Thessalonians 2:3c-4 ³ᶜthe man of sin is revealed, the son of perdition, ⁴who opposes and exalts himself above all that is called God or that is worshiped, so that he sits as God in the temple of God, showing himself that he is God.
Daniel 11:21b He will invade the kingdom when its people feel secure, and he will seize it through intrigue. [NIV]
Daniel 11:36-37 ³⁶"The king will do as he pleases. He will exalt and magnify himself above every god and will say unheard-of things against the God of gods. He will be successful until the time of wrath is completed, for what has been determined must take place. ³⁷He will show no regard for the gods of his fathers or for the one desired by women, nor will he regard any god, but will exalt himself above them all. [NIV]

Chapter 6 Verse 2
References Commentary

V. 2
Daniel 9:27a The Antichrist will deceive many people into thinking that there could be no more war if there is only one nation in the world, no other nation with which to have war, a one-world-government. *One week* in Hebrew translates to seven years.

The Antichrist/lawless one is described in 2 Thessalonians 2:3c-4 in agreement with Daniel 11:36-37 where he appears as the **king**.
2 Thessalonians 2:3 and 2:7-8 confirm the Antichrist will not be revealed until after two major occurrences:

First, the falling away of faith (by many):
2 Thessalonians 2:3b: ³ᵇ*that Day will not come unless the falling away comes first...*

and **Second,** not until after the Rapture:
2 Thessalonians 2:7-8a: ⁷*For the mystery* [hidden truth] *of the lawlessness is already at work; only He who now restrains will do so until He is taken out of the way.* ⁸ᵃ*And then the lawless one will be revealed...*
He (the indwelling Holy Spirit *who is restraining the Antichrist is taken out of the way*) when **He**, with the Church, is raptured away to heaven.

76

Chapter 6 Verses 3-4

³When He opened the second seal, I heard the second living creature saying, "Come and see." ⁴Another horse, fiery red, went out. And it was granted to the one who sat on it to take peace from the earth, and that *people* should kill one another; and there was given to him a great sword.

Chapter 6 Verses 3-4
Commentary

6:3-4
The **second seal describes war and lack of peace. The **sword** is for conflict,** and takes peace from earth. (Ezekiel 38:1-23; Joel 1:15; Daniel 11:33)

-VERSES 3-4 ARE REPEATED WITH DETAILED COMMENTARY, REFERENCES AND REFERENCES COMMENTARY ON THE NEXT SET OF PAGES-

Chapter 6 Verses 3-4
References

Overview of Ezekiel 38
Ezekiel 38 Previews the Broken Peace in the Seven-Year Tribulation

As the Antichrist begins by making a seven-year covenant promising peace, he becomes the supposed leader of the world.

Daniel 9:27a *Then he shall confirm a covenant* [peace treaty] *with many for one week.*
The word *week* in the Hebrew language means *seven years*.

Ezekiel Chapter 38 prophesies how this peace will be broken when the Lord sends *Gog of the land of Māgog* to Israel at an undisclosed time after the onset of the Seven-year Tribulation. Gog is the prince (or head) of Rosh (possibly Russia). Gog rules over two Scythian tribes named Mēshech and Tūbal. The name *Scythian* often included all the barbaric, Scythian tribes, who dwelt mostly near the Caucasus Mountains between the Black Sea and Caspian Sea, Rosh might stretch straight north of Jerusalem to Moscow and even further northeast into Asia. There were (and still are) other tribes south of Israel in northeastern Africa: Libya, Egypt, Sudan and Ethiopia.

During the seven years the Lord Jesus will display His mighty power *at the same time* He sends the Scythians (Ezekiel 38:18). All these people, have provoked Him to jealousy and anger (Ezekiel 38:19).

Chapter 6 Verses 3-4
References Commentary

Overview of Ezekiel 38
Continued

At the mid-point of the seven years, three-and-a-half years, the Antichrist will have gotten a "big head" and will attempt to take over not only the entire world, but will also appoint himself as God over everything (Matthew 24:15; 2 Thessalonians 2:4).

The Lord Jesus will end this Battle of Gog and Māgog. The Antichrist will likely take credit for defeating Gog (Revelation 13:4). This Battle of Gog and Māgog is not the Battle of Armageddon. That conflict will most definitely be won by Christ, the Lord of lords, when He returns at His Second Coming to end the Tribulation Period (Revelation 16:15-17; 19:19-21).

Revelation Chapter 16 tells us the Battle of Armageddon is finished; Chapter 17 describes the fall and consequences of the Babylon religious system; and chapter 18 depicts the collapse of Babylon's commercial structure. Chapter 19 gives a more detailed account of how the Lord Jesus will triumph.

Eventually—at the end of the Millennial Reign—Satan, Gog and Māgog will be totally defeated; utterly destroyed and cast into the eternal lake of fire (Revelation 20:8-10).

Chapter 6 Verses 3-4	Chapter 6 Verses 3-4 Commentary
VERSES 3-4 REPEATED FROM PREVIOUS PAGE-	**-VERSES 3-4 COMMENTARY REPEATED FROM PREVIOUS PAGE-**
³When He opened the second seal, I heard the second living creature saying, "Come and see." ⁴Another horse, fiery red, went out. And it was granted to the one who sat on it to take peace from the earth, and that *people* should kill one another; and there was given to him a great sword.	**6:3-4** The **second seal describes war and lack of peace. The **sword** is for conflict,** and takes peace from earth. (Ezekiel 38:1-23; Joel 1:15; Daniel 11:33)

Chapter 6 Verses 3-4 References	Chapter 6 Verses 3-4 References Commentary
Vv. 3-4	**Vv. 3-4**
Ezekiel 38:1-3 ¹The word of the LORD came to me: ²"Son of man, set your face against Gog, of the land of Māgog, the chief prince of Mēshech, and Tūbal; prophesy against him, ³and say: 'This is what the Sovereign LORD says: I *am* against you, O Gog, chief prince of Mēshech, and Tūbal. [NIV]	Ezekiel 38:2: [Mēshech, and Tūbal are two of Noah's grandsons—Jāpheth's sons (Gen. 10:2)]. William Kelly explains: "For as '*nasi*' regularly means the head of a tribe, or a prince in general, so Meshech and Tubal fix 'rosh' as meaning a Gentilic name (Rosh). They were in fact three great tribes, by the ancients called Scythians."
	Today, from this compiler's opinion, the Scythians (barbarians, *according to Kelly, as far back as Alexander the Great*) live between the Black and Caspian Seas, and as far west as eastern Turkey and Armenia, then east to Iran and Afghanistan. They might go as far north as Moscow (Māgog?) and as far east as western Siberia.
	The Lord is quoted, saying how He would remove these barbarians back to the north of Israel:
	Joel 2:20 *"But I will remove far off from you the northern army, and will drive him into a land barren and desolate, with his face toward the east sea* [Caspian Sea]*, and his hinder part toward the utmost sea* [Black Sea]*; and his stink shall come up, and his ill savour shall come up, because he hath done great things."* [KJV]
	The *eastern sea* is the Caspian Sea and the *western sea* is the Black Sea; about 700km apart. The Caucasus Mountain range rises between the seas and runs WNW to ESE.
Ezekiel 38:4 And I will turn thee back, and put hooks into thy jaws, and I will bring thee forth, and all thine army, horses and horsemen, all of them clothed with all sorts of armour, even a great company with bucklers and shields, all of them handling swords: [KJV]	Ezekiel 38:4: Bucklers in verse 4 are shields with sharp, piercing points, and the swords represent weapons of any kind. The Lord God will lead Gog and Māgog from the north to come up and attack Israel.
-CONTINUED ON NEXT SET OF PAGES UNDER REFERENCES!-	**-CONTINUED ON NEXT SET OF PAGES UNDER REFERENCES COMMENTARY!-**

Chapter 6 Verses 3-4

VERSES 3-4 REPEATED FROM PREVIOUS PAGE-

³When He opened the second seal, I heard the second living creature saying, "Come and see." ⁴Another horse, fiery red, went out. And it was granted to the one who sat on it to take peace from the earth, and that *people* should kill one another; and there was given to him a great sword.

Chapter 6 Verses 3-4
Commentary

-VERSES 3-4 COMMENTARY REPEATED FROM PREVIOUS PAGE-

6:3-4
The ****second seal describes war and lack of peace. The sword is for conflict,**** and takes peace from earth. (Ezekiel 38:1-23; Joel 1:15; Daniel 11:33)

| Chapter 6 Verses 3-4 References | Chapter 6 Verses 3-4 References Commentary |

-CONTINUED FROM PREVIOUS PAGE-

-CONTINUED FROM PREVIOUS PAGE-

Vv. 3-4
Ezekiel 38:5 "Persia, Cush and Put will be with them, all with shields and helmets, [NIV]

Vv. 3-4
Ezekiel 38:5: Verse 5 speaks of Persia, which is today's Turkey and Iran. Ethiopia (Hebrew for Cush), was the settling place of Cush, a grandson of Noah—and son of Ham. Libya was where Put, another son of Ham, settled. Genesis 10:1-8 gives this genealogy. Put hired mercenary soldiers. Even as recent as 2012, terrorists fiercely attacked the US Embassy for 13 hours in Banghāzi, in NE Libya, killing the US ambassador, his diplomatic helper and two of his armed guards. Banghāzi is on the south coast of the Mediterranean Sea, only about 600km west of the Egyptian border.

Ethiopia, with varying borders yet today, is a war-torn country in NE Africa; east of Sudan and west of Somalia. Somalia separates Ethiopia from the Indian Ocean. Two smaller countries, Eritrea and Djibouti, narrowly keep Ethiopia's northern border from the Gulf of Aden and southern entrance of the Red Sea from the Indian ocean. The western section of Ethiopia lies in a line almost directly south of Jerusalem.

Ezekiel 38:6 "also Gōmer with all its troops, and Beth Togarmah from the far north with all its troops—the many nations with you." [NIV]

Ezekiel 38:6: **Gōmer** [grandson of Noah and a son of Jāpeth] **with all its troops;** the house of **Tōgarmah**, whose settling place was, as some suggest, eastern Turkey, Iran and Armenia.] **from the far north with all its troops—many nations** [people] **with you** [that is, Gog, Mēshech, and Tūbal]. Those with him will come *from* the far north with all their troops; plus, as we read on, they will also come from the south, east, and west. In the first part of the Tribulation, when they attack, *all of* Israel will be found dwelling *safely*.

-CONTINUED ON NEXT SET OF PAGES UNDER REFERENCES!-

-CONTINUED ON NEXT SET OF PAGES UNDER REFERENCES COMMENTARY!-

Chapter 6 Verses 3-4	Chapter 6 Verses 3-4 Commentary
VERSES 3-4 REPEATED FROM PREVIOUS PAGE-	**-VERSES 3-4 COMMENTARY REPEATED FROM PREVIOUS PAGE-**

6:3-4

³When He opened the second seal, I heard the second living creature saying, "Come and see." ⁴Another horse, fiery red, went out. And it was granted to the one who sat on it to take peace from the earth, and that *people* should kill one another; and there was given to him a great sword.

The **second seal describes war and lack of peace. The **sword** is for conflict,** and takes peace from earth. (Ezekiel 38:1-23; Joel 1:15; Daniel 11:33)

Chapter 6 Verses 3-4 References	Chapter 6 Verses 3-4 References Commentary
-CONTINUED FROM PREVIOUS PAGE-	-CONTINUED FROM PREVIOUS PAGE-

Vv. 3-4

Ezekiel 38:7 " 'Get ready; be prepared, you and all the hordes gathered about you, and take command of them. [NIV]

Ezekiel 38:8-11 ⁸After many days you will be called to arms. In future years you will invade a land that has recovered from war, whose people were gathered from many nations to the mountains of Israel, which had long been desolate. They had been brought out from the nations, and now all of them live in safety. ⁹You and all your troops and the many nations with you will go up, advancing like a storm; you will be like a cloud covering the land." ¹⁰" 'This is what the Sovereign LORD says: On that day thoughts will come into your mind and you will devise an evil scheme. ¹¹You will say, 'I will invade a land of unwalled villages; I will attack a peaceful and unsuspecting people – all of them living without walls and without gates and bars. [NIV]

Ezekiel 38:12 I will plunder and loot and turn my hand against the resettled ruins and the people gathered from the nations, rich in livestock and goods, living at the center of the land." [NIV]

Ezekiel 38:13 Shēba and Dēdan and the merchants of Tarshish and all her villages will say to you, "Have you come to plunder? Have you gathered your hordes to loot, to carry off silver and gold, to take away livestock and goods and to seize much plunder?" [NIV]

Vv. 3-4

Ezekiel 38:7: Verse 7 quotes God urging the Scythians to be prepared to attack Israel.

Ezekiel 38:8: In Verse 8, **a land**, refers to Israel, and those who were **brought back out from the nations** are the Jews who had previously been scattered to many nations.

Ezekiel 38:12: To take plunder means to rob forcibly putting the victim in fear and to take booty is seizing even with violence.

Ezekiel 38:13: **Shēba, Dēdan** are possibly towns in Ethiopia or sons of Raamah, sons of Cush (Genesis 10:7; 1 Chronicles1:9), and nephews of Nimrod who began the kingdom of Bābel in the land of Shīnar (Babylon; Genesis 10:8-10), the merchants of Tarshish are probably sea-going ships. **All her villages** probably translate metaphorically, to a fierce, evil enemy.

-CONTINUED ON NEXT SET OF PAGES UNDER REFERENCES!-

-CONTINUED ON NEXT SET OF PAGES UNDER REFERENCES COMMENTARY!-

Chapter 6 Verses 3-4	Chapter 6 Verses 3-4 Commentary

VERSES 3-4 REPEATED FROM PREVIOUS PAGE-

-VERSES 3-4 COMMENTARY REPEATED FROM PREVIOUS PAGE-

³When He opened the second seal, I heard the second living creature saying, "Come and see." ⁴Another horse, fiery red, went out. And it was granted to the one who sat on it to take peace from the earth, and that *people* should kill one another; and there was given to him a great sword.

6:3-4
The ****second seal describes war and lack of peace. The sword is for conflict,**** and takes peace from earth. (Ezekiel 38:1-23; Joel 1:15; Daniel 11:33)

Chapter 6 Verses 3-4 References	Chapter 6 Verses 3-4 References Commentary
-CONTINUED FROM PREVIOUS PAGE-	**-CONTINUED FROM PREVIOUS PAGE-**

Vv. 3-4

Ezekiel 38:14-15 ¹⁴"Therefore, son of man, prophesy and say to God, 'Thus says the Lord GOD: "On that day when My people Israel dwell safely, will you not know *it*? ¹⁵Then you will come from your place out of the far north, you and many peoples with you, all of them riding on horses, a great company and a mighty army."

Ezekiel 38:16 "You will come up against My people Israel like a cloud, to cover the land. It will be in the latter days that I will bring you against My land, so that the nations may know Me, when I am hollowed in you, Gog, before their eyes."

Ezekiel 38:17 'Thus says the Lord GOD; "Are *you* he of whom I have spoken in former days by My servants the prophets of Israel, who prophesied for years in those days that I would bring you against them?"'

Ezekiel 38:18 "And it will come to pass at the same time, when Gog comes against the land of Israel," says the Lord GOD, "*that* My fury will show in My face."

Ezekiel 38:19 "For in My jealousy *and* in the fire of My wrath I have spoken: 'Surely in that day there shall be a great earthquake in the land of Israel."

Vv. 3-4

Ezekiel 38:14-15:   The **son of man** is Ezekiel throughout the Book of Ezekiel, and **you** in v. 15 is Gog of Māgog.

Ezekiel 38:16 is proving the end times prophecy of God being the Source of all this turmoil (Revelation 20:8-10).

Ezekiel 38:17:   Gog is referred to as **you**, and **them** is Israel.

Ezekiel 38:18:   The **fury** that will **show in** God's **face** is His enraged wrath that will bring on the 1st defeat of Gog and Magog.

Ezekiel 38:19:   The **great earthquake in the land of Israel** coincides with the **great earthquake** we read of in Revelation 6:12. (There will later be an even greater earthquake in Revelation 16:18 following the end of the Battle of Armageddon, God will win this first battle against Gog and Māgog (Ezekiel 38:21-22) during the first half of the Tribulation Period. Gog and Māgog will reappear after the Millennial Reign. Revelation 20:8)

-CONTINUED ON NEXT SET OF PAGE UNDER REFERENCES!-   **-CONTINUED ON NEXT SET OF PAGES UNDER REFERENCES COMMENTARY!-**

| Chapter 6 Verses 3-4 | Chapter 6 Verses 3-4 Commentary |

VERSES 3-4 REPEATED FROM PREVIOUS PAGE-

-VERSES 3-4 COMMENTARY REPEATED FROM PREVIOUS PAGE-

³When He opened the second seal, I heard the second living creature saying, "Come and see." ⁴Another horse, fiery red, went out. And it was granted to the one who sat on it to take peace from the earth, and that *people* should kill one another; and there was given to him a great sword.

6:3-4
The **second seal describes war and lack of peace. The sword is for conflict,** and takes peace from earth. (Ezekiel 38:1-23; Joel 1:15; Daniel 11:33)

Chapter 6 Verses 3-4 References	Chapter 6 Verses 3-4 References Commentary
-CONTINUED FROM PREVIOUS PAGE-	**-CONTINUED FROM PREVIOUS PAGE-**

Vv. 3-4

Ezekiel 38:20 'so that the fish of the sea, the birds of the heavens, the beasts of the field, all creeping things that creep on the earth, and all men who *are* on the face of the earth shall shake at My presence. The mountains shall be thrown down, the steep places shall fall, and every wall shall fall to the ground.'

Ezekiel 38:21 "I will call for a sword against Gog throughout all My mountains," says the Lord GOD. "Every man's sword will be against his brother."

Ezekiel 38:22 "And I will bring him to judgment with pestilence and bloodshed; I will rain down on him, on his troops, and on the many peoples who *are* with him, flooding rain, great hailstones, fire, and brimstone."

Vv. 3-4

Ezekiel 38:20: **All men will shake at** God's **presence**, (Revelation 6:15), and **the mountains shall be thrown down** again at the end of the Tribulation Period in a more intense earthquake in Revelation 16:20.

Ezekiel 38:21: In the chaos, God will stir up these particular earlier named descendants of Noah to fight and slaughter each other; similar to what He did with the Philistines in 1 Samuel 14:20b *and, behold, every man's sword was against his fellow, and there was very great discomfiture* [confusion]. [KJV]

Ezekiel 38:22: Other remarkable, truth confirming comparisons of Ezekiel's prophecy compare to John's vision in Revelation 6:15-17. Examples include the **many peoples who are with** Gog (Revelation 19:14-15), the flooding rain (Revelation 12:15), great hailstones (Revelation 16:21), fire, and brimstone (Revelation 19:20; 20:10; 21:8).

Zechariah 14:12 describes the later end of Armageddon: *And this shall be the plague wherewith the LORD will smite* [strike] *all the people that have fought against Jerusalem; Their flesh shall consume away while they stand upon their feet, and their eyes shall consume away in their holes, and their tongue shall consume away in their mouth.* [KJV]

All prophecies that have been given up to today's date have been fulfilled. Those who will continue to reject our Almighty Creator and Savior will experience these dreadful future events. Israel will finally see the truth and will be saved by God's chastening.

-CONTINUED ON NEXT SET OF PAGES UNDER REFERENCES!-	**-CONTINUED ON NEXT SET OF PAGES UNDER REFERENCES COMMENTARY!-**

Chapter 6 Verses 3-4	Chapter 6 Verses 3-4 Commentary
VERSES 3-4 REPEATED FROM PREVIOUS PAGE-	**-VERSES 3-4 COMMENTARY REPEATED FROM PREVIOUS PAGE-**
³When He opened the second seal, I heard the second living creature saying, "Come and see." ⁴Another horse, fiery red, went out. And it was granted to the one who sat on it to take peace from the earth, and that *people* should kill one another; and there was given to him a great sword.	**6:3-4** The **second seal describes war and lack of peace. The **sword** is for conflict,** and takes peace from earth. (Ezekiel 38:1-23; Joel 1:15; Daniel 11:33)

Chapter 6 Verses 3-4 References	Chapter 6 Verses 3-4 References Commentary
-CONTINUED FROM PREVIOUS PAGE-	**-CONTINUED FROM PREVIOUS PAGE-**
Vv. 3-4 **Ezekiel 38:23** "Thus I will magnify Myself, and I will be known in the eyes of many nations. Then they shall know that I *am* the LORD.'"	**Vv. 3-4** Ezekiel 38:23: The survivors of Gog and Māgog will return to the land of Māgog. After the Millennial Reign they will come back to Israel for the last battle (Revelation 20:7-10). All should hunger to know the Lord Jesus Christ right now, before it's too late. We, the Lord's people, should not be complacent in informing the lost about the truth of these prophecies.
Joel 1:15 Alas for the day! For the day of the LORD *is* at hand; it shall come as destruction from the Almighty.	Joel 1:15: *…the day of the Lord…* This expression refers to any time when God steps forth in judgment, … In the future, the Day of The Lord includes the Tribulation Period, the Second Advent, the Millennial Reign of Christ, and the final destruction of the heavens and earth with fire.*
Daniel 11:33 "Those who are wise will instruct many, though for a time they will fall by sword or be burned or captured or plundered. [NIV]	Daniel 11:33 speaks of Gog forces swarming over the land and meeting with the blazing wrath and jealousy of God. There will be a great earthquake, pestilence, bloodshed, flooding rain, hailstones, fire, and brimstone.

Chapter 6 Verses 5-8

⁵When He opened the third seal, I heard the third living creature say, "Come and see." So I looked, and behold, a black horse, and he who sat on it had a pair of scales [a symbol of famine since the grain was rationed] in his hand. ⁶And I heard a voice in the midst of the four living creatures saying, "A quart [about one quart] of wheat for a denarius [one day's wages for a worker—represents tremendous inflation]; and do not harm the oil and the wine."

⁷When He opened the fourth seal, I heard the voice of the fourth living creature saying, "Come and see." ⁸So I looked, and behold, a pale horse. And the name of him who sat on it was Death, and Hādēs followed with him. And power was given to them over a fourth of the earth, to kill with sword, with hunger, with death, and by the beasts of the earth.

Chapter 6 Verses 5-8
Commentary

6:5-6
The **third seal represents enormous inflation and famine. (Matthew 24:7) **

6:7-8
The **fourth seal describes death to a quarter of the earth's population through war, famine, and pestilence.** (Luke 21:11)

Death takes bodies and **Hādēs** holds their spirits and souls for judgment.**

Chapter 6 Verses 5-8
References

Vv.: 6-5
Matthew 24:7   Nation will rise against nation, and kingdom against kingdom. There will be famines and earthquakes in various places. [NIV]

Vv.: 7-8
Luke 21:11   There will be great earthquakes, famines and pestilences in various places, and fearful events and great signs from heaven. [NIV]

Chapter 6 Verses 5-8
References Commentary

Chapter 6 Verses 9-14

⁹When He opened the fifth seal, I saw under the altar the souls of those who had been slain for the word of God and for the testimony which they held. ¹⁰And they cried with a loud voice, saying, "How long, O Lord, holy and true, until You judge and avenge our blood on those who dwell on the earth?" ¹¹Then a white robe was given to each of them; and it was said to them that they should rest a little while longer, until both *the number of* their fellow servants and their brethren, who would be killed as they *were*, was completed. ¹²I looked when He opened the sixth seal, and behold, there was a great earthquake; and the sun became black as sackcloth of hair, and the moon became like blood. ¹³And the stars of heaven fell to the earth, as a fig tree drops its late figs when it is shaken by a mighty wind. ¹⁴Then the sky receded as a scroll when it is rolled up, and every mountain and island was moved out of its place.

Chapter 6 Verses 9-14
Commentary

6:9-14
The fifth seal presents the first martyrdom of the Tribulation saints throughout the world. The sixth seal describes huge natural disasters:
Matthew 24:29 *"Immediately after the tribulation of those days the sun will be darkened, and the moon will not give its light; the stars will fall from heaven, and the powers of the heavens will be shaken."*
[And the unbelievers will hate the believers because of Jesus' name (Matthew 24:9).]
(Luke 21:25a; Joel 2:30-31; Zechariah 14:1-5)

Chapter 6 Verses 9-14
References

Vv. 9-14
Matthew 24:9 *"Then they will deliver you up to tribulation and kill you, and you will be hated by all nations for My name's sake."*

Luke 21:25a *"There will be signs in the sun, moon and stars"* [NIV]

Joel 2:30-31 ³⁰And I will shew wonders in the heavens and in the earth, blood and fire, and pillars of smoke. ³¹The sun shall be turned into darkness, and the moon into blood, before the great and the terrible day of the LORD come. [KJV]

Zechariah 14:1-5 Behold, the day of the LORD is coming, and your spoil will be divided in your midst. ²For I will gather all the nations to battle against Jerusalem; the city shall be taken, the houses rifled, and the women ravished. Half of the city will go into captivity, but the remnant of the people shall not be cut off from the city. ³Then the LORD will go forth and fight against those nations, as He fights in the day of battle. ⁴And in that day His feet will stand on the Mount of Olives, which faces Jerusalem on the East. And the Mount of Olives shall be split in two, from east to west, making a very large valley; half of the mountain shall move toward the north and half of it toward the south. ⁵Then you shall flee through My mountain valley, for the mountain valley shall reach Azal. Yes, you shall flee as you fled from the earthquake in the days of Uzziah king of Judah. Thus the LORD my God will come, and all the saints with You.

Chapter 6 Verses 9-14
References Commentary

Vv. 9-14
In Matthew 24:9 *faithful believers (who have come to believe during the Tribulation Period) will experience great personal testing during the Tribulation. This verse seems to have particular reference to the 144,000 Jewish believers who will have a special ministry during this period.*

Luke 21:25a says *there will be disturbances involving **the sun...moon, and stars** that will be clearly visible on earth. Heavenly bodies will be moved out of their orbits. This might cause the gravitational pull to change and the earth could tilt on its axis.*

Joel 2:30-31: **the great and the terrible day of the LORD** refers to a judgment of the Lord = a Day of the Lord.

Zechariah 14:1-5 The prophets, Ezekiel, Isaiah, Daniel, Joel, Zechariah, and John are all miraculously in agreement about this prophecy of the Lord's Second Coming bringing the end of the Great Tribulation with His victory in the Battle of Armageddon.

All the saints with Him is in agreement with Revelation 19:14.

Chapter 6 Verses 15-17	**Chapter 6 Verses 15-17** **Commentary**
¹⁵And the kings of the earth, the great men, the rich men, the commanders, the mighty men, every slave and every free man, hid themselves in the caves and in the rocks of the mountains, ¹⁶and said to the mountains and rocks, "Fall on us and hide us from the face of Him who sits on the throne and from the wrath of the Lamb! ¹⁷For the great day of His wrath has come, and who is able to stand?"	**6:15-17** See Ezekiel 32:6-8, Joel 1:15; 2:1, 11, 31. People will want to die but can't. **The great day of His wrath** begins Christ's judgment—a "Day of the Lord."

Chapter 6 Verses 15-17
References

Vv. 15-17
Ezekiel 32:6-8 ⁶I will drench the land with your flowing blood all the way to the mountains, and the ravines will be filled with your flesh. ⁷When I snuff you out, I will cover the heavens and darken their stars; I will cover the sun with a cloud, and the moon will not give its light. ⁸All the shining lights in the heavens I will darken over you; I will bring darkness over your land, declares the LORD. [NIV]

Joel 1:15 Alas for the day! For the day of the LORD is at hand; it shall come as destruction from the Almighty.

Joel 2:1 Blow the trumpet in Zion, and sound an alarm in My holy mountain! Let all the inhabitants of the land tremble; for the day of the LORD is coming, for it is at hand:
Joel 2:11 The LORD gives voice before His army, for His camp is very great; for strong *is the One* who executes His word. For the day of the LORD *is* great and very terrible; who can endure it? ...
Joel 2:31 The sun shall be turned into darkness, and the moon into blood, before the great and the terrible day of the LORD come. [KJV]

Chapter 6 Verses 15-17
References Commentary

Vv. 15-17
Ezekiel 32:6-8 concerns the sun, moon and stars, and Ezekiel's prophecy lines up with the words of our Lord Jesus Christ in Matthew 24:29, Luke 21:5, and Joel 2:31; and with the opening of the sixth seal in Revelation 6:12.

In Joel 1:15, again, the prophecies relating to the beginning of the Great Tribulation are all in miraculous agreement.

In Joel 2:1, 11 and 31 **the **trumpet** is used to **alarm** the people to the seriousness of the crisis that is upon them. A double figure of locusts and a future invading army may be intended in verses 1-11. Nature has not gone awry; the locusts are not beyond God's control. They move at His specific command.** We read of this also in Exodus when Pharaoh's heart was hardened: Exodus 10:4: *"Or else, if you refuse to let My people go, behold, tomorrow I will bring locusts into your territory."* **The great and the terrible day of the LORD** spoken of in verse 31 *will be preceded by wonders in the heavens. Some of these predicted signs are **blood**, fire, pillars of smoke, **the sun** turning **into darkness and the moon into blood**. All who turn to Jesus as Messiah (Christ, Savior), calling **on His name**, will **be saved** to enter the Millennium with Him.* The Lord Jesus in Matthew 24:37-43, like Joel, informs us of the breathtaking might **before the coming of the great and the terrible day of the LORD**.

Chapter 7 Verses 1-3

Chapter 7 Verses 1-3
Commentary

The Saved Ones During the Tribulation

Chapter 7, like a parenthesis, comes between the sixth and seventh revealing seals and shows God's grace and salvation during the Tribulation Period.

¹After this I saw four angels standing at the four corners of the earth, holding back the four winds of the earth to prevent any wind from blowing on the land or on the sea or on any tree. ²Then I saw another angel coming up from the east, having the seal of the living God. He called out in a loud voice to the four angels who had been given power to harm the land and the sea: ³"Do not harm the land or the sea or the trees until we put a seal on the foreheads of the servants of our God." [NIV]

7:1-3
The four **winds depict God's judgment of the earth** (Daniel 7:2).

The four **angels are restraining agents who are holding back judgment of the earth (Revelation 9:15) until God's special **144,000** Jewish servants can be sealed.** **They must be sealed with the seal of God on their foreheads before the Tribulation judgments begin**. The seal is Father God's name written on their foreheads.

Jeremiah 32:37-41 and Zechariah 10:6-8 tells how the LORD God promised to bring them back.

Chapter 7 Verses 1-3 References	Chapter 7 Verses 1-3 References Commentary
Vv. 1-3 **Daniel 7:2** Daniel said: "In my vision at night I looked, and there before me were the four winds of heaven churning up the great sea. [NIV]	**Vv. 1-3** In Daniel 7:2 *the **Great Sea** is the Mediterranean* Sea and the **four winds** are obviously strong winds powered by God from heaven, coming from every direction to **churning up** the **sea** (which could be the *nations*).
Revelation 9:15 And the four angels who had been kept ready for this very hour and day and month and year were released to kill a third of mankind. [NIV]	**The **four angels** in Revelation 9:15 are fallen angels or demons who have been temporarily bound up by God. They are let loose for the purpose of killing a "third" of the population of the world.**
Jeremiah 32:37-41 ³⁷'Behold, I will gather them out of all countries where I have driven them in My anger, in My fury, and in great wrath; I will bring them back to this place, and I will cause them to dwell safely. ³⁸They shall be My people, and I will be their God; ³⁹then I will give them one heart and one way, that they may fear Me forever, for the good of them and their children after them. ⁴⁰And I will make an everlasting covenant with them, that I will not turn away from doing them good; but I will put My fear in their hearts so that they will not depart from Me. ⁴¹Yes, I will rejoice over them to do them good, and I will assuredly plant them in this land, with all My heart and with all My soul.'	Jeremiah 32:37-41: In these verses Jeremiah was probably concerned for getting the Israelites back from Babylon, but the God of gods and Lord of lords goes beyond just getting them back home in this temporary life. He makes an everlasting covenant with them. God told him in Jeremiah 32:26: *"Behold, I am the LORD, the God of all flesh. Is there anything too hard for Me?* Here in Revelation, we see that God will continue, as always, to keep every one of His promises ... forever. He will bring them back to their homeland from where they have been scattered.
Zechariah 10:6-8 ⁶I will strengthen the house of Judah, and I will save the house of Joseph, and I will bring them again to place them; for I have mercy upon them: and they shall be as though I had not cast them off: for I am the LORD their God, and will hear them. ⁷And they of Ephraim shall be like a mighty man, and their heart shall rejoice as through with wine: yea, their children shall see it, and be glad; their heart shall rejoice in the LORD. ⁸I will hiss for them, and gather them; for I have redeemed them: and they shall increase as they have increased. [KJV]	Zechariah 10:6-8: The Lord is promising to bring the Jews back to Israel and it surely will happen. Jeremiah 3:18: *In those days the house of Judah will join the house of Israel, and together they will come from a northern land to the land I gave your forefathers as an inheritance.* [NIV] Ezekiel 37:21: *and say to them, 'This is what the Sovereign LORD says: "I will take the Israelites out of the nations where they have gone. I will gather them from all around and bring them back into their own land."* [NIV]

Chapter 7 Verses 4-8	Chapter 7 Verses 4-8 Commentary
⁴Then I heard the number of those who were sealed: 144,000 from all the tribes of Israel. ⁵From the tribe of Judah 12,000 were sealed, from the tribe of Reuben 12,000, from the tribe of Gad 12,000, ⁶from the tribe of Asher 12,000, from the tribe of Naphtalī 12,000, from the tribe of Manasseh 12,000, ⁷from the tribe of Simēon 12,000, from the tribe of Levi 12,000, from the tribe of Issachar 12,000, ⁸from the tribe of Zebūlun 12,000, from the tribe of Joseph 12,000, from the tribe of Benjamin 12,000. [NIV]	**7:4-8** **The seal shows ownership and security, as a king's signet ring was used to authenticate and protect official documents** (like a notary). **The 144,000 are all Jews from the twelve tribes** (Genesis 49:1, 28; Romans 11:26). The Antichrist at this juncture has not yet taken over the temple. The four winds could be holding him back, along with the nations, until this remnant of Israel is saved and secured (Revelation 12:14). Then, in Revelation 13:1 the Antichrist commits the Abomination of Desolation, and ten nations are with him. There was always a remnant from all the tribes of the nation (Acts 26:6-8; Acts 23:6-8). The **144,000** will be converted and be a light to the Gentiles during the Tribulation. In verse 8 the tribe of Joseph represents Ephraim (the northern kingdom). In this passage the tribe of Dan is missing, possibly because it was the first to go into idolatry and apostacy (Judges 18:1-2, 14-17, 30-31). Ephraim was also a leader in idolatry as we read of their wicket kings beginning with Jeroboam, followed by the kings that walked in his sins (1 Kings 12:20, 28-31; 14:9; 15:25-26).

Chapter 7 Verses 4-8
References

Vv. 4-8
Genesis 49:1 And Jacob called unto his sons, and said, Gather yourselves together, that I may tell you that which shall befall you in the last days. [KJV]
Genesis 49:28 All these are the twelve tribes of Israel: and this is it that their father spake unto them, blessed them; every one according to his blessing he blessed them. [KJV]

Deuteronomy 4:30 "When you are in distress, and all these things come upon you in the latter days, when you turn to the LORD your God and obey His voice"

Romans 11:26 And so all Israel will be saved, as it is written: "The Deliverer will come out of Zion, and He will turn away ungodliness from Jacob;"

Acts 26:6-8 ⁶"And now it is because of my hope in what God has promised our fathers that I am on trial today. ⁷This is the promise our twelve tribes are hoping to see fulfilled as they earnestly serve God day and night. O king, it is because of this hope that the Jews are accusing me. ⁸Why should any of you consider it incredible that God raises the dead?" [NIV]

Acts 23:6-8 ⁶Then Paul, knowing that some of them were Sadducees and the others Pharisees, called out in the Sanhedrin, "My brothers, I am a Pharisee, the son of a Pharisee. I stand on trial because of my hope in the resurrection of the dead." ⁷When he said this, a dispute broke out between the Pharisees and the Sadducees, and the assembly was divided. ⁸(The Sadducees say that there is no resurrection, and that there are neither angels nor spirits, but the Pharisees acknowledge them all. [NIV]

Chapter 7 Verses 4-8
References Commentary

Vv. 4-8
Jacob's last words to his sons in Genesis 49 were both a prophecy (Genesis 49:1) and a blessing (Genesis 49:28). The verses of Genesis 49 describe Jacob's vision of what will happen to his sons who are renamed in Revelation Chapter 7. Believers will also be blessed—or rewarded—at the judgment seat of Christ according to their service.
**In the last days refers to Israel's future in two ways:
1. the time of their occupation of Canaan, and
2. the status of Israel during the Great Tribulation. Deuteronomy 4:30:**

Romans 11:26: During the Tribulation all believing Israel saints will be saved before the second coming of Christ. But this will only happen after the Spiritual Temple—the Church—has been completed by the *fullness of the Gentiles* having come in—and the Church having been raptured. (Romans 11:25)

Acts 26:6-8 tells us that the **hope** and the **promise** is for the coming Messiah to deliver the nation of Israel and it is the hope in the resurrection of the dead. This "hope" *then, was Paul's crime! He asked Agrippa and all those who were with him, "What was so **incredible** about this?*

In Acts 23:6-8 *the **Sadducees** did not believe in the **resurrection**, and neither did they believe in the existence of spirits or angels. The **Pharisees**, being very orthodox, believed in both, so in Acts 23:8 some of the scribes of the **Pharisees** defended Paul's innocence.*
Angels are spoken of in the Bible over 300 times, resurrection over 40 times, and spirit over 500 times.

Chapter 7 Verses 9-15

⁹After these things I looked, and behold, a great multitude which no one could number, of all nations, tribes, peoples, and tongues, standing before the throne and before the Lamb, clothed with white robes, with palm branches in their hands, ¹⁰and crying out with a loud voice, saying, "Salvation *belongs* to our God who sits on the throne, and to the Lamb!" ¹¹All the angels stood around the throne and the elders and the four living creatures, and fell on their faces before the throne and worshiped God, ¹²saying: "Amen! Blessing and glory and wisdom, thanksgiving and honor and power and might, *be* to our God forever and ever. Amen." ¹³Then one of the elders answered, saying to me, "Who are these arrayed in white robes, and where did they come from?" ¹⁴And I said to him, "Sir, you know." So he said to me, "These are the ones who come out of the great tribulation, and washed their robes and made them white in the blood of the Lamb. ¹⁵Therefore they are before the throne of God, and serve Him day and night in His temple. And He who sits on the throne will dwell among them.

Chapter 7 Verses 9-15
Commentary

7:9-15

Verses 9-14 compared to Revelation 5:11, in which tens of thousands who had already been raptured will, at the end of the Tribulation, witness a new **great multitude** arriving before the throne. These will be the resurrected martyrs, both Gentiles and Jews. (Romans 11:25-26a)

In verse 10 it will be all believers cheering with joy for Israel and other new believers. The ones who have been raptured are able to see the many Jews and Gentiles who will be saved during the Tribulation. **White robes portray a standing of righteousness and the multitude praises God for their salvation** (Psalm 3:8).

They will be God's servants day and night and God will wipe away every tear from their eyes.

Verse 12 has a noticeable seven-fold praise: As a hymn writer said, "Angels never felt the joy that our salvation brings." But they do chant His praises and pronounce Him worthy of seven distinct forms of honor.

The newly redeemed multitude of all nations (Gentiles), tribes (including the 144.000 of all the tribes of Israel—Romans 11:26) of this vision are new believers who will either be martyred or have survived the Tribulation and be on the earth upon Christ's return at His Second Coming. They will be temporarily left on earth for being Christ's servants during His Millennial Reign (Ezekiel Chapters 40-44).

Chapter 7 Verses 9-15 References	Chapter 7 Verses 9-15 References Commentary
Vv. 9-15 **Revelation 5:11** Then I looked, and I heard the voice of many angels around the throne, the living creatures, and the elders; and the number of them was ten thousand times ten thousand, and thousands of thousands,	**Vv. 9-15** In Revelation 5:11 even ***many angels** joined **the living creatures and the elders*** to praise the Lamb for His glory, power and wisdom. Verses 9-14 with Revelation 5:11 confirms that the Rapture takes place prior to the Tribulation.
Romans 11:25-26a ²⁵For I do not desire, brethren, that you should be ignorant of this mystery, lest you should be wise in your own opinion, that blindness in part has happened to Israel until the fullness of the Gentiles has come in. ²⁶ᵃAnd so all Israel will be saved...	Romans 11:25 agrees with Revelation 4:1 that the Church has been raptured and will return with Christ to witness the multitude who will be saved during the Tribulation. And Romans 11:26a agrees with the chronological order that after the fullness of the Gentiles have come in—have come into the Church and have been raptured into heaven; then—after the last Gentile has come in, then all Israel will also be saved. Since the Church Age believers have already been praising the Lamb since Chapter 5, here in Chapter 7 are the 144,000 (and possibly others saved during the Tribulation) arrayed in white robes who come out of the Great Tribulation (Revelation 7:13-14).
Psalm 3:8 Salvation belongs to the LORD, Your blessing *is* upon Your people. Sēlah	David is in prayer in Psalm 3:8 asking God to bless His **people** by continuing to show them His marvelous deliverance. **Sēlah**: is possibly a pause for contemplation.

Chapter 7 Verses 16-17	**Chapter 7 Verses 16-17** **Commentary**
¹⁶Never again will they hunger; never again will they thirst. The sun will not beat down on them, nor any scorching heat. ¹⁷For the Lamb at the center of the throne will be their shepherd; 'he will lead them to springs of living water.' 'And God will wipe away every tear from their eyes.' [NIV]	**7:16-17** The blessings will be great: no hunger, no thirst, perfect security as the sun shall not strike them, nor any heat; perfect guidance as the Lamb will be there to shepherd them and lead them; and perfect joy: **God will wipe away every tear from their eyes**. (Psalm 23:1; 121:5-6; Isaiah 25:8a; 49:10; 51:11; Matthew 5:4; Revelation 21:4).

Chapter 7 Verses 16-17 References	Chapter 7 Verses 16-17 References Commentary
Vv. 16-17 **Psalm 23:1** A psalm of David. The LORD is my shepherd, I shall not want. [NIV]	**Vv. 16-17** The first verse of the 23rd Psalm, with the pronoun **my**, applies only to those who actually believe on Him to truly be their Shepherd.
Psalm 121:5-6 ⁵The LORD watches over you- the LORD is your shade at your right hand; ⁶the sun will not harm you by day, nor the moon by night. [NIV]	Psalm 121:5-6 guarantees that the great Sovereign of the universe is personally involved in the security of the most obscure saint, protecting us from every evil influence. These verses promise welcome protection and freedom from the chains of demon possession.
Isaiah 25:8a he will swallow up death forever. The Sovereign LORD will wipe away the tears from all faces; [NIV] **Isaiah 49:10** "They shall neither hunger nor thirst, neither heat nor sun shall strike them; for He who has mercy on them will lead them, even by the springs of water He will guide them."	Isaiah 25:8a; 49:10; and 51:11 tell us that Christ conquers **death** (by His resurrection and by raising the Tribulation saints who have died), abolishes sorrow, protects His chosen.
Isaiah 51:11 So the ransomed of the Lord shall return, And come to Zion with singing, With everlasting joy on their heads. They shall obtain joy and gladness; Sorrow and sighing shall flee away.	And in Isaiah 51:11 Christ will summon all of Israel to return to the land. (Revelation 7:1-3; Romans 11:26)
Matthew 5:4 "Blessed are those who mourn, for they will be comforted." [NIV]	The mourning in Matthew 5:4 does not refer to normal loss of human life. *It is the sorrow one experiences because of fellowship with the Lord Jesus. It is an active sharing of the world's hurting, killings, and sinning against Jesus. Therefore, it includes, not only sorrow for one's own sin, but also sorrow because of the world's rejection of the Savior.*
Revelation 21:4 "And God will wipe away every tear from their eyes; there shall be no more death, nor sorrow, nor crying. There shall be no more pain, for the former things have passed away."	Revelation 21:4 confirms the last verse of this Chapter seven.

Chapter 8 Verses 1-2	Chapter 8 Verses 1-2 Commentary
	Seventh Seal is Opened
	First Four Trumpets will Signal the Beginning of the Tribulation on the Earth
¹When He opened the seventh seal, there was silence in heaven for about half an hour. ²And I saw the seven angels who stand before God, and to them were given seven trumpets.	**8:1-2** Beginning where Chapter 6 left off, the **seventh seal contains the seven trumpets**. The Lamb opens the **seventh seal**, and then **silence** is held **for about half an hour** to **indicate the beginning of these further series of judgments.** The first four trumpets will be blasted in this Chapter 8.

Chapter 8 Verses 1-2
References

Chapter 8 Verses 1-2
References Commentary

Chapter 8 Verses 3-6

³Another angel, who had a golden censer, came and stood at the altar. He was given much incense to offer, with the prayers of all the God's people, on the golden altar in front of the throne. ⁴The smoke of the incense, together with the prayers of God's people, went up before God from the angel's hand. ⁵Then the angel took the censer, filled it with fire from the altar, and hurled it on the earth; and there came peals of thunder, rumblings, flashes of lightning and an earthquake. ⁶Then the seven angels who had the seven trumpets prepared to sound them. [NIV]

Chapter 8 Verses 3-6
Commentary

8:3-6

**Incense is often an illustration of prayer (Revelation 5:8). A censer is a pan which holds a small fire for burning the incense oil.

The trumpet judgments may be God's response to the prayers of the saints in Revelation 6:10—a cry for revenge against the enemies of Christ (Psalm 94:1;** Deuteronomy 32:35; **Romans 12:19).

The throwing of the censer to earth represents the coming judgment of the earth. Christ will use the angels to administer the trumpets. The blast of each trumpet symbolizes the execution of God's judgment.** (2 Samuel 22:8-10)

Chapter 8 Verses 3-6
References

Vv. 3-6
Revelation 5:8 Now when He had taken the scroll, the four living creatures and the twenty-four elders fell down before the Lamb, each having a harp, and golden bowls full of incense, which are the prayers of the saints.

Psalm 94:1 O LORD, the God who avenges, O God who avenges, shine forth. [NIV]

Deuteronomy 32:35 "Vengeance is Mine, and recompense; their foot shall slip in *due* time; for the day of their calamity *is* at hand, and the things to come hasten upon them."

Romans 12:19 Beloved, do not avenge yourselves, but *rather* give place to wrath; for it is written, "*Vengeance is Mine, I will repay,*" says the Lord.

2 Samuel 22:8-10 ⁸"Then the earth shook and trembled; the foundations of heaven quaked and were shaken, because He was angry. ⁹Smoke went up from His nostrils, and devouring fire from His mouth; coals were kindled by it. ¹⁰He bowed the heavens also, and came down with darkness under His feet.

Chapter 8 Verses 3-6
References Commentary

Vv. 3-6
Revelation 5:8 refers to coming judgment in the **scroll**. Due to His First and Second Comings—His work as Savior and as Sovereign Judge, Christ has the right to judge, possess, and rule the earth because of His submission to the death of the cross (Philippians 2:8-11).

The faithful remnant of Israel appeal to God in Psalm 94 to bring His **vengeance** to reveal Himself in His hatred of evil. The gloating of the wicked will soon be silenced.

In Deuteronomy 32:35 *God's **vengeance** upon the nations that were used to punish Israel was carried out. As a result, God's people and all the nations were to rejoice, because God avenged Himself and made atonement for His land and His people.*

Concerning Romans 12:19 ***vengeance** is God's prerogative. We **give place to wrath** because God will take care of it for us. Lenski writes, "God has long ago settled the whole matter about exacting justice from wrongdoers. Not one of them will escape. Perfect justice will be done in every case. If any of us interfered, it would be the height of presumption."*

2 Samuel 22:8-10 describe the Lord's vengeance with **His triumphant march from Sinai to the Jordan River.** The description appears to be a prelude to the vengeance that He will be accomplishing prior to His Second Coming.

Chapter 8 Verses 7-11

⁷The first angel sounded his trumpet, and there came hail and fire mixed with blood, and it as hurled down on the earth. A third of the earth was burned up, a third of the trees were burned up, and all the green grass was burned up. [NIV]

⁸The second angel sounded his trumped, and something like a huge mountain, all ablaze, was thrown into the sea. A third of the sea turned into blood, ⁹a third of the living creatures in the sea died, and a third of the ships were destroyed. [NIV]

¹⁰The third angel sounded his trumped, and a great star, blazing like a torch, fell from the sky on a third of the rivers and on the springs of water— ¹¹the name of the star is Wormwood. A third of the waters turned bitter, and many people died from the waters that had become bitter. [NIV]

Chapter 8 Verses 7-11
Commentary

8:7
The **first trumpet brings literal **fire and hail**, and causes the destruction of much of the vegetation on earth. Famine and shortage of oxygen will result.** (Ezekiel 38:22; Revelation 9:4)

8:8-9
The **second trumpet turns one **third** of the **sea** into **blood** and one **third** of the sea creatures and **ships** will be **destroyed**.** Commerce will suffer.

8:10-11
The **third trumpet makes one **third** of the earth's fresh **water** turn bitter causing widespread thirst and death.** Prolonged sustainability of life on the earth's land will end. **Wormwood is literally *undrinkable*** (Deuteronomy 30:18-20).

Chapter 8 Verses 7-11
References

V. 7
Ezekiel 38:22 "And I will bring him to judgment with pestilence and bloodshed; I will rain down on him, on his troops, and on the many peoples who *are* with him, flooding rain, great hailstones, fire, and brimstone."
Revelation 9:4 They were told not to harm the grass of the earth or any plant or tree, but only those people who did not have the seal of God on their foreheads. [NIV]

Vv. 10-11
Deuteronomy 30:18-20 ¹⁸"I announce to you today that you shall surely perish; you shall not prolong *your* days in the land which you cross over the Jordan to go in and possess. ¹⁹I call heaven and earth as witnesses today against you, *that* I have set before you life and death, blessing and cursing; therefore choose life, that both you and your descendants may live; ²⁰that you may love the LORD your God, that you may obey His voice, and that you may cling to Him, for He *is* your life and the length of your days; and that you may dwell in the land which the LORD swore to your fathers, to Abraham, Isaac, and Jacob, to give them."

Chapter 8 Verses 7-11
References Commentary

V. 7
Ezekiel 38:22 and Revelation 9:4:
depicting the destruction of the enemies [Gog and Magog in first half of Tribulation] of God's people and reminds us of the Lord's promise in Isaiah 54:17:
"No weapon formed against you shall prosper.. This is the heritage of the servants of the LORD."

God's enemy will be unable to prevail against these supernatural disasters.

Vv. 10-11
In Deuteronomy 30:18-20 *the people were called to choose between **life** and good on the one hand, and **death** and evil on the other—**life** for obedience, but **death** for disobedience. Moses strongly pleaded with them to prefer **blessing** over **cursing**—to **choose life** so **that both** them **and** their **descendants may live**. The desired response (choosing to obey and live) brought good results, including **length of...days** and abundant spiritual **life**, implied by the words **that you may cling to Him**. The only alternative was that of **cursing**.*

Chapter 8 Verses 12-13

¹²The fourth angel sounded his trumpet, and a third of the sun was struck, a third of the moon, and a third of the stars, so that a third of them turned dark. A third of the day was without light, and also a third of the night. [NIV]

¹³As I watched, I heard an eagle that was flying in midair call out in a loud voice: "Woe! Woe! Woe to the inhabitants of the earth, because of the trumpet blasts about to be sounded by the other three angels!" [NIV]

Chapter 8 Verses 12-13
Commentary

8:12
The **fourth trumpet takes away one **third** of the light from the heavens both **day** and **night** (Matthew 24:29; Luke 21:25).**

8:13
The last three trumpets will bring such severity that trumpets five and six will be in Chapter 9, but **trumpet** number seven will be reserved until Revelation 11:15. **Here in 8:13 we find that these last three are so severe that there is a three-fold **woe** expressed to initially describe them.**

A single **woe** can be defined as sadness, despair, misery, distress, affliction, mournfulness...all due to a catastrophic calamity. A triple **woe** must be exceedingly miserable.

Chapter 8 Verses 12-13
References

V. 12

Matthew 24:29 "Immediately after the tribulation of those days the sun will be darkened and the moon will not give its light; the stars will fall from heaven, and the powers of the heavens will be shaken."

Luke 21:25 "There will be signs in the sun, moon and stars. On the earth, nations will be in anguish and perplexity at the roaring and tossing of the sea." [NIV]

Chapter 8 Verses 12-13
References Commentary

V. 12

Matthew 24:29 and Luke 21:25 promise a sad situation on this earth. *After the close of the Great Tribulation there will be terrifying disturbances in the heavens. Since the moon's light is only a reflection of the sun's, there will be only darkness—no light. The vast cosmic upheavals will undoubtedly affect the earth's weather, tides, and seasons.*

We thank our God for the promise to send His Son to the air to take us up to be with Him prior to these seven years of Tribulation trials, temptations, deceptions, and persecutions; and before the last three-and-a-half years of enormous sufferings in the Great Tribulation.

Chapter 9 Verses 1-3

**Chapter 9 Verses 1-3
Commentary**

Trumpets Five and Six will Blast the First Two of Three Coming Woes

¹Then the fifth angel sounded his trumpet, and I saw a star that had fallen from the sky to the earth. The star was given the key to the shaft of the Abyss. ²When he opened the Abyss, smoke rose from it like the smoke from a gigantic furnace. The sun and sky were darkened by the smoke from the Abyss. ³And out of the smoke locusts came down on the earth and were given power like that of scorpions of the earth. [NIV]

9:1-3
The first woe will come as a result of this fifth trumpet. The **fifth** trumpet blasts a **star** (an angel) from **the sky to the earth** that has been **given the key to the** bottomless pit (Hādēs—the *abyss* in Greek—the dwelling place of demons). The emitted **smoke** darkens the sun and air, (Joel 2:1-2, 10-11; Matthew 24:29), locusts come out of the **Abyss** (pit) having the power of scorpions to torment, but not kill the unbelievers on the earth for five months.

The sounding of the seventh trumpet in Revelation 11:14-15 will begin the third woe.

The locusts compare to those in the seventh plague against Egypt and the Pharaoh in Exodus 10:4.
In verse 2 the **Abyss** (bottomless pit) is an immeasurable depth underworld abode of demons (Luke 8:31). Jesus casts out demons from people possessing them and locked in the demons (Revelation 20:1, 3).

Chapter 9 Verses 1-3
References

Vv. 1-3
Joel 2:1-2 ¹Blow the trumpet in Zion, and sound an alarm in My holy mountain! Let all the inhabitants of the land tremble; for the day of the LORD is coming, for it is at hand: ²A day of darkness and gloominess, a day of clouds and thick darkness, like the morning *clouds* spread over the mountains...

Joel 2:10-11 ¹⁰The earth quakes before them, the heavens tremble; the sun and moon grow dark, and the stars diminish their brightness. ¹¹The LORD gives voice before His army, for His camp is very great; for strong *is the One* who executes His word. For the day of the LORD *is* great and very terrible; who can endure it?

Matthew 24:29 "Immediately after the tribulation of those days the sun will be darkened and the moon will not give its light; the stars will fall from heaven, and the powers of the heavens will be shaken."

Exodus 10:4 'Or else if you refuse to let My people go, behold, tomorrow I will bring locusts into your territory.'

Chapter 9 Verses 1-3
References Commentary

Vv. 1-3
In Joel 2:1-2 **the **trumpet** is used to **alarm** the people to the seriousness of the crisis that is upon them.**

Joel 2:10-11 Referring to Christ's Second Coming at the end of the seven years, Joel predicts the greatness of **the Day of the Lord**.

Matthew 24:29 previews beyond to the Second Advent—the Day of the Lord—at the close of the Great Tribulation. *There will be terrifying disturbances in the heavens. The sun will be darkened, the moon will not have the sun's light to give light at night, the stars will plunge from heaven and planets will be moved out of their orbits. Such vast cosmic upheavals will probably affect gravity, tides, seasons,* tsunamis, tornadoes, hurricanes, floods, fires, earthquakes, volcanoes and more.

Exodus 10:4: The locusts in Exodus 10 ate trees and herbs, not men; but the locusts in Revelation 9:3 tormented *men* but not grass or trees.

Chapter 9 Verses 4-6

⁴They were told not to harm the grass of the earth or any plant or tree, but only those people who did not have the seal of God on their foreheads. ⁵They were not allowed to kill them but only to torture them for five months. And the agony they suffered was like that of a scorpion when it strikes. [NIV]

⁶During those days people will seek death but will not find it; they will long to die, but death will elude them. [NIV]

Chapter 9 Verses 4-6 Commentary

9:4-5
Back in Revelation 8:7 all green grass was burned up. But obviously this only acted to fertilize the soil for the grass to return. The locusts' stings do not kill people, but it inflicts torment that lasts for five months. It produces such intense suffering that men will want to die, but they can't. The effect of scorpions will be brought out again in Revelation 16:2. However, the 144,000 men of Israel who **have the seal of God on their foreheads** (from Revelation 7:2-4) are not to be harmed.

9:6
In Revelation 9:6 [much like Revelation 6:15-17) the unbelievers wanted to hide and even choose **death** to escape the torment (Jeremiah 8:3).

The king of those in the bottomless pit is named *Abaddon* (Destruction) in Hebrew, but *Apollyon* (Destroyer) in Greek. This would be Satan.

Chapter 9 Verses 4-6
References

Vv. 4-5
Revelation 7:2-4 ²Then I saw an angel coming up from the east, having the seal of the living God. He called out in a loud voice to the four angels who had been given power to harm the land and the sea: ³"Do not harm the land or the sea or the trees until we put a seal on the foreheads of the servants of our God." ⁴Then I heard the number of those who were sealed: 144,000 from all the tribes of Israel. [NIV]

V. 6
Revelation 6:15-17 ¹⁵And the kings of the earth, the great men, the rich men, the commanders, the mighty men, every slave and every free man, hid themselves in the caves and in the rocks of the mountains, ¹⁶and said to the mountains and rocks, "Fall on us and hide us from the face of Him who sits on the throne and from the wrath of the Lamb! ¹⁷For the great day of His wrath has come, and who is able to stand?"

Jeremiah 8:3 And death shall be chosen rather than life by all the residue of them that remain of this evil family, which remain in all the places whither I have driven them," saith the LORD of hosts. [KJV]

Chapter 9 Verses 4-6
References Commentary

Vv. 4-5
Revelation 7:2-4 is John's vision of *the **four** (fallen) **angels** standing at the four corners of the earth and holding back the four winds that will burst a great storm onto the world. However, the angels are commanded to delay this terrible destruction until **the servants of God** have been given the seal **of God on their foreheads**. Twelve thousand persons from each of **the** twelve **tribes of Israel** are then **sealed**.*

The believers of the Church Age are already sealed: 2 Timothy 2:19a: *Nevertheless the solid foundation of God stands, having this seal: "The Lord knows those who are His,"*

Ephesians 1:13: *In Him you also trusted, after you heard* [absorbed] *the word of truth, the gospel of your salvation; in whom also, having believed, you were sealed with the Holy Spirit of promise.*

2 Corinthians 1:22: *Who hath also sealed us, and given the earnest of the Spirit in our hearts.* [KJV]

V. 6
Revelation 6:15 calls to our attention, *not surprisingly, all classes of society will be seized with panic. They prefer to be crushed by tumbling rocks than to endure the judgment of **the wrath of the Lamb!*** (Revelation 6:16-17)

In Jeremiah 8:1 *the Babylonian invaders dig up the graves of the previous believing kings, princes, priests, prophets, and inhabitants of Jerusalem exposing their bones to the heavens. Then in Jeremiah 8:3 those Jewish observers who chose to sin and not to repent wished they could die.*

Chapter 9 Verses 7-12

⁷The locusts looked like horses prepared for battle. On their heads they wore something like crowns of gold, and their faces resembled human faces. ⁸Their hair was like women's hair, and their teeth were like lions' teeth. ⁹They had breastplates like breastplates of iron, and the sound of their wings was like the thundering of many horses and chariots rushing into battle. ¹⁰They had tails with stingers, like scorpions, and in their tails they had power to torment people for five months. ¹¹They had as king over them the angel of the Abyss, whose name in Hebrew is Abaddon and in Greek is Apollyon (that is, Destroyer). [NIV]

¹²The first woe is past; two other woes are yet to come. [NIV]

Chapter 9 Verses 7-12
Commentary

9:7-11
Where here 9:7 says **resembled human faces** implies they were creatures of intelligence. **Hair like women's** suggests they were attractive and seductive. **Lion**-like **teeth** connote they were ferocious and cruel. The **iron breastplates** made them difficult to attack and destroy.

*Their noisy **wings** created a terrifying and demoralizing atmosphere. The **tails like scorpions** equipped them to torture both physically and mentally.* Arabs remove locusts' heads, wings, legs, and stew them with butter. The locusts appear as monsters representing satanic agencies. (The locusts life span is *five months*).

Verse 10 confirms God's plan for what His Word says in verse 5—**to torment** men **for five months**.

In verse 11 ***Abaddon** is Hebrew for *Destruction*, but in **Greek the name is Apollyon** meaning *Destroyer*. It is Satan!*

9:12
*The first of three woes (Revelation 8:13) **is past** (Revelation 9:2-11). The worst is yet to come. The judgments increase in intensity.*

The second woe will begin in Revelation 9:13 when the sixth angel will sound the trumpet.

The third and final woe will begin in Revelation 11:13-14 and end in Revelation 16:17.

Chapter 9 Verses 7-12
References

Chapter 9 Verses 7-12
References Commentary

Chapter 9 Verses 13-14   **Chapter 9 Verses 13-14**
                                                                            Commentary

9:13-14

[13] The sixth angel sounded his trumpet, and I heard a voice coming from the four horns of the golden altar that is before God. [14] It said to the sixth angel who had the trumpet, "Release the four angels who are bound at the great river Eūphratēs." [NIV]

The **sixth** trumpet blasts and God commands the **sixth angel** to **release the four angels who are bound at the river Eūphratēs.** (Revelation 16:12-14).

We are reminded in Revelation 7:3 that they are not to harm the 144,000 of the tribes of Israel.

Chapter 9 Verses 13-14
References

Vv. 13-14
Revelation 16:12-14 ¹²The sixth angel poured out his bowl on the great river Eūphrātēs, and its water was dried up to prepare the way for the kings from the East. ¹³Then I saw three evil spirits that looked like frogs; they came out of the mouth of the dragon, out of the mouth of the beast and out of the mouth of the false prophet. ¹⁴They are spirits of demons performing miraculous signs, and they go out to the kings of the whole world, to gather them for the battle on the great day of God Almighty. [NIV]

Revelation 7:3 "Do not harm the land or the sea or the trees until we put a seal on the foreheads of the servants of our God." [NIV]

Chapter 9 Verses 13-14
References Commentary

Vv. 13-14
Here in Chapter 9 we read of the command for **the sixth angel** to sound his trumpet, and in Revelation 16:12-14 the situation is going to be, if one could possibly imagine, greatly worsened.
In verse 13 **three evil spirits** is representing the false trinity, the **dragon** Satan, the **beast** Antichrist, and the false prophet.
Of course Chapter 16 is still to come, but here is a preview to see what happens when the sixth **bowl** is **poured out**. *The **water** of the **Eūphrātēs** River will be **dried up**, allowing the armies **from the East** to march toward the land of Israel. John sees **three** frog-like **spirits coming out of the mouth of the dragon, ... the beast and ... the false prophet**—Satan's false trinity* — Satan playing the part of God, the Antichrist man the part of Christ, and the False Prophet the part of the Holy Spirit. These three counterfeits are *demonic **spirits, performing** miracles to deceive the world's rulers, and to lure them to a climactic soon coming **battle** against the Second Coming of the Lord Jesus Christ on the **great day of God Almighty**.*
The seventh angel is yet to sound his trumpet...in Chapter 11:15. But first, in Chapter 10, the next chapter, *another angel* will cry out resulting in *seven thunders*.

Revelation 7:3 begins the protection of the saved Jews. Once saved, they are no longer appointed to wrath. In agreement, Revelation 9:4: *They were told not to harm the grass of the earth or any plant or tree, but only those people who did not have the seal of God on their foreheads.* [NIV]
God's protection continues throughout the Great Tribulation—the last three-and-a-half years as confirmed in Revelation 12:14: *The woman* [the Israelis] *was given the two wings of a great eagle, so that she might fly to the place prepared for her in the desert, where she would be taken care of for a time, times and half a time,* [the last 3½ years] *out of the serpent's reach.* [NIV]
Therefore, the demonic spirits of Chapter 16 will have neither influence nor negative effect upon the 144,000 sealed forever believers.

Chapter 9 Verses 15-21

¹⁵And the four angels who had been kept ready for this very hour and day and month and year were released to kill a third of mankind. ¹⁶The number of the mounted troops was twice ten thousand times ten thousand. I heard their number. ¹⁷The horses and riders I saw in my vision looked like this: Their breastplates were fiery red, dark blue, and yellow as sulfur. The heads of the horses resembled the heads of lions; and out of their mouths came fire, smoke, and sulfur. ¹⁸A third of mankind was killed by the three plagues of fire, smoke and sulfur that came out of their mouths. ¹⁹The power of the horses was in their mouths and in their tails; for their tails were like snakes, having heads with which they inflict injury. [NIV]

²⁰The rest of mankind who were not killed by these plagues still did not repent of the work of their hands; they did not stop worshiping demons, and idols of gold, silver, bronze, stone and wood—idols that cannot see or hear or walk. ²¹Nor did they repent of their murders, their magic arts, their sexual immorality or their thefts. [NIV]

Chapter 9 Verses 15-21
Commentary

9:15-19
These **four angels** will be **released to kill** one **third of** remaining **mankind** with the use of three plagues from an army (**troops**)—the Lord's army—**of two hundred million horsemen**. The **horses**—*not the riders*—issue *three plagues: **fire**, **smoke**, and **brimstone** to kill one **third of mankind**. Not only do the **horses** kill with their **mouths**, but they also wound with their serpent-like **tails**.* This is the **power** of our God! His power will be even more realized when He returns for the Battle of Armageddon:
In Zechariah 13:8 *"And it shall come to pass in all the land, says the LORD, that two-thirds in it shall be cut off and die, but one-third shall be left in it:"*
During the entire Seven-year Tribulation, two-thirds of all Jews will be slaughtered.

9:20-21
But the rest of mankind who were not killed by these plagues still did not repent (Jeremiah 8:6).

*They continued worshipping lifeless and impotent **idols** made with their own hands. And they did not **repent** of their **murders** or their **magic arts** (witchcrafts; pretenders to magic powers; sorceries) or their **sexual immorality** or their **thefts**.*
Only by believing, repenting and being born again with a new heart can a sinner's character change.

Chapter 9 Verses 15-21
References

Chapter 9 Verses 15-21
References Commentary

Vv. 20-21
Jeremiah 8:6 I have listened attentively, but they do not say what is right. No one repents of his wickedness, saying, "What have I done?" Each pursues his own course like a horse charging into battle. [NIV]

Vv. 20-21
Jeremiah 8:6 is mirrored here by Revelation 9:21.

Chapter 10 Verses 1-3	Chapter 10 Verses 1-3 Commentary
	Another Angel with the Little Book and Seven Thunders
¹I saw still another mighty angel coming down from heaven, clothed with a cloud. And a rainbow *was* on his head, his face *was* like the sun, and his feet like pillars of fire. ²He had a little book open in his hand. And he set his right foot on the sea and *his* left *foot* on the land, ³and cried with a loud voice, as *when* a lion roars. When he cried out, seven thunders uttered their voices.	**10:1-3** **Another mighty angel** comes down to earth **from heaven** *holding a **little book**—possibly containing a record of impending judgments.* **The description of this angel *resembles* that of Christ (Revelation 1:13-16),** but the text does not confirm it is Him. *The angel cries out in a loud voice and **seven thunders** are heard.*

Chapter 10 Verses 1-3 References	Chapter 10 Verses 1-3 References Commentary

Vv. 1-3

Revelation 1:13-16 ¹³and in the midst of the seven lampstands *One* like the Son of Man, clothed with a garment down to the feet and girded about the chest with a golden band. ¹⁴His head and hair *were* white like wool, as white as snow, and His eyes like a flame of fire; ¹⁵His feet *were* like fine brass, as if refined in a furnace, and His voice as the sound of many waters; ¹⁶He had in His right hand seven stars, out of His mouth went a sharp two-edged sword, and His countenance *was like* the sun shining in its strength.

Vv. 1-3

Revelation 1:13-16 **is a description of Jesus Christ as Judge (John 5:22, 27).

The **seven lampstands** are identified in Revelation 1:20 as the seven churches mentioned in Revelation 1:11.

The Son of Man is a Messianic title from Daniel 7:13,** and, since He, God Himself, was born in the flesh of Mary in the lineage to Adam through [David's son Nathan (2 Samuel 5:14)], this ****Son of Man** was Jesus' most used designation for Himself.** However, He also referred to Himself as the "only begotten Son of God" (John 3:16).

The **garment is a judge's robe. His **white hair** symbolizes justice, purity, and glory. **Fire** is also a symbol of judgment. The **brass** and the **sound** of the **voice** show Christ's authority and power. The **seven stars** are identified in verse 20 as the angels of the seven churches. The **sword** also represents Christ's judgment (Revelation 19:15) of the churches and the world through His Word. His **countenance** or face was **like the sun** as the glory of God shone forth.**

Chapter 10 Verses 4-7

⁴Now when the seven thunders uttered their voices, I was about to write; but I heard a voice from heaven saying to me, "Seal up the things which the seven thunders uttered, and do not write them." ⁵The angel whom I saw standing on the sea and on the land raised up his hand to heaven ⁶and swore by Him who lives forever and ever, who created heaven and the things that are in it, the earth and the things that are in it, and the sea and the things that are in it, that there should be delay no longer, ⁷but in the days of the sounding of the seventh angel, when he is about to sound, the mystery of God would be finished, as He declared to His servants the prophets.

Chapter 10 Verses 4-7
Commentary

10:4-7
John is told not to write what he hears from the **thunders**. Daniel was also told not to write the vision that God had given him:
Daniel 8:26   *"The vision of the evenings and mornings that has been given you is true, but seal up the vision, for it concerns the distant future."* [NIV]
Daniel 12:4   *"But you, Daniel, close up and seal the words of the scroll until the time of the end. Many will go here and there to increase knowledge."* [NIV]
Daniel 12:9   *He replied, "Go your way, Daniel, because the words are closed up and sealed until the time of the end."* [NIV]
The time of the end has come; the *words* are no longer **sealed**:
Revelation 22:10   *Then he told me, "Do not seal up the words of the prophecy of this book, because the time is near."* [NIV]
The eternally vital importance of this verse cannot be overemphasized. The **angel** swears to God in heaven that He, the Lord Jesus Christ, has the authority to perform these judgments (John 5:22, 26-27) because He is omnipotent (all powerful), omnipresent (everywhere all the time), omniscient (knowledgeable of all things past, present and future), even able to know our thoughts (Psalm 139:1-16; Luke 5:22; 6:8; 11:17; 24:38), and because He is the Creator (Psalm 19:1; Hebrews 1:8a, 10), and that **there should be no more delay**.
The **seventh** and final trumpet will be blasted soon. (Revelation 11:15).

Here in 10:7, when the two prophet witnesses finish giving the testimony of the mystery of God, they will be killed, left to be seen for three-and-a-half days, and then be seen ascending to heaven (Revelation 11:3-12.)

Chapter 10 Verses 4-7
References

Vv. 4-7
John 5:22 *"For the Father judges no one, but has committed all judgment to the Son."*
John 5:26-27 *²⁶"For as the Father has life in Himself, so He has granted the Son to have life in Himself, ²⁷ and has given Him authority to execute judgment also, because He is the Son of Man."*
Luke 5:22 *But when Jesus perceived their thoughts, He answered and said to them, "Why are you reasoning in your hearts?"*
Luke 6:8 *But He knew their thoughts, and said to the man who had the withered hand, "Arise and stand here." And he arose and stood.*
Luke 11:17 *But He, knowing their thoughts, said to them: "Every kingdom divided against itself is brought to desolation, and a house divided against a house falls."*
Luke 24:38 *And He said to them, "Why are you troubled? And why do doubts arise in your hearts?"*

Psalm 19:1
Hebrews 1:8a
Hebrews 1:10
Revelation 11:15

-CONTINUED ON NEXT SET OF PAGES UNDER REFERENCES!-

Chapter 10 Verses 4-7
References Commentary

Vv. 4-7
*For the Lord Jesus to be able to do this judging (John 5:22; John 5:26-27), He must also be God as the Father is God. He must have the knowledge, perfect righteousness, and **authority**. He must be able to discern the thoughts and motives of men's hearts* (Matthew 15:19; Mark 7:21; Luke 5:22; 6:8; 11:17; 24:38; 1 Corinthians 3:20; Hebrews 4:12).

How strange it was that the Judge of all the earth should stand being judged before the Jews, asserting His authority, and yet they did not recognize Him!

-CONTINUED ON NEXT SET OF PAGES UNDER REFERENCES COMMENTARY!-

Chapter 10 Verses 4-7   **Chapter 10 Verses 4-7**
Commentary

-VERSES 4-7 REPEATED FROM PREVIOUS PAGE-

-PART OF COMMENTARY VERSES 4-7 REPEATED FROM PREVIOUS PAGE-

10:4-7

⁴Now when the seven thunders uttered their voices, I was about to write; but I heard a voice from heaven saying to me, "Seal up the things which the seven thunders uttered, and do not write them." ⁵The angel whom I saw standing on the sea and on the land raised up his hand to heaven ⁶and swore by Him who lives forever and ever, who created heaven and the things that are in it, the earth and the things that are in it, and the sea and the things that are in it, that there should be delay no longer, ⁷but in the days of the sounding of the seventh angel, when he is about to sound, the mystery of God would be finished, as He declared to His servants the prophets.

The eternally vital importance of verses 5-6 cannot be overemphasized. The **angel** swears to God in heaven that He, the Lord Jesus Christ, has the authority to perform these judgments (John 5:22, 26-27) because He is omnipotent (all powerful), omnipresent (everywhere all the time), omniscient (knowledgeable of all things past, present and future), even able to know our thoughts (Psalm 139:1-16; Luke 5:22; 6:8; 11:17; 24:38), and because He is the Creator (Psalm 19:1; Hebrews 1:8a, 10), and that **there should be no more delay**.

The **seventh** and final trumpet will be blasted soon. (Revelation 11:15).

Here in 10:7, when the two prophet witnesses finish giving the testimony of the mystery of God, they will be killed, left to be seen for three-and-a-half days, and then be seen ascending to heaven (Revelation 11:3-12.)

| Chapter 10 Verses 4-7 | Chapter 10 Verses 4-7 |
| References | References Commentary |

-CONTINUED FROM PREVIOUS PAGE-   -CONTINUED FROM PREVIOUS PAGE-

Vv. 4-7

Vv. 4-7

Psalm 19:1 THE heavens declare the glory of God; and the firmament shows His handiwork.
Hebrews 1:8a But to the Son *He says*: ...
Hebrews 1:10 And: *"You LORD, in the beginning laid the foundation of the earth, and the heavens are the work of Your hands."*

Psalm 19:1, Hebrews 1:8a and 10 not only tell us that God is our Creator, but the Father Himself is quoted in Hebrews 1 confirming that all of creation was done by the hands of God the Son, Jesus Christ. John 1:2-3 and Colossians 1:16-17 further clarify these truths.

Revelation 11:15 Then the seventh angel sounded: And there were loud voices in heaven, saying, "The kingdoms of this world have become *the kingdoms* of our Lord and of His Christ, and He shall reign forever and ever!"

The **seventh** trumpet in Revelation 11:15 *reveals that the Great Tribulation is over [(in this first of four chronological versions)] and the reign of Christ in His millennial kingdom has begun.* **The vials (or bowls; Revelation 16:1) are probably contained in the judgment of the **seventh** trumpet. They will occur in a very brief period of time at the end of the Great Tribulation. The Second Coming of Christ, while a great blessing for believers, will be God's most severe judgment of the earth. The **kingdoms of this world** will be completely overthrown by the coming kingdom of Christ (Revelation 19:11-21; Daniel 2:34-35, 44) who will **reign forever and ever** (Daniel 7:13-14, 27).**

Chapter 10 Verses 8-11

⁸Then the voice that I heard from heaven spoke to me once more: "Go, take the scroll that lies open in the hand of the angel who is standing on the sea and on the land." ⁹So I went to the angel and asked him to give me the little scroll. He said to me, "Take it and eat it. It will turn your stomach sour, but 'in your mouth it will be as sweet as honey.'" ¹⁰I took the little scroll from the angel's hand and ate it. It tasted as sweet as honey in my mouth but when I had eaten it, my stomach turned sour. [NIV]

¹¹Then I was told, "You must prophesy again about many peoples, nations, languages, and kings." [NIV]

Chapter 10 Verses 8-11
Commentary

10:8-10
The angel commanded John to **eat** the **little book** which would be **sweet** in his **mouth** but **bitter** in his **stomach**. The LORD caused Ezekiel to **eat** the scroll with writings on it, and it was like **honey** in sweetness in Ezekiel's **mouth** (Ezekiel 3:1-3).

It is **sweet** to read of God's triumph over Satan and how all sin will be done away with, but it is **bitter** to contemplate the eternal doom of all who reject the Savior. We, too, need to *eat*, that is, absorb and digest God's Word. When we set our hearts to know and understand God, and pray to Him in His will, He hears us just as He did in Jeremiah 15:16 and Daniel 10:11-12. (Acts 8:30-31)

10:11
John is told to **prophesy** a second time (key to understanding the chronology of the Book of Revelation is that the prophecy and its warnings will be repeated, but in more detail) to better enhance understanding of the personages and movements of the Tribulation Period. Chapters 12 to 19 fulfill this repeated second prophecy mandate. (Ephesians 1:17-18)

Chapter 10 Verses 8-11
References

Vv. 8-10
Ezekiel 3:1-3 ¹Moreover He said to me, "Son of man, eat what you find; eat this scroll, and go, speak to the house of Israel." ²So I opened my mouth, and He caused me to eat that scroll. ³And He said to me, "Son of man, feed your belly, and fill your stomach with this scroll that I give you." So I ate, and it was in my mouth like honey in sweetness.

Jeremiah 15:16 Your words were found and I ate them, and Your word was to me the joy and rejoicing of my heart; for I am called by Your name, O LORD God of hosts.

Daniel 10:11-12 ¹¹He said, "O Daniel, you who are highly esteemed, consider carefully the words I am about to speak to you, and stand up, for I have now been sent to you." And when he said this to me, I stood up trembling. ¹²Then he continued, "Do not be afraid, Daniel. Since the first day that you set your mind to gain understanding and to humble yourself before your God, your words were heard, and I have come in response to them." [NIV]

Acts 8:30-31 ³⁰Then Phillip ran up to the chariot and heard the man reading Isaiah the prophet. "Do you understand what you are reading?" Philip asked. ³¹"How can I," he said, "unless someone explains it to me?" So he invited Philip to come up and sit with him. [NIV]

V.11
Ephesians 1:17-18 ¹⁷that the God of our Lord Jesus Christ, the Father of glory, may give to you the spirit of wisdom and revelation in the knowledge of Him, ¹⁸the eyes of your understanding being enlightened; that you may know what is the hope of His calling, what are the riches of the glory of His inheritance in the saints,

Chapter 10 Verses 8-11
References Commentary

Vv. 8-10
Ezekiel **ate** the **scroll**, as commanded in Ezekiel 3:1-3. As we see here in Revelation 10:8-10, John did the same thing. *Every prophet, that is, preacher, needs to absorb the Word of God, making it part of his own life* —in order to be worthy and able to transmit it to others in truth which would please, honor, and glorify God.

Jeremiah 15:16 reveals that even though Jeremiah had been so faithful and yet suffered and was persecuted, he **found joy and rejoicing in** his **heart** with God's **words**.

Daniel 10:11-12: **he** in verse 11 is Michael the angel. Daniel 10:11-12 also depicts the tremendous value of us being humble and hungering and thirsting for God's Word just as we are now doing in this study of *The Revelation of Jesus Christ*. It goes right back to Revelation 1:3: *Blessed is he who reads and those who hear the words of this prophecy, and keep those things which are written in it; for the time is near.*
(Also confirmed in Revelation 22:7)

Acts 8:30-31 gives a perfect example of how all of us who need the help can benefit from gifted Bible teachers to better understand, know, and love our God (Romans 10:14). Verse 31 is speaking of the Ethiopian eunuch who had great authority.

V.11
Ephesians 1:17-18: John is told to repeat the prophecy and Paul, the apostle, also repeats it here in Ephesians and in 1 Corinthians 2:13-14. God truly wants us to *know* Him.

Chapter 11

Chapter 11
Commentary

First Half of Tribulation Ends in this Chapter

Note:

All the things we've been reading since the beginning of chapter 6 and right through to the end of this upcoming chapter 11 will take place without the presence of those who believed in the Messiah, the Savior—our Lord Jesus Christ. These, who are called saints, will have been raptured (in Revelation 4:1) and will be in heaven during all this dreadful, horrifying time of the Seven-year Tribulation (Romans 5:9).

Arriving here in Chapter 11, coming to the end of the first half of Tribulation, it would be well to look back concerning some of the sequence of events thus far: 2 Thessalonians 2:7-8; Romans 5:9; 1 Thessalonians 5:9; 1 Thessalonians 1:10; John 3:36

Chapter 11
References

Chapter 11
References Commentary

2 Thessalonians 2:7-8 ⁷For the mystery of lawlessness is already at work; only He who now restrains will do so until He is taken out of the way. ⁸And then the lawless one will be revealed, whom the Lord will consume with the breath of His mouth and destroy with the brightness of His coming.

Romans 5:9 Much more then, having now been justified by His blood, we shall be saved from wrath through Him.

1 Thessalonians 5:9 For God did not appoint us to suffer wrath but to receive salvation through our Lord Jesus Christ. [NIV]

2 Thessalonians 2:7-8; Romans 5:9; and 1 Thessalonians 5:9 confirm that the Church, indwelled by the Holy Spirit, will be raptured before the Antichrist can be revealed. When the Antichrist promises peace, he will be revealed to those who missed the Rapture.

In Romans 5:9 where it says **justified**, believers are justified (saved) to be seen as righteous in the eyes of God simply because they had faith and belief in the Lord Jesus Christ (Romans 3:22). Being righteous means being perfect; but since none of us are perfect, the Lord Jesus was—and is—perfectly righteous for those who believe in Him is—perfectly righteous, and upon believing in Him dying in our place, that we are forgiven by His shed blood, that by the power of God, He was raised back to life from being dead—and God promises to also raise us who believe this truth (Romans 3:21-26). Further, once saved, Christ does not allow His betrothed bride to be handed over to wrath—neither the wrath of God nor the wrath of Satan and his Antichrist:

Revelation 12:12: *"Therefore rejoice, you heavens and you who dwell in them! But woe to the earth and the sea, because the devil has gone down to you! He is filled with fury, because he knows that his time is short."* [NIV]

Chapter 11 Verse 1	**Chapter 11 Verse 1** **Commentary**
¹I was given a reed like a measuring rod and was told, "Go and measure the temple of God and the altar, with its worshipers. [NIV]	**11:1** Zechariah 2:1-2 is a precursor to measuring Millennial Jerusalem compared to the Tribulation temple here in verse 1 and the city, its gates and walls in Revelation 21:15. The temple that was built in 515BC (Ezra 6:15) was destroyed in AD 70 (Luke 21:24) and will be rebuilt during the Tribulation Period (2 Thessalonians 2:4).

Chapter 11 Verse 1 References	Chapter 11 Verse 1 References Commentary
V. 1 **Zechariah 2:1-2** "¹I lifted up mine eyes again, and looked, and behold, a man with a measuring line in his hand. ²Then said I, Whither goest thou? And he said unto me, To measure Jerusalem, to see what is the breadth thereof, and what is the length thereof." [KJV]	**V. 1** Zechariah 2:1-2: Zechariah prophecies the rebuilding of Jerusalem in the Millennium.
Revelation 21:15 The angel who talked with me had a measuring rod of gold to measure the city, its gates and its walls. [NIV]	Revelation 21:15 begins the fulfillment of the prophecy.
Ezra 6:15 The temple was completed on the third day of the month of Ādar, in the sixth year of the reign of King Darīus. [NIV]	Ezra 6:15 date: In his commentary *Revive Us Again*, pg. 66. Warren Henderson researched the exact date to be "March 12, 515 BC, approximately four and a half years after they had resumed construction (verses 15-16)." However, this rebuilt temple was destroyed in AD70.
Luke 21:24 "They will fall by the sword and will be taken as prisoners to all the nations. Jerusalem will be trampled on by the Gentiles until the times of the Gentiles are fulfilled." [NIV]	*In Luke 21:24 Jesus prophesies the destruction of the temple and fall of Jerusalem in AD70.* The Jews **will fall by the sword**. The **times of the Gentiles** is not the same as the *fullness* of the Gentiles. *The *fullness* of the Gentiles refers to the Rapture in Romans 11:25. **The times of the Gentiles** refers to the time which began with the Babylonian captivity in 586 BC and continues to the time when Gentile nations will no longer have control over Jerusalem.* So **these times of the Gentiles** control is still ongoing today.

Chapter 11 Verse 2

²But exclude the outer court; do not measure it, because it has been given to the Gentiles. They will trample on the holy city for 42 months. [NIV]

**Chapter 11 Verse 2
Commentary**

11:2
The **outer court outside the temple represents control of Jerusalem and Israel being trampled by **the Gentiles**.** (Ezekiel 40:3, 17)

***The altar** [in verse one] probably pictures the means by which the worshipers approach God—that is—by believing in the work of Christ at Calvary.*

The **forty-two months show that Jerusalem will continue to be under **Gentile** control for the last three-and-a-half years of the Seven-year Tribulation Period (Daniel 7:25; 9:24a, 26a, 27a; 12:7; Revelation 12:6; 13:5-6).**

| Chapter 11 Verse 2 References | Chapter 11 Verse 2 References Commentary |

V. 2

Daniel 7:25 He shall speak pompous words against the Most High, shall persecute the saints of the Most High, and shall intend to change times and law. Then the saints shall be given into his hand for a time and times and half a time.

Daniel 9:24a "Seventy weeks [KJV]

Daniel 9:26a "And after the sixty-two weeks Messiah shall be cut off,"

Daniel 9:27a "Then he shall confirm a covenant with many for one week".

Daniel 12:7 then I heard the man clothed in linen, who was above the waters of the river, when he held up his right hand and his left hand to heaven, and swore by Him who lives forever, that it shall be for a time, times, and half time; and when the power of the holy people has been completely shattered, all these things shall be finished.

Revelation 12:6 The woman fled into the desert to a place prepared for her by God, where she might be taken care of for 1,260 days. [NIV]

Revelation 13:5-6 ⁵And he was given a mouth speaking great things and blasphemies, and he was given authority to continue for forty-two months. ⁶Then he opened his mouth in blasphemy against God, to blaspheme His name, His tabernacle, and those who dwell in heaven.

V. 2

Daniel 7:25; 9:24a, 26a, 27a; and Daniel 12:7 is a highly complex and amazingly accurate prophecy including time of the Savior's death and beyond to the future-soon-coming Seven-year Tribulation Period. In Hebrew one week represents seven years. The Hebrew context here of *seven sevens* [weeks] translates to *49 YEARS*. Daniel prophesied a total of 7 x 70 *weeks* = 490 years. Seven weeks—or 49 years—after the release of the Jews from captivity in 468 BC brings us to 419BC when Nehemiah's work of rebuilding the Jerusalem wall was completed. Then 62 *weeks*— or 434 more years—from the end of Jerusalem being rebuilt (49 + 434 totaling 483 years from when the Jews were released) takes us to near the exact time of Christ's Triumphal Entry—the tenth day of the month of Nisan exactly four days before He was crucified or, as Daniel put it: **Messiah shall be cut off** (Daniel 9:26a). All that prophecy has been fulfilled. In Daniel 9:27a: **he** is the Antichrist. The Church Age began 50 days (Pentecost) after Christ's death, resurrection, and ascension, and only the Father knows when He will send His Son to the air to rapture the saints; and subsequently, back to earth for His Second Coming.

Revelation 12:6 reveals how Israel will be protected during the last half of the Tribulation Period. The woman in 12:6 represents Israel.

Revelation 13:5-6 agree with Matthew 24:15-16 ¹⁵*"Therefore when you see the abomination of desolation spoken of by Daniel the prophet, standing in the holy place"* (whoever reads, let him understand), ¹⁶*"then let those who are in Judea flee to the mountains."* This further describes the Antichrist desecrating the temple.

But, when the Rapture occurs, Daniel's prophecy of the seventieth week (the Seven-year Tribulation) will begin. Christ's Second Coming is based on the completion of seven years of Tribulation (Matthew 24:36; Mark 13:32; Zechariah 14:6-7).

Chapter 11 Verses 3-6

³And I will appoint my two witnesses, and they will prophesy for 1,260 days, clothed in sackcloth." ⁴They are "the two olive trees" and the two lampstands, and "they stand before the Lord of the earth." ⁵This is how anyone who wants to harm them must die. ⁶They have power to shut up the heavens so that it will not rain during the time they are prophesying; and they have power to turn the waters into blood and to strike the earth with every kind of plague as often as they want. [NIV]

Chapter 11 Verses 3-6
Commentary

God's Two Witnesses Testify (Vv. 3-12)

11:3-6
God gives power to two witnesses for 1,260 days (also three-and-a-half years based on prophetical years of 360 days each). **The sackcloth symbolizes mourning, confession, and repentance** —due to Israel's rejection of Jesus Christ during the entire present church age. **The witnesses** (possibly Moses and Elijah) **will proclaim a message of judgment and the need for repentance. They bear similarities to John the Baptist, and will be the ultimate fulfillment of the promised return of Elijah (Malachi 4:4-6).**

They are also identified as **the two olive trees and the two lampstands** (relating to Zechariah 4:1-3; 4:9, 11-14) where Zerubbabel and Joshua the priest are pictured as two olive trees for a lampstand (Israel).

The two witnesses will perform miracles similar to those performed by *Moses* (Exodus 7:14-20; 9:33) *and Elijah* (1 Kings 17:1, 7; 18:1; 2 Kings 1:10-12; Luke 4:25; James 5:17). They are protected from harm for three-and-a-half years. Their miraculous powers are apparently for the purpose of authenticating their divine message as in the case of Jesus and His apostles.

To this day no one has found the grave of Moses (Deuteronomy 34:5-6). Elijah was previously taken up (*raptured*) and seen ascending by Elisha in 2 Kings 2:11-12. Moses and Elijah actually appear during the Transfiguration in Matthew 17:3; Mark 9:4; Luke 9:32-33; and 2 Peter 1:16. Peter, James and John also witnessed the appearance of Jesus and His garments being supernaturally changed; thus the Transfiguration named as it is. All this does not prove that the two witnesses are in fact Moses and Elijah, but these verses and passages certainly point to this possibility. We will only know when we meet them in heaven.

Chapter 11 Verses 3-6
References

Vv. 3-6

Malachi 4:4-6 ⁴"Remember the Law of Moses, My servant, which I commanded him in Hōreb for all Israel, *with* the statutes and judgments, ⁵"Behold, I will send you Elijah the prophet before the coming of the great and dreadful day of the LORD. ⁶And he will turn the hearts of the fathers to the children, and the hearts of the children to their fathers, lest I come and strike the earth with a curse."

Zechariah 4:1-3 And the angel that talked with me came again, and waked me, as a man that is wakened out of his sleep, ²And said unto me, What seest thou? And I said, I have looked, and behold a candlestick all of gold, with a bowl on top of it, and his seven lamps thereon, and seven pipes to the seven lamps, which are upon the top thereof: ³And two olive trees by it, one upon the right side of the bowl, and the other upon the left side thereof. [KJV]

Zechariah 4:9 "The hands of Zerubbabel have laid the foundation of this temple; his hands shall also finish it. Then you will know that the LORD of hosts has sent Me to you."

Zechariah 4:11-14 ¹¹Then answered I, and said unto him, What are these two olive trees upon the right side of the candlestick and upon the left side thereof? ¹²And I answered again, and said unto him, What be these two olive branches which through the two golden pipes empty the golden oil out of themselves? ¹³And he answered me and said, Knowest thou not what these be? And I said, No, my lord. ¹⁴Then said he, These are the two anointed ones, that stand by the Lord of the whole earth. [KJV]

Chapter 11 Verses 3-6
References Commentary

Vv. 3-6

The LORD is quoted in Malachi 4:4-6 giving us the strong possibility that He will send Moses and Elijah as His two witnesses to proclaim a message of judgment and the need for repentance. (In v.4 Hōreb translates to Sinai.)

In Zechariah 4:1-3, 4:9 and 4:11-14 Zerubbabel, the head of the tribe of Judah, and Joshua (Joshua in Zechariah 3:7) the priest are pictured as the two olive trees for a lampstand (Israel). They will witness to the world during the first half of the Tribulation Period. They can only fulfill their function as a light to the world by the *oil*, i.e., by the Holy Spirit. The Holy Spirit will remove difficulties just as He did for Zerubbabel when he and his men finished rebuilding the temple. (Ezra 3:2, 8-10)

Chapter 11 Verses 7-10

⁷Now when they have finished their testimony, the beast that comes up from the Abyss will attack them, and overpower and kill them. [NIV]

⁸Their bodies will lie in the public square of the great city—which is figuratively called Sodom and Egypt—where also their Lord was crucified. ⁹For three and a half days some from every people, tribe, language and nation will gaze on their bodies and refuse them burial. ¹⁰The inhabitants of the earth will gloat over them and will celebrate by sending each other gifts, because these two prophets had tormented those who live on the earth. [NIV]

Chapter 11 Verses 7-10
Commentary

The Two Witnesses (Vv. 3-12)

11:7
The **beast is the Antichrist [will be revealed coming out of the sea] (Revelation 13:1-2, 7-8; Daniel 7:21) or false messiah under the control of Satan.

11:8-10
At the end of the three-and-a-half years of preaching, the witnesses (Moses and Elijah?) will finally be killed by the beast in the **great city (Jerusalem), *where also our Lord was crucified*** (John 19:20; Hebrews 13:12).

Since it will be at this Tribulation time under the control of Satan, it will be **called **Sodom**, referring to uncleanness and immorality **and Egypt**, depicting oppression and bondage. Not allowing their dead bodies to be buried is the ultimate indignity. The unbelievers of the earth, having submitted to the authority of the beast, **will rejoice**, because they hate the plagues and the message of the **two prophets** (1 Kings 18:22; John 16:20).**

The Antichrist will undoubtedly rejoice along with those who dwell on the earth because he has successfully silenced the Word of God just prior to the arrival of Satan to earth (having been defeated by Michael the archangel) in the next chapter: Revelation 12:12-13.

Chapter 11 Verses 7-10
References

V. 7
Revelation 13:1-2 ¹Then I stood on the sand of the sea. And I saw a beast rising up out of the sea, having seven heads and ten horns, and on his horns ten crowns, and on his heads a blasphemous name. ²Now the beast which I saw was like a leopard, his feet were like *the feet of* a bear, and his mouth like the mouth of a lion. The dragon gave him his power, his throne, and great authority. ...
Revelation 13:7-8 ⁷It was granted to him to make war with the saints and to overcome them. And authority was given him over every tribe, tongue, and nation. ⁸All who dwell on the earth will worship him, whose names have not been written in the Book of Life of the Lamb slain from the foundation of the world.
Daniel 7:21 "As I watched, this horn was waging war against the saints and defeating them, [NIV]

Vv. 8-10
John 19:20 Many of the Jews read this sign, for the place where Jesus was crucified was near the city, and the sign was written in Aramaic, Latin and Greek. [NIV]
Hebrews 13:12 Therefore Jesus also, that He might sanctify the people with His own blood, suffered outside the gate.

1 Kings 18:22 Then said Elijah unto the people, I even I only, remain a prophet of the LORD; but Baal's prophets are four hundred and fifty men. [KJV]

John 16:20 "I tell you [His disciples] the truth, you will weep and mourn while the world rejoices. You will grieve, but your grief will turn to joy." [NIV]

Chapter 11 Verses 7-10
References Commentary

V.7
In Revelation 13:1-2, 7-8; and Daniel 7:21 **the **sea** represents the Gentile nations of the world, from one of which the **beast**, the Antichrist comes.**
The **seven heads** are said in Revelation 17:9-10 to be seven kings, or rulers, or seven different stages of the empire.
Ten horns are predicted by Daniel 7:24 to be a ten-kingdom form.
The **ten crowns** speak of the power to rule, from a **throne** with great **authority** which was given to the Antichrist by Satan, the **dragon**. The Antichrist **beast** is **worshiped** by men. They are not only amazed at him; they actually worship him thinking he is God the Savior (2 Thessalonians 2:4-12). The **beast** will persecute the saints of God and all whose names are not in the Book of Life of the Lamb will be deceived and worship Satan and the Antichrist.

Vv. 8-10
In Revelation 11:8 we read *where also our Lord was crucified*. In John 19:20 and Hebrews 13:12 it is confirmed that the Lord Jesus Christ was crucified just outside Jerusalem.

1 Kings 18:22: In Chapter 18 Elijah, the lone prophet of the Lord, defeated Baal's prophets of four hundred and fifty men.
(1 Kings 18:40 *And Elijah said unto them, Take the prophets of Baal; let not one of them escape. And they took them: and Elijah brought them down to the brook Kishon, and slew them there.* [KJV])

John 16:20: Jesus told them their future of which we read here in the Book of Revelation. "There will be no more **sorrow**" (Revelation 21:4).

Chapter 11 Verses 11-14	Chapter 11 Verses 11-14 Commentary

Chapter 11 Verses 11-14

¹¹But after the three-and-a-half days the breath of life from God entered them, and they stood on their feet, and terror struck those who saw them. ¹²Then they heard a loud voice from heaven saying to them, "Come up here." And they went up to heaven in a cloud, while their enemies looked on. ¹³At that very hour there was a severe earthquake, and a tenth of the city collapsed. Seven thousand people were killed in the earthquake, and the survivors were terrified and gave glory to the God of heaven. ¹⁴The second woe has passed; the third woe is coming soon. [NIV]

Chapter 11 Verses 11-14 Commentary

11:11-14
These verses are a demonstration of God's mighty power and brings further warnings.
In verse 11 **terror struck those who saw them**. (Proverbs 9:10; Revelation 14:7b)

**The two witnesses are brought back to life and taken up into heaven (2 Kings 2:11-12a).

Their enemies react in **fear**, since the two witnesses' resurrection and ascension is absolute proof their message was true and Jesus is God and Messiah. An **earthquake** kills **seven thousand men**. [Is it the same earthquake that was prophesied in Revelation 6:12a?]

Compare to the earthquake that opened tombs and allowed many to be raised after Christ's resurrection (Matthew 27:51-53).

The **remnant** are those who are not killed by the earthquake. Many of them repent and give **glory to God**. The parenthesis begun with Chapter 10 ends here. The **third woe** begins with the **seventh trumpet** which comes next in verse 15.**

Of the 3 woes spoken of in Revelation 8:13:
1. the first woe passed on after the locusts tormented men for five months in Revelation 9:10,
2. the second woe ended with the earthquake in Revelation 11:13,
3. the third ends with the seventh and last bowl poured out in Revelation 16:17.

Chapter 11 Verses 11-14
References

Vv. 11-14
Proverbs 9:10 The fear of the LORD is the beginning of wisdom, and knowledge of the Holy One is understanding. [NIV]
Revelation 14:7b "fear God and give glory to Him, for the hour of His judgment has come; and worship Him who made heaven and earth, the sea and springs of water."

2 Kings 2:11-12a And it came to pass, as they still went on, and talked, that, behold, there appeared a chariot of fire, and horses of fire, and parted them both asunder; and Elijah went up by a whirlwind into heaven. ¹²ªAnd Elisha saw it,… [KJV]

Revelation 6:12a I looked when He opened the sixth seal, and behold, there was a great earthquake;

Matthew 27:51-53 ⁵¹Then, behold, the veil of the temple was torn in two from top to bottom; and the earth quaked, and the rocks were split, ⁵²and the graves were opened; and many bodies of the saints who had fallen asleep were raised; ⁵³and coming out of the graves after His resurrection, they went into the holy city and appeared to many.

Chapter 11 Verses 11-14
References Commentary

Vv. 11-14
Proverbs 9:10; Revelation 14:7b: The effects of the Lord's mighty power can result in fear. In Revelation 11:13 the earthquake killed seven thousand people, *and the rest were afraid and gave glory to God in heaven.*

2 Kings 2:11-12a: 2 Kings 2:12 points out Elisha witnessed Elijah ascending, and here in Revelation 11:12 their enemies saw the two witnesses ascend.

The sixth seal in Revelation 6:12a reveals that there will be an earthquake and here in Chapter 11:13 another one. After the seventh seal is opened in Revelation 8:1, we read of an earthquake in 8:5. We will come across a different one in Revelation 11:19, and yet one more, greater than all prior, in Revelation 16:18.

Matthew 27:51-53 makes known two miracles: First, the curtain that blocked the entrance to the Most Holy place (Exodus 26:33; Hebrews 9:3) into God's presence was torn open **from top to bottom**, and now the way was opened by Him for a new and living way to God for believers. Second, Matthew is the only writer to mention the **saints** who came **out of the graves** and nothing more is said about these believers except that they **appeared to many**. Great fear probably fell on those who saw them.

Chapter 11 Verse 15

Chapter 11 Verse 15
Commentary

The First Prophecy Preview of the Seven Years End

The Seventh Trumpet and Christ's Return

¹⁵Then the seventh angel sounded: And there were loud voices in heaven, saying, "The kingdoms of this world have become *the kingdoms* of our Lord and of His Christ, and He shall reign forever and ever!"

11:15
The **seventh trumpet brings closer the soon coming war of Armageddon and the Millennial Kingdom of **Christ**. The seven vials or bowls (Revelation 16:1) are probably contained in the judgment of the **seventh trumpet**. They will occur in a very brief period of time at the end of the Great Tribulation. The Second Coming of Christ, while a great blessing for believers, will be God's most severe judgment of the earth. The prophecy temporarily goes all the way to Christ's Millennial Reign. The **kingdoms of this world** will be completely overthrown by the coming kingdom of Christ (Revelation 19:11, 20-21; Daniel 2:34-35a, 44), who will **reign forever and ever** (Daniel 7:13a, 14b, Daniel 7:27).**

Chapter 11 Verse 15
References

Chapter 11 Verse 15
References Commentary

V. 15
Revelation 16:1 Then I heard a loud voice from the temple saying to the seven angels, "Go, pour out the seven bowls of God's wrath on the earth." [NIV]

Revelation 19:11 Now I saw heaven opened, and behold, a white horse. And He who sat on him *was* called Faithful and True, and in righteousness He judges and makes war. ...
Revelation 19:20-21 ²⁰Then the beast was captured, and with him the false prophet who worked signs in his presence, by which he deceived those who received the mark of the beast and those who worshiped his image. These two were cast alive into the lake of fire burning with brimstone. ²¹And the rest were killed with the sword which proceeded from the mouth of Him who sat on the horse. And the birds were filled with their flesh.

Daniel 2:34-35a ³⁴"While you were watching, a rock was cut out, but not by human hands. It struck the statue on its feet of iron and clay and smashed them. ³⁵ᵃThen the iron, the clay, the bronze, the silver and the gold were broken to pieces at the same time and became like chaff on a threshing floor in the summer. The wind swept them away without leaving a trace." ... [NIV]
Daniel 2:44 "In the time of those kings, the God of heaven will set up a kingdom that will never be destroyed, nor will it be left to another people. It will crush all those kingdoms and bring them to an end, but it will itself endure forever." [NIV]
Daniel 7:13a "I was watching in the night visions, and behold, *One* like the Son of Man, coming with the clouds of heaven!
Daniel 7:14b His dominion *is* an everlasting dominion, which shall not pass away."

V. 15
In Revelation 16:1; 19:11 and 19:20-21 **the bowls of the wrath of God** represent the climax of God's punishment of sinners during the Tribulation Period. **The **white horse** here is not the same one as in Revelation 6:2.**

In 19:11 **He who sat on him *was* called Faithful and True** reveals that this is the Second Coming of Christ, arriving on earth for the Battle of Armageddon, to win the war and to begin His Millennial Reign.

Daniel 2:34-35a, 44; 7:13a and 7:14b go with Daniel 7:27, preceded by Daniel 2:28 where Daniel informed King Nebuchadnezzar that God in heaven reveals the secrets of the king's dream of what will be occurring in *the latter days*.
What we read in Daniel 2:34-35 describes how the **feet of iron** foreshadow the Roman Empire and how the latter weakness is represented by poor mixture of **iron** and **clay**. The **rock** that was **cut out without hands** that will destroy the last kingdom represents Jesus Christ, who, at His return, will destroy Gentile world power, and in Daniel 2:44 Christ **will set up a kingdom which shall never be destroyed**.

Chapter 11 Verses 16-19

¹⁶And the twenty-four elders who sat before God on their thrones fell on their faces and worshiped God, ¹⁷saying: "We give You thanks, O Lord God Almighty, the One who is and who was and who is to come, because You have taken Your great power and reigned. ¹⁸The nations were angry, and Your wrath has come, and the time of the dead, that they should be judged, and that You should reward Your servants the prophets and the saints, and those who fear Your name, small and great, and should destroy those who destroy the earth." ¹⁹Then the temple of God was opened in heaven, and the ark of His covenant was seen in His temple. And there were lightnings, noises, thunderings, an earthquake, and great hail.

Chapter 11 Verses 16-19
Commentary

11:16-19
Verses 16 and 17 bring out the fact that not only is Jesus Christ called **God** with the Father, but also He is **Lord God Almighty**. This is the third of seven times in this last Book of the Bible that He is recognized as being **Almighty God**. The Lord Jesus in Matthew 19:28 also prophesied about the elders who were on their thrones before God. ****God** is **worshiped** by the **elders** because what He promised is now accomplished. Their gratitude is for the establishment of the Millennial kingdom (1 Corinthians 15:24). The **dead** of all ages will be **judged** at the future Great White Throne (1 Corinthians 15:24; Revelation 20:11a, 20:15; Daniel 12:2; Matthew Chapter 25).

Those who have tried to **destroy the earth** will themselves be destroyed by God. **The ark of His covenant** (testament) is a symbol of the presence of God and of His faithfulness in fulfilling His covenant promises.**
In reference to Revelation 11:18 see Psalm 2:1-6.

The Gentile **nations** will be overpowered. The **wrath** of God will take vengeance on His enemies (2 Thessalonians 1:7-8).

The Tribulation saints who have died will be raised to life (Isaiah 26:19a) and, with the Old Testament saints, enjoy the marriage supper with the raptured Church. God will take revenge upon those who have rejected Him—their very Creator (Daniel 7:10).

Chapter 11 Verses 16-19
References

Vv. 16-19

1 Corinthians 15:24 Then *comes* the end, when He delivers the kingdom to God the Father, when He puts an end to all rule and all authority and power.

Revelation 20:11a Then I saw a great white throne and Him who sat on it ...

Revelation 20:15 And anyone not found written in the Book of Life was cast into the lake of fire.

Daniel 12:2 Multitudes who sleep in the dust of the earth will awake: some to everlasting life, others to shame and everlasting contempt. [NIV]

2 Thessalonians 1:7-8 ⁷and to *give* you who are troubled rest with us when the Lord Jesus is revealed from heaven with His mighty angels, ⁸in flaming fire taking vengeance on those who do not know God, and on those who do not obey the gospel of our Lord Jesus Christ.

Isaiah 26:19a But your dead will live; their bodies will rise. ... [NIV]

Daniel 7:10 A fiery stream issued and came forth from before Him. A thousand thousands ministered to Him; ten thousand times ten thousand stood before him. The court was seated, and the books were opened.

Chapter 11 Verses 16-19
References Commentary

Vv. 16-19

1 Corinthians 15:24, Revelation 20: 11a, 15, and Daniel 12:2 all refer to the following: At the end of Christ's Millennial Reign, all who have died in unbelief will be resurrected to be judged at the Great White Throne to hear their doom. The reign of Christ will then give way to His eternal kingdom. 2 Peter 3:10-13 explains that His kingdom will not be on this present earth nor the present heaven: *¹⁰But the day of the Lord will come as a thief in the night, in which the heavens will pass away with a great noise, and the elements will melt with fervent heat, both the earth and the works that are in it will be burned up. ¹¹Therefore, since all these things will be dissolved, what manner of persons ought you to be in holy conduct and godliness, ¹²looking for and hastening the coming of the day of God, because of which the heavens will be dissolved, being on fire, and the elements will melt with fervent heat? ¹³Nevertheless we, according to His promise, look for new heavens and a new earth in which righteousness dwells.*

2 Thessalonians 1:7-8 gives an example of those in the Church Age who are **troubled**—that is, persecuted—but makes known that we will be given rest **when the Lord Jesus is revealed from heaven**. Verse 8 tells us that God will avenge.

Isaiah 26:19a: This prophecy in about 700 BC could be giving the same kind of hope we have: Hope for not just rewards, but for life everlasting. It could possibly be used metaphorically in speaking of Israel's restoration (Romans 11:26); it could even refer to those who will be saved during the Tribulation, prior to Christ's Second Coming.

Daniel 7:10 prophecy agrees with the number of saints who were praising the Lord at His throne in Revelation 5:11. Here they are seated within the court to watch **the books** being **opened** for the judgment of those who would be tried later at the Great White Throne (Revelation 20:12).

Chapter 12 Verses 1-2

Chapter 12 Verses 1-2
Commentary

Satan Identified and Described

Returning to Key Figures of the Last Half of the Tribulation

Chapters 12-14
These Chapters further explain prophesies pertaining to the major personages and movements of the latter half of the Tribulation Period. God will remember His new Covenant.

¹A great sign appeared in heaven: a woman clothed with the sun, with the moon under her feet and a crown of twelve stars on her head. ²She was pregnant and cried out in pain as she was about to give birth. [NIV]

12:1-2
The **woman** is Israel and her **Child** is Christ, the Messiah (Revelation 12:5; Isaiah 7:14; 9:6a; Isaiah 66:7-8; Micah. 5:2; Romans 9:4a-5).

Isaiah 26:17-18 clarifies that the woman is Israel:

The woman is not the Church, since the Church did not bring forth Christ. Rather, Christ brought forth the Church. ** The **woman is the 12 tribes of *Israel*. The **child** is Jesus. Psalm 2:7b: *You are My Son, today I have begotten You.* **Twelve stars on her head** are the twelve patriarch sons of Israel (Jacob) and their 12 tribes; **sun** around her head represents the *new everlasting covenant* (Hebrews 13:20) which permits her to be reconciled to God. The **moon under her feet** reflects the terms of the *old covenant* (Exodus 19:5-6) Israelites had to keep all Ten Commandments in order to be saved. In Romans 11:25-26, and Revelation 7:4-8, *all the tribes of the children of Israel were sealed.* Genesis 17:19 spells out God's promise.*God promised all this for the coming kingdom (John 16:21), just as they pictured Joseph's ultimate rule over his father, mother, and brothers (Genesis 37:9, 11).*

The **birth pains refer to the period before the birth of Christ when Israel was waiting for redemption by the Messiah.** They themselves brought on the sharp pains with stubbornness that led to suffering during the Church Age.

Chapter 12 Verses 1-2 References	Chapter 12 Verses 1-2 References Commentary

Vv. 1-2

Isaiah 7:14 "Therefore the Lord Himself will give you a sign: Behold, the virgin shall conceive and bear a Son, and shall call His name Immanüel."

Isaiah 9:6a "For unto us a Child is born, unto us a Son is given."

Vv. 1-2

Isaiah 7:14 and 9:6a are two of the most heard verses during the celebration of Jesus' incarnate birth every Christmas. **In Isaiah's prophetic view the scene is present as he sees the pregnant virgin about to bear a Son. That this prophecy must refer to the virgin birth of Christ is obvious since the virgin is pregnant and is still a virgin! **Immanuel** is a symbolic name, meaning "God with us"** —in other words, the Divine Child. **Everlasting Father** (Isaiah 9:6b) literally means Father of Eternity. As the **Prince of Peace**, Christ Jesus will bring eternal peace to the hearts of all believers through the establishment of His kingdom.**

Micah 5:2 "But you, Bethlehem Ephrathah, *though* you are little among the thousands of Judah, *yet* out of you shall come forth to Me the One to be Ruler in Israel, whose goings forth *are* from of old, from everlasting.

Micah 5:2 confirms the birth place of Jesus to be the same as David in Judah. **From everlasting** clearly indicates the past eternality of Christ.**

Romans 9:4a the people of Israel ... [NIV]
Romans 9:5 Theirs are the patriarchs, and from them is traced the human ancestry of Christ, who is God over all, forever praised! Amen. [NIV]

Romans 9:4a, 5: *Abraham, Isaac, Jacob, and the twelve sons of Jacob are the **patriarch** fathers. The Messiah is an Israelite from their lineage, but more, He is also the Sovereign of the universe, **the eternally blessed God**. This gives us a positive statement both of the humanity and of the deity of the Savior.*

Isaiah 26:17-18; Genesis 17:19; John 16:21; Genesis 37:9, 11

-CONTINUED ON NEXT SET OF PAGES UNDER REFERENCES!-

-CONTINUED ON NEXT SET OF PAGES UNDER REFERENCES COMMENTARY!-

Chapter 12 Verses 1-2	Chapter 12 Verses 1-2 Commentary

-VERSES 1-2 REPEATED FROM PREVIOUS PAGE-

-PART OF COMMENTARY VERSES 1-2 REPEATED FROM PREVIOUS PAGE-

12:1-2

¹A great sign appeared in heaven: a woman clothed with the sun, with the moon under her feet and a crown of twelve stars on her head. ²She was pregnant and cried out in pain as she was about to give birth. [NIV]

Isaiah 26:17-18 clarifies that the woman is Israel:

The woman is not the Church, since the Church did not bring forth Christ. Rather, Christ brought forth the Church. The **woman** is the 12 tribes of *Israel*. The **child** is Jesus. Psalm 2:7b: *You are My Son, today I have begotten You.* **Twelve stars on her head** are the twelve patriarch sons of Israel (Jacob) and their 12 tribes; **sun** around her head represents the *new everlasting covenant* (Hebrews 13:20) which permits her to be reconciled to God. The **moon under her feet** reflects the terms of the *old covenant* (Exodus 19:5-6) Israelites had to keep all Ten Commandments in order to be saved. In Romans 11:25-26, and Revelation 7:4-8, *all the tribes of the children of Israel were sealed.* Genesis 17:19 spells out God's promise.*God promised all this for the coming kingdom (John 16:21), just as they pictured Joseph's ultimate rule over his father, mother, and brothers (Genesis 37:9, 11).*

The **birth pains refer to the period before the birth of Christ when Israel was waiting for redemption by the Messiah.** They themselves brought on the sharp pains with stubbornness that led to suffering during the Church Age.

| Chapter 12 Verses 1-2 References | Chapter 12 Verses 1-2 References Commentary |

-CONTINUED FROM PREVIOUS PAGE-

Vv. 1-2

Isaiah 26:17-18 ¹⁷As a woman with child is in pain and cries out in her pangs, when she draws near the time of her delivery, so have we been in Your sight, O LORD. ¹⁸We have been with child, we have been in pain; we have, as it were, brought forth wind; we have not accomplished any deliverance in the earth, nor have the inhabitants of the world fallen.

Isaiah 26:18: "But Israel's suffering was so drawn out that it seemed that she could give birth only to wind, meaning she could not deliver herself from her ongoing sorrows." (Warren Henderson, "Sorrow And Comfort" *A Devotional Study of Isaiah*, pg. 161)

Genesis 17:19 Then God said: "No, Sarah your wife shall bare you a son, and you shall call his name Isaac; I will establish My covenant with him for an everlasting covenant, and with his descendants after him."

Genesis 17:19: God keeps His promises and He even repeats in Genesis 22:18: *"and through your offspring all nations on earth will be blessed, because you have obeyed me."* [NIV]

John 16:21 "A woman giving birth to a child has pain because her time has come; but when her baby is born she forgets the anguish because of her joy that a child is born into the world." [NIV]

In John 16:21 it's remarkable how quickly a mother can recover from the labor pains after giving birth to a child. It will also be so for the Israelites after the regret of being disconnected from our God for so long, but then how their sorrow will soon be forgotten and they will be comforted when they—the 144,000—are sealed.

Genesis 37:9 And he dreamed yet another dream, and told it his brethren, and said, Behold, I have dreamed a dream more; and, behold, the sun and the moon and the eleven stars made obeisance to me [bowed down to me]. [KJV]
Genesis 37:11 And his brethren envied him; but his father observed the saying. [KJV]

Genesis 37:9, 11: Joseph was the twelfth star! As a "type" of the coming Messiah Joseph dreamt that the **eleven stars** were under his control. The Savior created the heavens with His own hands, and **eleven** of His disciples during His ministry on earth became apostles of the Lamb.

Chapter 12 Verses 3-4

³Then another sign appeared in heaven: an enormous red dragon with seven heads and ten horns and seven crowns on its heads. ⁴Its tail swept a third of the stars out of the sky and flung them to the earth. The dragon stood in front of the woman who was about to give birth, so that it might devour her child the moment he was born. [NIV]

Chapter 12 Verses 3-4 Commentary

12:3-4

The dragon, dwelling at this time **in heaven**, **is identified as Satan**, prince of this world (John 12:31; 14:30; 16:11), **in verse 9. His red color reveals his murderous character (John 8:44)**.

The third part of the stars of heaven are probably the fallen angels who followed Satan in his original rebellion against God (Isaiah 14:12-13a, 14b-15)**. Shortly after the incarnate **birth of Christ, Satan was ready to kill Him (Matthew 2:13-16)**.

His **seven heads, ten horns, and seven** *crowns* are telling us that the **dragon** had, in his mass of forces, seven wicked and idolatress national leaders ruling over ten nations. Satan would use these emperors in an attempt to overthrow the Lord Jesus and Israel. In verse 4 he stands **before the woman**, waiting for her to deliver her Child so that he might devour Him immediately upon His birth. His **ten horns** show Satan's connection with the fourth beast (the Roman Empire of Daniel 7:7, 24) and with the beast from the sea (the Antichrist having seven heads and ten horns: Revelation 13:1; 17:3; 17:7; 17:9)

Chapter 12 Verses 3-4
References

Vv. 3-4
John 8:44 "You belong to your father the devil, and you want to carry out your father's desire. He was a murderer from the beginning, not holding to the truth, for there is no truth in him. When he lies, he speaks his native language, for he is a liar and the father of lies." [NIV]

Isaiah 14:12-13a ^{12}How you have fallen from heaven, O morning star, son of the dawn! You have been cast down to the earth, you who once laid low the nations! ^{13a}You said in your heart, "I will ascend to heaven; I will raise my throne above the stars of God;" [NIV]
Isaiah 14:14b-15 ^{14b}"I will make myself like the Most High" ^{15}But you are brought down to the grave, to the depths of the pit." [NIV]

Daniel 7:7 "After that, in my vision at night I looked, and there before me was a fourth beast- terrifying and frightening and very powerful. It had large iron teeth; it crushed and devoured its victims and trampled underfoot whatever was left. It was different from all the former beasts, and it had ten horns." [NIV]

Daniel 7:24 The ten horns *are* ten kings *who* shall arise from this kingdom. And another shall rise after them; he shall be different from the first *ones* and shall subdue three kings.

Chapter 12 Verses 3-4
References Commentary

Vv. 3-4
In John 8:44 Jesus tells it like it is. He is saying that these Jews imitate the devil. *The devil was *a murderer from the beginning*. He brought death to Adam and the whole human race. Not only was he a **murderer**, but he was **a liar** as well. The Jews were murderers because the intention of their hearts was to kill the Son of God. They were liars saying that God was their Father. They pretended to be godly, spiritual men, but they were wicked.*

Isaiah 14:12-13a and 14b-15 describe how Satan was cast out of heaven in the beginning and how he will be defeated in the end. (Ezekiel 28:12-16; 2 Peter 2:4; Jude 6)

Daniel 7:7 prophesied that the Roman Empire *would follow the Grecian Empire, would cease, and then, after a considerable space of time [the present Church Age], would be revived.* The **fourth beast** is quite likely the Roman Empire, and the three **beasts** who *were* **before it** are the Babylonian, Medo-Persian and Greek Empires.

Daniel 7:24 is a prophecy that a new empire will emerge consisting of ten nations. **Another "king" shall arise and subdue three** of the ten (Daniel 7:42-43). This ruler will be the Antichrist.

Old Testament Prophecies are in total agreement with the Book of Revelation prophecies and reinforce the pure, miraculous agreement of these truths given by the Spirit in thousands of years-wide time span.

Chapter 12 Verses 5-6

⁵She gave birth to a son, a male child, who "will rule all the nations with an iron scepter." And her child was snatched up to God and to his throne. ⁶The woman fled into the wilderness to a place prepared for her by God, where she might be taken care of for 1,260 days. [NIV]

Chapter 12 Verses 5-6
Commentary

12:5-6
The **male child is Christ the Messiah,** Almighty God (Psalm 2:7-9; Revelation 19:15; Isaiah 11:4).

In verse 5 He **was caught up to God and His throne** (Acts 1:9; 7:55-56; Mark 16:19, Luke 24:51).

The woman, Israel, will flee at mid-tribulation. **The **wilderness** represents anywhere outside** Israel (Some commentators believe their place of refuge will be in Petra about 55 miles south of the Dead Sea.).
In verse 6, **during the last half of the Tribulation Period (1,260 days = three-and-a-half years), Israel will take refuge among the Gentile nations, where God will care for them (possibly through Gentile believers** —(Mark 9:41).
Daniel 12:9 refers to the same 1,260 days as the **time of the end**—the last three-and-a-half years of Tribulation.
Then Daniel 12:10-12 tell of the subsequent 30 and 45 days which occur prior to the Millennial.
Chronologically, Revelation 12:6 occurs after verses 12:7-12, and is equivalent to verse 12:14. (Verse 12:14 repeats verse 12:6.)

Chapter 12 Verses 5-6
References

Vv. 5-6
Psalm 2:7-9 "I will declare the decree: The LORD has said to Me, 'You *are* My Son, today I have begotten You. ⁸Ask of Me, and I will give *You* the nations *for* Your inheritance, and the ends of the earth *for* Your possession. ⁹You shall break them with a rod of iron; You shall dash them to pieces like a potter's vessel.' "

Revelation 19:15 Now out of His mouth goes a sharp sword, that with it He should strike the nations. And He Himself will rule them with a rod of iron. He Himself treads the winepress of the fierceness and wrath of Almighty God.

Acts 1:9 Now when He had spoken these things, while they watched, He was taken up, and a cloud received Him out of their sight.
Mark 16:19 So then, after the Lord had spoken to them, He was received up into heaven, and sat down at the right hand of God.

Chapter 12 Verses 5-6
References Commentary

Vv. 5-6
Christ was the **Son** of God from all eternity in Psalm 2:7-9, and the Psalm also tells us that Jesus was **begotten**—by His incarnate birth in the flesh. Prior to Christ's inauguration as King, He, at the Great White Throne Judgment, will destroy those who do not know God and do not obey the gospel.

Then, in the Millennium, He will rule **with a rod of iron**, punishing rebellion when it raises its head (Revelation 19:15-20:10-15).

Jesus reminded His chosen apostles of all this before they witnessed Him ascending Acts 1:9; Mark 16:19; Luke 24:51.

Chapter 12 Verses 7-10   **Chapter 12 Verses 7-10**
                                                                    Commentary

12:7-10

⁷Then war broke out in heaven. Michael and his angels fought against the dragon; and the dragon and his angels fought back. ⁸But he was not strong enough, and they lost their place in heaven. ⁹The great dragon was hurled down—that ancient serpent called the devil, or Satan, who leads the whole world astray. He was hurled to the earth, and his angels with him. ¹⁰Then I heard a loud voice in heaven say: "Now have come the salvation and the power and the kingdom of our God, and the authority of his Messiah. For the accuser of our brothers and sisters, who accuses them before our God day and night, has been hurled down. [NIV]

In mid-tribulation **war** breaks out in heaven with **Michael and his angels** on one side and **the dragon,** Satan (who has been up in heaven acting like he is God) **and his angels** on the other. Michael is associated with the nation of Israel (Daniel 12:1-2).

The dragon (**serpent, devil,** deceiver -Genesis 3:1, 4) *is so thoroughly defeated that he and his followers are **cast down** to earth* where they will later join the Antichrist and False Prophet. (Revelation 19:20) *However, this isn't his final fate* as we will see when we arrive at Revelation 20:1-3, 10.

In verse10 the **loud** rejoicing **in heaven** is heard in the vision that both Jesus Christ and the seven Spirits have given to John to write (Revelation 1:4b-5).

Where verse 10 says **Now have come the salvation and the power and the kingdom of our God, and the authority of his Messiah**, it is pointing toward Christ's soon coming Millennial Reign. At the end of the Millennium He will raise the dead who rejected Him and judge them for their disobedience and immoral acts (Revelation 20:11-15).

Chapter 12 Verses 7-10
References

Vv. 7-10

Daniel 12:1-2 ¹"At that time Michael, the great prince who protects your people, will arise. There will be a time of distress such as has not happened from the beginning of nations until then. But at that time your people-everyone whose name is found written in the book-will be delivered. ²Multitudes who sleep in the dust of the earth will awake: some to everlasting life, others to shame and everlasting contempt. [NIV]

Revelation 20:11-15 ¹¹Then I saw a great white throne and Him who sat on it, from whose face the earth and the heaven fled away. And there was found no place for them. ¹²And I saw the dead, small and great, standing before God, and books were opened. And another book was opened, which is *the Book* of Life. And the dead were judged according to their works, by the things which were written in the books. ¹³The sea gave up the dead who were in it, and Death and Hādēs delivered up the dead who were in them. And they were judged, each one according to his works. ¹⁴Then Death and Hādēs were cast into the lake of fire. This is the second death. ¹⁵And anyone not found written in the Book of Life was cast into the lake of fire.

Chapter 12 Verses 7-10
References Commentary

Vv. 7-10

In Daniel 12:1-2 **during the Great Tribulation there will be an unprecedented attack on the Jews, but **Michael** will deliver them.** However, the greater multitude of those who continued refusing to believe, will suffer for eternity (Matthew 7:13-14; Revelation 9:21; 20:11-15; 21:8).

Revelation 20:11-15 reveals to us that it is a shocking, dreadful thing for a man to go to his grave with unforgiven sins. The Old Testament believers who died having faith in God (Hebrews 11:39-40; 12:23) will either be with the Lord and His Church upon the Rapture or will be resurrected with the Tribulation martyrs who will have died believing in Christ. (See "End Times Major Events Time Line": next to last page of this study guide.)

Chapter 12 Verses 11-13

¹¹They triumphed over him by the blood of the Lamb and by the word of their testimony; they did not love their lives so much as to shrink from death. ¹²Therefore rejoice, you heavens and you who dwell in them! But woe to the earth and the sea, because the devil has gone down to you! He is filled with fury, because he knows that his time is short." ¹³When the dragon saw that he had been hurled to the earth, he pursued the woman who had given birth to the male child. [NIV]

Chapter 12 Verses 11-13 Commentary

More Details of Last Half of the Tribulation

12:11-13

The reason for the cheering in v. 12 is because the accuser (Satan) of the brothers and sisters in Christ has just been evicted from among them! They overcame **him**, the devil, and his world! Their victory was based upon Christ's shed **blood** and His resurrection. This testimony gives the value of His death out of the unconditional love He has for all. Also their testimony is sealed by their faithfulness to shed their own blood. They **did not love their** own **lives**, even all the way **to death**. They were Christian martyrs, like those in the church of Smyrna, who obviously believed in the resurrection (Revelation 2:10). The woman mentioned in verse 13 represents the nation of Israel.

The last half of the Tribulation Period will be a time of terrible trouble on earth (Jeremiah 30:7; Daniel 9:27; 12:1; Zephaniah 1:15; Matthew 24:15-22; Revelation 13-19).

In verse 12 Satan's **wrath** is **great** because he *had been* prince of the world, and he knows his time is running out. The **short time** becomes one day in Revelation 18:8, and one hour in 17:12; 18:10, and 18:17. **It will be Satan's final attempt in his awareness of a **short time** to prevent the return and the reign of Christ.** Therefore, in Revelation verses 12:13-17, we learn Satan, when he had been cast to the earth, will become enraged and will intensify his persecution of God's chosen nation. Israel. Confirming the blessed hope for believers that they will not suffer Satan's **wrath**, let alone His *furious* **wrath**, which is given in four beautiful verses: We are told that we are not appointed to wrath, but to salvation: Romans 5:9; 1 Thessalonians 5:9; 1:10; and John 3:36. We are saved from wrath through the shed blood of the Lamb. The confirmation is also evidenced in Revelation 5:9-11 as we will already be in heaven, again worshiping and praising Him.

In Chapters 13 to 17 Satan sets up his own counterfeit kingdom through the beast, the false messiah (Revelation 13:1-17).

Chapter 12 Verses 11-13
References

Vv. 11-13

Jeremiah 30:7 How awful that day will be! None will be like it. It will be a time of trouble for Jacob, but he will be saved out of it. [NIV]

Daniel 9:27 Then he shall confirm a covenant with many for one week; but in the middle of the week he shall bring an end to sacrifice and offering. And on the wing of abominations shall be one who makes desolate, even until the consummation, which is determined, is poured out on the desolate.

Zephaniah 1:15 That day is a day of wrath, a day of trouble and distress, a day of wasteness and desolation, a day of darkness and gloominess, a day of clouds and thick darkness. [KJV]

Matthew 24:15-22 ¹⁵"Therefore when you see the *'abomination of desolation,'* spoken of by Daniel the prophet, standing in the holy place" (whoever reads, let him understand), ¹⁶then let those who are in Judea flee to the mountains. ¹⁷Let him who is on the housetop not go down to take anything out of his house. ¹⁸And let him who is in the field not go back to get his clothes. ¹⁹But woe to those who are pregnant and to those who are nursing babies in those days! ²⁰And pray that your flight may not be in winter or on the Sabbath. ²¹For then there will be great tribulation, such as has not been since the beginning of the world until this time, no, nor ever shall be. ²²And unless those days were shortened, no flesh would be saved; but for the elect's sake those days will be shortened."

Chapter 12 Verses 11-13
References Commentary

Vv. 11-13

Jeremiah 30:7: Even through the desolation, fear, darkness, gloom, earthly and celestial phenomena, devastation and destruction, wrath and death, of the Great Tribulation—**Jacob's trouble**—or *Israel's sufferings* will be ended and their future promised blessing will come about.

Daniel 9:27: The Antichrist will, during the first three-and-a-half years, deceive people into believing he is the great peace maker, but the peace will be broken by Gog and Māgog (Ezekiel 38). He will show his true colors and temper tantrums during the last three-and-a-half years. The seven years will end in the Antichrist's defeat when Christ returns to establish His kingdom.

Zephaniah 1:15: *The **day of** God's wrath is pictured because of the spiritual complacency; especially the wickedness, of the men of Judah.*

Matthew 24:15-22: The abomination of desolation marks the beginning of the Great Tribulation (last three-and-a-half years) when the Antichrist *sits as God in the temple of God showing himself that he is God* (2 Thessalonians 2:4). The words of the Lord Jesus are confirmation of Daniel's prophecy in Daniel 9:27 that, as Jesus states in Matthew 24:21:
"For then there will be great tribulation, such as has not been since the beginning of the world until this time, no, nor ever shall be."
In verse 22, **the elect's** are God's Jewish chosen ones.

Chapter 12 Verse 14

¹⁴The woman was given the two wings of a great eagle, so that she might fly to the place prepared for her in the wilderness, where she would be taken care of for a time, times and half a time, out of the serpent's reach. [NIV]

Chapter 12 Verse 14
Commentary

12:14
Revelation 12:14 here tells us much: The time and times and half a time is three-and-a-half years (verse 6). The believers in heaven can rejoice over the dragon's departure, but it is bad news for the earth and the sea! But *the faithful Jewish remnant on earth is given **two wings of a great eagle**, enabling them to quickly escape to a **wilderness** hideout*
(Matthew 24:16-21: ¹⁶*then let those who are in Judea flee to the mountains. ¹⁷Let him who is on the housetop not go down to take anything out of his house. ¹⁸And let him who is in the field not go back to get his clothes. ¹⁹But woe to those who are pregnant and to those who are nursing babies in those days! ²⁰And pray that your flight may not be in winter or on the Sabbath. ²¹For then there will be great tribulation, such as has not been since the beginning of the world until this time, no, nor ever shall be.*)

*(Some have *supposed* that these **wings** speak of a great Air Force.) The Jewish remnant is cared for and protected* until the end of the Tribulation (Matthew 24:31) by angels who are possibly Gentile believers on earth *from the serpent's attacks in this **wilderness** for three-and-a-half years* {**for a time and times and half a time** (Daniel 7:25; 12:7)} the time of "Great Tribulation" (Matthew 24:21).

According to Zechariah 13:7-9, however, two thirds of the Jews will die.

159

Chapter 12 Verse 14 References	Chapter 12 Verse 14 References Commentary
V. 14 **Matthew 24:31** "And He will send His angels with a great sound of a trumpet, and they will gather together His elect from the four winds, from one end of heaven to the other."	**V. 14** Matthew 24:31: At the end of the Tribulation Period, *when the Savior descends, **He will send His angels** throughout the earth to **gather together His elect** people—the newly converted believing Jews, to the land of Palestine. From all the earth they will gather to greet their Messiah and to enjoy His glorious* reign.
Daniel 7:25 He shall speak *pompous* words against the Most High, shall persecute the saints of the Most High, and shall intend to change times and law. Then *the saints* shall be given into his hand for a time and times and half a time. **Daniel 12:7** Then I heard the man clothed in linen, who *was* above the waters of the river, when he held up his right hand and his left hand to heaven, and swore by Him who lives forever, that *it shall be* for a time, times, and half *a time*; and when the power of the holy people has been completely shattered, all these *things* shall be finished.	Daniel 7:25 and 12:7: **A time, times, and half *a* time** is an expression used in Daniel and in Revelation to refer to three-and-a-half years, or 1,260 days, or 42 months.** The Antichrist's **Pompous** words in 7:25 are showy words with grandeur, splendid, magnificent—but deceiving—promise. **Change times** means re-writing history, and **the law** means there will be lawlessness. As this is being written, there is already a head-start in schools changing history and in lawlessness. During the first half of the Tribulation period will be a time of trouble for the Jewish people due to an invasion by ten nations including Gog and Māgog. The Antichrist will have promised peace—the promised peace will abruptly be ended. Then, as we read in Daniel 12:7, the latter last three-and-a-half years, there will be tremendous persecution and suffering.
Zechariah 13:7-9 ⁷"Awake, O sword, against My Shepherd, against the Man who is My Companion," says the LORD of hosts. "Strike the Shepherd, and the sheep will be scattered; then I will turn My hand against the little ones. ⁸And it shall come to pass in all the land," says the LORD, "that two-thirds in it shall be cut off *and* die, but *one*-third shall be left in it: ⁹I will bring the *one*-third through the fire, will refine them as silver is refined, and test them as gold is tested. They will call on My name, and I will answer them. I will say, 'This is My people'; and each one will say, 'The LORD *is* my God.'"	In Zechariah 13:7-9 **the sword is the symbol of judicial power (Romans 13:4) and indicates the power that God has entrusted to human government.** Here in Zechariah, *Father God is quoted as He orders His **sword** to **awake** ... against His only begotten Son, the Lord Jesus. The **Shepherd** was struck at Calvary by crucifixion on the cross, and **the Jewish sheep** have been **scattered** ever since.*

Chapter 12 Verses 15-17

¹⁵Then from his mouth the serpent spewed water like a river, to overtake the women and sweep her away with the torrent. ¹⁶But the earth helped the woman by opening its mouth and swallowing the river that the dragon had spewed out of his mouth. [NIV]

¹⁷Then the dragon was enraged at the woman and went off to wage war against the rest of her offspring—those who keep God's commands and hold fast their testimony about Jesus. [NIV]

Chapter 12 Verses 15-17
Commentary

12:15-16
*In an effort to foil Israel's escape, **the serpent** causes a great **flood** to follow the people, but an apparent earthquake swallows the water and the devil is outwitted.*
(2 Thessalonians 2:9-12 confirms that Satan has *power, signs, and lying wonders*; and gives a vital warning to anyone who refuses *to receive the love of truth*

12:17
*Furious over this humiliation, the devil seeks to wreak vengeance on some Jews who had not escaped—Jews who showed the reality of their faith by keeping **the commandments of God and have the testimony of Jesus Christ**.*
(Revelation 12:11)

Chapter 12 Verses 15-17
References

V. 15-16
2 Thessalonians 2:9-12 ⁹The coming of the lawless one will be in accordance with the work of Satan displayed in all kinds of counterfeit miracles, signs and wonders, ¹⁰and in every sort of evil that deceives those who are perishing. They perish because they refused to love the truth and so be saved. ¹¹For this reason God sends them a powerful delusion so that they will believe the lie ¹²and so that all will be condemned who have not believed the truth but have delighted in wickedness. [NIV]

Chapter 12 Verses 15-17
References Commentary

V. 15-16
In 2 Thessalonians 2:9-12 Satan has enormous power, but God always overpowers and humiliates him. Verses 10-12 warrant observation:

Once the Rapture leaves them behind, the naysayers who've actually heard the Gospel message and yet adopted the lies about the truth; it leaves one wondering whether they have a path to be redeemed to God. Will God give these yet another chance after He has given His verdict of condemnation here in the Age of Grace?

Hebrews 6:4-6: ⁴*For it is impossible for those who were once enlightened, and have tasted the heavenly gift, and have become partakers of the Holy Spirit, ⁵and have tasted the good word of God and the powers of the age to come, ⁶if they fall away, to renew them again to repentance, since they crucify again for themselves the Son of God, and put Him to an open shame.*

I believe it is important to notice the word *taste* in this passage. These people have only *tasted*; they have not *absorbed* the indwelling Holy Spirit who *seals* the true believer.

Revelation Chapters 6-12 have formed previews of the Seven-year Tribulation *warnings*.

Chapter 13 focuses on the last half of the Tribulation Period. We will see that people will suffer the wrath of the false trinity by being forced to worship Satan, the Antichrist *and his image (artificial look-alike and sound-alike intelligence*???), and the False Prophet—or else— have no means to survive.

Chapter 13 begins describing a *one-world-government*. We see huge strides in these last days of the Church Age in powerful organizations for this *globalization* movement

Chapter 13 Verses 1-18

Chapter 13 Verses 1-18
Commentary

**The Two Beasts from the Sea and the Land:
The Antichrist and the False Prophet**

INTRODUCTION

Chapter 13 introduces us to how Satan (the dragon) blasphemously sets up his own false "trinity". Satan acts as the Father, the Antichrist as the Son, and the False Prophet as the Spirit who attempts to bring glory to the Antichrist. Satan appoints two great beasts (men): the first beast rising up out of the sea (the nations)—the Antichrist and his empire—and the second beast out of the earth or land—the False Prophet— possibly a Jew. The land could be anywhere on the literal earth, or, possibly, the land of Israel.

These beasts symbolize men who will play prominent roles during the Tribulation Period. They combine the features of the four beasts of Daniel 7:3-9.

In Daniel 7:3, metaphorically speaking, the sea symbolizes Gentile nations.

Revelation 17:1 *One of the seven angels who had the seven bowls came and said to me, "Come, I will show you the punishment of the great prostitute, who sits on many waters."* [NIV]

Revelation 17:15 *Then the angel said to me, "The waters you saw, where the prostitute sits, are peoples, multitudes, nations and languages."* [NIV]

REVELATION 13:1-18 VERSES, COMMENTARY, REFERENCES AND REFERENCES COMMENTARY CAN BE FOUND ON THE FOLLOWING SETS OF PAGES.

Chapter 13 Verses 1-18
References

Chapter 13 Verses 1-18
References Commentary

Daniel 7:3-8 ³"Four great beasts, each different from the others, came up out of the sea. ⁴The first was like a lion, and it had the wings of an eagle. I watched until its wings were torn off and it was lifted from the ground so that it stood on two feet like a man, and the heart of a man was given to it. ⁵And there before me was a second beast, which looked like a bear. It was raised up on one of its sides, and it had three ribs in its mouth between its teeth. It was told, 'Get up and eat your fill of flesh!' ⁶After that, I looked, and there before me was another beast, one that looked like a leopard. And on its back it had four wings like those of a bird. The beast had four heads, and it was given authority to rule. ⁷After that, in my vision at night I looked, and there before me was a fourth beast-terrifying and frightening and very powerful. It had large iron teeth; it crushed and devoured its victims and trampled underfoot whatever was left. It was different from all the former beasts, and it had ten horns. ⁸While I was thinking about the horns, there before me was another horn, a little one, which came up among them; and three of the first horns were uprooted before it. This horn had eyes like the eyes of a man and a mouth that spoke boastfully." [NIV]

Daniel 7:3-8: The **four great beasts**—all rising **up out of the sea**, just like the Antichrist will rise from the sea (Revelation 13:1) *represent the four world empires*: Babylonian, Medo-Persian, Greek, and Roman; none of which honored God's chosen people Israel. *The **lion** stands for *Babylon*. The **eagle's wings** suggest swiftness of conquest. **The wings... plucked** may refer to Nebuchadnezzar's insanity, and the rest of verse 4 to his recovery and conversion* —becoming a believer in God (Daniel 4:16, 34). *The **bear** [the second beast] pictures *Medo-Persia*. The **three ribs**, North, Lydia; East, Babylon; South, Egypt, which it held **in its mouth** perhaps represent the three previous sections of the Babylonian Empire which were overtaken by the Medes and Persians under King Cyrus—Babylon in the east; Egypt in the south; and the Lydian kingdom in NW Asia Minor* (today's western Turkey). *The **leopard** symbolizes *the Greek Empire* with rapid expansion by Alexander the Great. The **four heads** apparently are Alexander's generals after his death. The **fourth beast, dreadful and terrible, exceedingly strong**, with **huge iron teeth**, speaks of the *Roman Empire* which followed the Greek Empire. In verse 8 a CONSIDERABLE SPACE OF TIME takes place [this is the Church Age which we are in right now] before the Roman Empire may be revived. Still future, it will have **ten horns**, that is ten kings, and a **little** [obscure] **horn**: the future head of the Roman Empire—the Antichrist.* The *three horns*, Egypt, Libya, and Ethiopia, to be *plucked out* (Daniel 11:42-43) leave seven kings.

Daniel 7:9 ⁹As I looked, "thrones were set in place, and the Ancient of Days took his seat. His clothing was as white as snow; the hair of his head was white like wool. His throne was flaming with fire, and its wheels were all ablaze." [NIV]

Daniel 7:9: In verse 9 Daniel pictures the fifth and final world empire—the glorious kingdom given to the Son by His Father—**the Ancient of Days** [as described much like the Son in Revelation 1:11-16]. In Daniel 7:13 and 22 we see **Ancient of Days** again..

Chapter 13 Verses 1-2

¹Then I stood on the sand of the sea. And I saw a beast rising up out of the sea, having seven heads and ten horns, and on his horns ten crowns, and on his heads a blasphemous name. ²Now the beast which I saw was like a leopard, his feet were like *the feet of* a bear, and his mouth like the mouth of a lion. The dragon gave him his power, his throne, and great authority.

Chapter 13 Verses 1-2
Commentary

13:1-2
The first **beast**, the Antichrist, who, although not known yet, will already be *among* the Church before the Rapture (1 John 4:3).

*He is the Gentile head of the revived Roman Empire, which will exist in a **ten**-kingdom form.* **The **sea** here represents the Gentile nations of the world, from one of which the Antichrist comes.** *The **seven heads** are said in Revelation 17:9-10 to be seven kings, or rulers, or seven different stages of the empire.*

The Antichrist will deceive many into thinking he is the messiah in 2 Thessalonians 2:3-4 and Daniel 11:36-37.

But the Antichrist will not be revealed until after a falling away of faith and until after the Holy Spirit indwelled Church is raptured (2 Thessalonians 2:7-8).

The pre-tribulation Rapture is confirmed in the following verses: John 14:1-3; 5:24; 3:36; Romans 5:9; 1 Thessalonians 4:13-18; 5:9; 1:10.

The **ten horns** were predicted by Daniel 7:24 to be a ten-kingdom form. The ten crowns on his horns speak of the power to rule from a throne with great authority, which was given to him by the dragon. **Satan is attempting to duplicate how God the Father gives all authority to the Son. The first **beast**—the Antichrist—will rule over the previous people and cultures of the three previous empires to the ancient Roman Empire of which Daniel's prophesies were fulfilled: Babylonian—**lion**; Medo-Persian—**bear**; Greek—**leopard**; all an outgrowth of the **iron toothed** Roman Empire.** *In short, the revived Roman Empire combines all the evil features of the preceding world empires. The empire and its ruler receive supernatural strength from Satan.*

Chapter 13 Verses 1-2 References	Chapter 13 Verses 1-2 References Commentary
Vv. 1-2 **1 John 4:3** and every spirit that does not confess that Jesus Christ has come in the flesh is not of God. And this is the *spirit* of the Antichrist, which you have heard was coming, and is now already in the world.	**Vv. 1-2** In 1 John 4:3 the **spirit of the Antichrist** which **is now already in the world** is a solid fact. *There are many *spirits* today who are willing to say good things about Jesus, but not to confess Him as God incarnate. They say that Christ is "divine," but not that He is *God*.*
2 Thessalonians 2:3-4 ³Let no one deceive you by any means; *for that Day will not come* unless the falling away comes first, and the man of sin is revealed, the son of perdition, ⁴who opposes and exalts himself above all that is called God or is worshiped, so that he sits as God in the temple of God, showing himself that he is God.	2 Thessalonians 2:3-4: *That Day* throughout much of God's Word refers to "The Day of the Lord [which] refers to Christ's second advent and the judgments immediately preceding it" (Ironside). *During the Tribulation those who refuse to worship the Antichrist will be persecuted and many will be martyred* (Revelation 20:4). Could the severe persecution which the Thessalonians were experiencing have driven them to thinking it had already begun?
Daniel 11:36-37 ³⁶The king will do as he pleases. He will exalt and magnify himself above every god and will say unheard-of things against the God of gods. He will be successful until the time of wrath is completed, for what has been determined must take place. ³⁷He will show no regard for the gods of his fathers or for the one desired by women, nor will he regard any god, but will exalt himself above them all. [NIV]	Daniel 11:36-37 is not only in complete agreement with 2 Thessalonians 2:4 but also reveals an even more startling description of the Antichrist (= **king** in verse 36).

2 Thessalonians 2:7-8
John 14:1-3; 5:24; 3:36
Daniel 7:24

-CONTINUED ON NEXT SET OF PAGES UNDER REFERENCES!-   **-CONTINUED ON NEXT SET OF PAGES UNDER REFERENCES COMMENTARY!-**

Chapter 13 Verses 1-2

-VERSES 1-2 REPEATED FROM PREVIOUS PAGE-

¹Then I stood on the sand of the sea. And I saw a beast rising up out of the sea, having seven heads and ten horns, and on his horns ten crowns, and on his heads a blasphemous name. ²Now the beast which I saw was like a leopard, his feet were like *the feet of* a bear, and his mouth like the mouth of a lion. The dragon gave him his power, his throne, and great authority.

Chapter 13 Verses 1-2
Commentary

-PART OF COMMENTARY VERSES 1-2 REPEATED FROM PREVIOUS PAGE-

13:1-2

But the Antichrist will not be revealed until after a falling away of faith and until after the Holy Spirit indwelled Church is raptured (2 Thessalonians 2:7-8).

The pre-tribulation Rapture is confirmed in the following verses: John 14:1-3; 5:24; 3:36; Romans 5:9; 1 Thessalonians 4:13-18; 5:9; 1:10.

The **ten horns** were predicted by Daniel 7:24 to be a ten-kingdom form. The ten crowns on his horns speak of the power to rule from a throne with great authority, which was given to him by the dragon. **Satan is attempting to duplicate how God the Father gives all authority to the Son. The first **beast**—the Antichrist—will rule over the previous people and cultures of the three previous empires to the ancient Roman Empire of which Daniel's prophesies were fulfilled: Babylonian—**lion**; Medo-Persian—**bear**; Greek—**leopard**; all an outgrowth of the **iron toothed** Roman Empire.** *In short, the revived Roman Empire combines all the evil features of the preceding world empires. The empire and its ruler receive supernatural strength from Satan.*

Chapter 13 Verses 1-2
References

Chapter 13 Verses 1-2
References Commentary

-CONTINUED FROM PREVIOUS PAGE-

-CONTINUED FROM PREVIOUS PAGE-

Vv. 1-2

Vv. 1-2

2 Thessalonians 2:7-8 ⁷For the mystery of the lawlessness is already at work; only He who now restrains *will* do so until He is taken out of the way. ⁸And then the lawless one will be revealed, whom the Lord will consume with the breath of His mouth and destroy with the brightness of His coming.

2 Thessalonians 2:7-8 combines with 2 Thessalonians 2:3 to reveal the two things which must happen before the Antichrist will be revealed: In verse 3 we see where *that Day will not come* unless the falling away comes first, and in verses 7-8 the lawless Antichrist cannot be revealed until after the Holy Spirit indwelled believers of the Church are raptured off the earth. And *then* the Antichrist will be revealed. Comparing Scripture to Scripture we see that the Church is raptured before the Antichrist begins the Seven-year Tribulation Period. It is in total agreement with 1 Thessalonians 5:1-9, and agrees with the chronological order in Revelation Chapters 2, 3, 4, 5, and 6.

John 14:1-3 *"Let not your heart be troubled; you believe in God, believe also in Me. ²In My Father's house are many mansions; if it were not so, I would have told you. I go to prepare a place for you. ³And if I go and prepare a place for you, I will come again and receive you to Myself; that where I am, there you may be also."*
John 5:24 *"Most assuredly, I say to you, he who hears My word and believes in Him who sent Me has everlasting life, and shall not come into judgment, but has passed from death into life."*
John 3:36 "Whoever believes in the Son has eternal life, but whoever rejects the Son will not see life, for God's wrath remains on him." [NIV]

John 14:1-3; 5:24; 3:36: These words of the Lord Jesus Christ and John the baptizer (3:36) confirm that the believers in the body of Christ, the Church, will not suffer any of God's wrath but will have eternal life from the moment when they first believed.

Daniel 7:24

-CONTINUED ON NEXT SET OF PAGES UNDER REFERENCES!-

-CONTINUED ON NEXT SET OF PAGES UNDER REFERENCES COMMENTARY!-

Chapter 13 Verses 1-2	Chapter 13 Verses 1-2 Commentary
-VERSES 1-2 REPEATED FROM PREVIOUS PAGE-	**-PART OF COMMENTARY VERSES 1-2 REPEATED FROM PREVIOUS PAGE-**

13:1-2

¹Then I stood on the sand of the sea. And I saw a beast rising up out of the sea, having seven heads and ten horns, and on his horns ten crowns, and on his heads a blasphemous name. ²Now the beast which I saw was like a leopard, his feet were like *the feet of* a bear, and his mouth like the mouth of a lion. The dragon gave him his power, his throne, and great authority.

The **ten horns** were predicted by Daniel 7:24 to be a ten-kingdom form.

The ten crowns on his horns speak of the power to rule from a throne with great authority, which was given to him by the dragon. **Satan is attempting to duplicate how God the Father gives all authority to the Son. The first **beast**—the Antichrist—will rule over the previous people and cultures of the three previous empires to the ancient Roman Empire of which Daniel's prophesies were fulfilled: Babylonian—**lion**; Medo-Persian—**bear**; Greek—**leopard**; all an outgrowth of the **iron toothed** Roman Empire.** *In short, the revived Roman Empire combines all the evil features of the preceding world empires. The empire and its ruler receive supernatural strength from Satan.*

Chapter 13 Verses 1-2 References	Chapter 13 Verses 1-2 References Commentary
-CONTINUED FROM PREVIOUS PAGE-	**-CONTINUED FROM PREVIOUS PAGE-**
Vv. 1-2	**Vv. 1-2**
Daniel 7:24 The ten horns are ten kings who will come from this kingdom. After them another king will arise, different from the earlier ones; he will subdue three kings. [NIV]	Daniel 7:24: The Antichrist will **subdue three kings**. Therefore, there will no longer be ten kings, but only seven. The Antichrist will overpower three of the ten nations: Egypt, Libya, and Ethiopia (Daniel 11:42-43).

Chapter 13 Verses 3-9

³And I saw one of his heads as if it had been mortally wounded, and his deadly wound was healed. And all the world marveled and followed the beast. ⁴So they worshiped the dragon who gave authority to the beast; and they worshiped the beast, saying, "Who *is* like the beast? Who is able to make war with him? ⁵And he was given a mouth speaking great things and blasphemies, and he was given authority to continue for forty-two months. ⁶Then he opened his mouth in blasphemy against God, to blaspheme His name, His tabernacle, and those who dwell in heaven. ⁷It was granted to him to make war with the saints and to overcome them. And authority was given him over every tribe, tongue, and nation. ⁸All who dwell on the earth will worship him, whose names have not been written in the Book of Life of the Lamb slain from the foundation of the world. ⁹If anyone has an ear, let him hear.

Chapter 13 Verses 3-9
Commentary

13:3-9
One of the beast's seven heads receives a **deadly wound**, and **all the world marveled** as the **wound was healed**. In John's vision the Antichrist was **wounded by the sword and lived** (Revelation 13:14).

Saying that *the **wound** is **healed** could possibly mean that the empire is revived—with an emperor—namely, the **beast*** —the **Antichrist**. *They also worship the **dragon**.*
In verse 4: worshipers will say, "**Who is able to make war with him?**" Deceiving them into thinking: *only one nation*, how could there be a war? The Antichrist will likely take credit for victory over the Battle of Gog and Māgog which will have already ended. (Ezekiel 38 and 39).
Verse 5 is the beginning of the second half of the Seven-year Tribulation Period. **The beast's authority to make war lasts 42 months (three-and-a-half years)**. *The **beast** is **worshiped** by men. They are not only amazed at him; **they actually worship him** thinking he is God* **the Savior (2 Thessalonians 2:1-3, 9-12).

Verse 7 is possibly pointing to the beginning of the war of Armageddon which will end in Revelation 16:17. At the end of verse 7, during this Great Tribulation the Antichrist will control a one world government—globalism. In verse 8 the **beast** will persecute the saints of God, and **all whose names are not in the Book of Life of the Lamb will be deceived to worship Satan** and the Antichrist**.
John writes of the Savior's plea, *"He who has an ear, let him hear what the Spirit says"*...

(Revelation 2:7, 11, 17, 29; 3:6, 13, 22: These verses illustrate Jesus' warnings to the seven churches.).

Chapter 13 Verses 3-9
References

Vv. 3-9
Revelation 13:14 Because of the signs he was given power to do on behalf of the first beast, he deceived the inhabitants of the earth. He ordered them to set up an image in honor of the beast who was wounded by the sword and yet lived. [NIV]

2 Thessalonians 2:1-3 Now, brethren, concerning the coming of our Lord Jesus Christ and our gathering together to Him, we ask you, ²not to be soon shaken in mind or troubled, either by spirit or by word or by letter, as if from us, as though the day of Christ had come. ³Let no one deceive you by any means; for *that Day will not come* unless the falling away comes first, and the man of sin is revealed, the son of perdition,

2 Thessalonians 2:9-12 ⁹The coming of the lawless one will be in accordance with the work of Satan displayed in all kinds of counterfeit miracles, signs and wonders, ¹⁰and in every sort of evil that deceives those who are perishing. They perish because they refused to love the truth and so be saved. ¹¹For this reason God sends them a powerful delusion so that they will believe the lie ¹²and so that all will be condemned who have not believed the truth but have delighted in wickedness. [NIV]

Chapter 13 Verses 3-9
References Commentary

Vv. 3-9
Revelation 13:14: *The Roman emperor [Antichrist by the will of Satan] gives unlimited authority to the False Prophet to act on his behalf. The purpose of his miracles (2 Thessalonians 2:9) is to deceive the people into worshiping a man (the Antichrist) as God.*

2 Thessalonians 2:1-3: Verse 2 of the KJV and NKJV both say, **as though the day of Christ had come**. The day of *Christ* in other Scriptures has to do with receiving rewards following the Rapture (1 Corinthians 1:8; 3:8, 14; 2 Corinthians 1:14; Philippians 1:6; 1:10; 2:16; Colossians 3:24; Hebrews 10:25; 2 John 8).
The NIV, NLT, ESV, and other versions, *instead of day of Christ*, have d*ay of the Lord*, which refers to God's wrath rather than rewards. Consider: **Christ *is* Lord** (Philippians 2:11).
Verse 1, **our gathering together to Him** (1 Thessalonians 4:17) is undeniably referring to the Rapture.
Verse 3 is referring to the Lord's wrath preceding and upon His coming.
Verse 2 is a transition from verse 1 (the Rapture) to verse 3 (the revealing of the Antichrist. (*that Day will not come unless*).
The Thessalonians had mistakenly thought the Day of the Lord—the Tribulation—had already begun. The Rapture had to take place first. (2 Thessalonians 2:7-8)

2 Thessalonians 2:9-12 confirms Satan has enormous deceptive power to conquer souls. These verses are essentially saying that anyone who had heard the truth but still outwardly rejected Christ, they would not be given another opportunity; they will neither be raptured nor be saved during the Tribulation. *The **lie**, of course is the Antichrist's claim to be God.*

Chapter 13 Verses 10-14

Chapter 13 Verses 10-14
Commentary

The False Prophet, Second Beast and the Mark of the Beast

¹⁰"If anyone is to go into captivity, into captivity they will go. If anyone is to be killed with the sword, with the sword they will be killed." This calls for patient endurance and faithfulness on the part of God's people. [NIV]

13:10
*The ones who have come to be true believers are assured that their persecutors, the Antichrist and his followers, **shall go into captivity** and **be killed with the sword** (Revelation 19:20-21). This enables **the saints** [holy ones] to wait **patiently** with **faith*** (Revelation 14:12; 2:10).

¹¹Then I saw a second beast, coming up out of the earth. It had two horns like a lamb, but it spoke like a dragon. ¹²It exercised all the authority of the first beast on its behalf, and made the earth and its inhabitants worship the first beast, whose fatal wound had been healed. ¹³And it performed great signs, even causing fire to come down from heaven on the earth in full view of the people. ¹⁴Because of the signs it was given power to perform on behalf of the first beast, it deceived the inhabitants of the earth. It ordered them to set up an image in honor of the beast who was wounded by the sword and yet lived. [NIV]

13:11-14
The second **beast** is the False Prophet symbolizing the "Holy Spirit of God" in Satan's false "trinity". *He comes up out of the land. If the land is Israel, he is likely a Jew. He has **two horns like a lamb**, giving the appearance of gentleness and harmlessness* (Matthew 7:15), *but also suggesting that he speaks for the Lamb of God. He converses **like a dragon**, indicating that he is directly inspired and empowered by Satan. He works closely with the Antichrist, first beast, even organizing an international campaign for the worship of the Antichrist, and makes an **image** [huge idol illustration; AI?]* of the Antichrist to show the Antichrist was **wounded—and lived**.
The Antichrist is the political ruler and the False Prophet is the priestly religious leader who promotes global worship of the Antichrist. With today's technology, artificial intelligent beings could be placed all over the globe.

*The False Prophet has even been given supernatural power from Satan to cause **fire** to fall **from heaven**. The purpose of his miracles is to deceive the people into worshiping a man as though the man is God* (Deuteronomy 13:1-3; Matthew 24:24; 2 Thessalonians 2:9).

The second beast—the False Prophet—has now been introduced.

Chapter 13 Verses 10-14 References	Chapter 13 Verses 10-14 References Commentary
V. 10 **Revelation 14:12** This calls for patient endurance on the part of the saints who obey God's commandments and remain faithful to Jesus. [NIV]	**V. 10** Revelation 14:12: The Tribulation Period will require much patience, perseverance, and endurance. But the difference between temporary suffering and eternal life will be worth whatever one must go through.
Vv. 11-14 **Matthew 7:15** "Watch out for false prophets. They come to you in sheep's clothing, but inwardly they are ferocious wolves." [NIV]	**Vv. 11-14** The Lord Jesus warned in Matthew 7:15 to **watch out for false prophets**, and the purpose of the Tribulation False Prophet's miracles is to deceive the people into worshiping a man as though the man is God. See also Acts 20:29.
Deuteronomy 13:1-3 ¹If a prophet, or one who foretells by dreams, appears among you and announces to you a miraculous sign or wonder of which he has spoken takes place, and he says, "Let us follow other gods" (gods you have not known) "and let us worship them," ³you must not listen to the words of that prophet or dreamer. The LORD your God is testing you to find out whether you love him with all your heart and with all your soul. [NIV]	Also, the LORD our God is quoted in Deuteronomy 13:1-3 for us **not to listen to** these kinds of deceivers.
Matthew 24:24 "For false christs and false prophets will rise and show great signs and wonders to deceive, if possible, even the elect."	Matthew 24:24: *Miracles are not necessarily from God. Miracles can be satanic in origin. The man of sin will be given satanic power to perform miracles (2 Thessalonians 2:9, 10)*.

Chapter 13 Verse 15

Chapter 13 Verse 15
Commentary

13:15

¹⁵The second beast was given power to give breath to the image of the first beast, so that the image could speak and cause all who refused to worship the image to be killed. [NIV]

Having been given power from Satan, the False Prophet gives a delusion to make the great **image** of the beast able to speak (2 Thessalonians 2:4, 9-11). Could this be A.I.?

The **image of the beast** not only appears able to speak, but also causes those who **would not worship the image** (idol) **to be killed**. It seems more and more probable that the **images of the beast** are likely artificial intelligence robots (AI).

Chapter 13 Verse 15
References

V. 15

2 Thessalonians 2:4   who opposes and exalts himself above all that is called God or that is worshiped, so that he sits as God in the temple of God, showing himself that he is God.

2 Thessalonians 2:9-11   ⁹The coming of the lawless one will be in accordance with the work of Satan displayed in all kinds of counterfeit miracles, signs and wonders, ¹⁰and in every sort of evil that deceives those who are perishing. They perish because they refused to love the truth and so be saved. ¹¹For this reason God sends them a powerful delusion so that they will believe the lie   [NIV]

Chapter 13 Verse 15
References Commentary

V. 15

In 2 Thessalonians 2:4 and 9-11 we learn that those who fall for all this unrighteous **deception** (and **believe the lie**) are led to perishing (into the eternal lake of fire), because God sends them a strong delusion, since **they refused to love the truth so be saved** (Revelation 19:20-21; 20:11-15). God controlled the minds and sent *strong delusion* to Pharaoh, Baalam, and Nebuchadnezzar (Exodus 7-11; Numbers 22-24; Daniel 4).

Chapter 13 Verses 16-17

¹⁶It also forced all people, great and small, rich and poor, free and slave, to receive a mark on their right hands or on their foreheads, ¹⁷so that they could not buy or sell unless they had the mark, which is the name of the beast or the number of its name. [NIV]

Chapter 13 Verses 16-17
Commentary

13:16-17
By mocking God's Word such as Romans 2:11 (and Galatians 3:28—one of Satan's most misused and abused verses in Scripture; and 2 Corinthians 3:17) by saying, "**both small and great, rich and poor, free and slave,**" the False Prophet requires all people **to receive** the **mark which is the name of the beast** (the Antichrist, possibly Roman Emperor) **or the number of its name...on their right hand or on their foreheads**. **Only the unbelievers will comply.**

In not submitting to the political and religious system of the Antichrist beast, the believers will not be able to **buy or sell**. This will be a severe economic and survival test, but true believers will prefer death to renouncing their Savior. This will be the consequence of earlier rejecting the Savior and accepting a "one world government" dictating to everyone in the world.

Chapter 13 Verses 16-17
References

Vv. 16-17
Romans 2:11 For God does not show favoritism. [NIV]

Galatians 3:28 There is neither Jew nor Greek, slave nor free, male nor female; for you are all one in Christ Jesus. [NIV]

2 Corinthians 3:17 Now the Lord is the Spirit; and where the Spirit of the Lord is, there is freedom. [NIV]

Chapter 13 Verses 16-17
References Commentary

Vv. 16-17
Romans 2:11 tells us plainly that **there is no partiality with God** to be saved. Some have been deceived into believing that this verse means there is no partiality for performing the responsibilities which God has prescribed in His Word for His way to conduct the assembly meeting. However, when comparing Scripture to Scripture, this verse is speaking plainly about salvation.

Galatians 3:28: We all need to be careful, to watch out not to be deceived. This verse can so easily be "misinterpreted" to contradict God's Word to say "it is really okay for women to be senior leaders in the Church," although 1 Corinthians 14:34-35 and 1 Timothy 2:11-12; 3:2, and 3:12 would then be contradicted. This would even further contradict God's pure, flawless Word. Proverbs 30:5 and Psalm 12:6 say that God's Word is pure. Isaiah 40:8 and 1 Peter 1:23, 25 say that it endures forever. Malachi 3:6 tells us that God does not change. Hebrews 4:12 informs us that His Word is alive.

Some might believe we've been given *liberty* to have God's Word tell us what would seem to be more convenient and have it say what we want it to mean instead of His original intent: 2 Corinthians 3:17, liberty *that is, **freedom** from the bondage of the law, freedom from obscurity in reading the Scriptures, and freedom to gaze upon His face without a veil between,*

We want to be cautious not to violate God's way. Some might be misinformed and mean well, but when the truth is revealed; we should "hear what the Spirit says to the churches."

Chapter 13 Verse 18

**Chapter 13 Verse 18
Commentary**

¹⁸This calls for wisdom. Let the person who has insight calculate the number of the beast, for it is the number of a man: That number is 666. [NIV]

13:18
**The number of the beast is 666—trinity of evil; (777 represents "Holy Trinity.")
The number of his name, of *mankind* is **666.****
Applying wisdom, we see that the Antichrist is *not* God, but rather *a man* (Psalm 118:8).

Those who take the **number** or the **image** will receive the wrath of God
(Revelation 14:9-11; 16:2, 19; 18:6; 19:20-21♦; 20:10♦; 2 Thessalonians 1:6♦).

Those who resist the mark and image will win victory over the number of his name and will sing the song of the Lamb to praise God (Revelation 15:2-3♦; Revelation 20:4b, 10).

♦Verses with this symbol ♦ also have to do with the subject of the mark of the beast

Chapter 13 Verse 18 References	Chapter 13 Verse 18 References Commentary
V. 18 **Psalm 118:8** It is better to trust in the LORD than to put confidence in man.	**V. 18** Psalm 118:8: If anyone takes the mark of man it then becomes a sign of *permanent* rejection of the Lord God and Savior. The mark of the beast spells eternal doom and suffering for those who accept the beast over Jesus Christ.
Revelation 14:9-11 ⁹Then a third angel followed them, saying with a loud voice, "If anyone worships the beast and his image, and receives *his* mark on his forehead or on his hand, ¹⁰he himself shall also drink of the wine of the wrath of God, which is poured out full strength into the cup of His indignation. He shall be tormented with fire and brimstone in the presence of the holy angels and in the presence of the Lamb. ¹¹And the smoke of their torment ascends forever and ever; and they have no rest day or night, who worship the beast and his image, and whoever receives the mark of his name."	By mocking God's Word, God will turn minds over to trusting in false teaching so sincerely that many will take the **mark** of the **beast** and will be **tormented** from then on **forever and ever** as told in Revelation 14:9-11.
Revelation 16:2 The first angel went and poured out his bowl on the land, and ugly and painful sores broke out on the people who had the mark of the beast and worshiped his image. [NIV]	Revelation 16:2 informs us that a **ugly and painful sores** will come **upon the people who** will take **the mark of the beast** and those **who worship his image**. What a thing to consider!
Revelation 19:20 Then the beast was captured, and with him the false prophet who worked signs in his presence, by which he deceived those who received the mark of the beast and those who worshiped his image.	Revelation 19:20 reminds all who read and understand this prophecy not to be **deceived** by the **signs** of a false prophet. The **beast** in this verse is, again, the Antichrist.
Revelation 20:4b And I saw the souls of those who had been beheaded because of their testimony for Jesus and because of the word of God. They had not worshiped the beast or his image and had not received his mark on their foreheads or their hands. They came to life and reigned with Christ a thousand years. [NIV] **Revelation 20:10** And the devil, who deceived them, was thrown into the lake of burning sulfur, where the beast and the false prophet had been thrown. They will be tormented day and night for ever and ever. [NIV]	Revelation 20:4b and 20:10 remind us that **those** who exercise much patience, perseverance, and endurance, who **had not received** *the deceiver's* **mark on their foreheads or on their hands**, will not perish to the lake of fire, but will live **and reign with Christ** for **a thousand years**. For the unbeliever an opposite destination is revealed in Revelation 20:10. Then those who rejected Christ who will be judged by the Son of God at the great white throne (Revelation 20:11) will join them: Revelation 20:15: *And anyone not found written in the Book of Life was cast into the lake of fire.*

Chapter 14 Verses 1-5

Chapter 14 Verses 1-5
Commentary

The Messages of Six Angels

¹Then I looked, and behold, a Lamb standing on Mount Zion, and with Him one hundred *and* forty-four thousand, having His Father's name written on their foreheads.

14:1
The **Lamb is Christ. **Mount Zion** is Jerusalem. This verse is looking forward to Christ's Second Coming for His Millennial Reign.** The **144,000** who will be in Jerusalem when He arrives are the same as the ones in Revelation 7:1-8. None of these are part of the *two-thirds* who will not survive the Tribulation (Zechariah 12:8).

²And I heard a voice from heaven, like the voice of many waters, and like the voice of loud thunder. And I heard the sound of harpists playing their harps. ³They sang as it were a new song before the throne, before the four living creatures, and the elders; and no one could learn that song except the hundred *and* forty-four thousand who were redeemed from the earth. ⁴These are the ones who were not defiled with women, for they are virgins. These are the ones who follow the Lamb wherever He goes. These were redeemed from *among* men, *being* firstfruits to God and to the Lamb. ⁵And in their mouth was found no deceit, for they are without fault before the throne of God.

14:2-5
The voice of many waters like the voice of loud thunder represents God's authority and audible power (Psalm 77:18).

The **four creatures and **elders** are the angels and elders of Revelation 4:4-8. That the 144,000 are **virgins** and **not defiled with women** may indicate either (literally) celibacy and sexual purity or (figuratively) moral and religious purity (refusal to submit to the False Prophet's system). The 144,000 are the **firstfruits** of the **redeemed**—the first to be saved—during the Tribulation Period (following the Rapture of the Church). That **they are without fault** means that they are ethically blameless (Ephesians 1:4; Ephesians 5:27; Philippians 2:15; Colossians 1:22; 1 Peter 1:19; Jude 24).**

Chapter 14 Verses 1-5
References

Chapter 14 Verses 1-5
References Commentary

Vv. 2-5
Psalm 77:18 Your thunder was heard in the whirlwind; your lightning lit up the world; the earth trembled and quaked. [NIV]

Vv. 2-5
Psalm 77:18 provides an electrifying example of our Almighty God's awesome power with which we can all simultaneously, physically and spiritually feel and sense. But when we hear God speaking to us individually, His indwelling Spirit is reminding us in our consciences of what we've heard or read in His guiding and saving Word.

Ephesians 1:4 just as He chose us in Him before the foundation of the world, that we should be holy and without blame before Him in love,

In Ephesians 1:4 we read of God's omniscience to know everything there is to know past present and future (Psalm 139:1-6). He even knew who would choose Him, love Him, and believe in Him to receive the holy righteousness of God through the Lord Jesus Christ (Romans 3:22-23.).

Philippians 2:15 so that you may become blameless and pure, children of God without fault in a crooked and depraved generation, in which you shine like stars in the universe [NIV]
Colossians 1:22 in the body of His flesh through death, to present you holy, and blameless, and above reproach in His sight—
1 Peter 1:19 but with the precious blood of Christ, a lamb without blemish or defect. [NIV]
Jude 24 Now to Him who is able to keep you from stumbling, and to present you faultless before the presence of His glory with exceeding joy,

Philippians 2:15, Colossians 1:22, 1 Peter 1:19, and Jude 24 give the wonderful truth and promise that being believers, we will all be seen as **holy, and blameless...***redeemed* **with the precious blood of Christ...without blemish or defect, children of God without fault** in the midst of a crooked and perverse **generation**, among whom we shine as lights in the world.

Chapter 14 Verses 6-8

⁶Then I saw another angel flying in the midst of heaven, having the everlasting gospel to preach to those who dwell on the earth—to every nation, tribe, tongue, and people— ⁷saying with a loud voice, "Fear God and give glory to Him, for the hour of His judgment has come; and worship Him who made heaven and earth, the sea and springs of water." ⁸And another angel followed, saying, "Babylon is fallen, that great city, because she has made all nations drink of the wine of the wrath of her fornication."

Chapter 14 Verses 6-8 Commentary

14:6-8
The announcement by the first two angels is the anticipation of coming events. **The **everlasting gospel** (Matthew 24:14) is that the "Good News" is not only of salvation through faith in Christ, but added here, that Christ will win and the Beast will be judged. The **everlasting gospel** definitely focuses on people being redeemed back to God through Christ and the coming of His eternal kingdom. For unbelievers there are three negative parts of this "News": **the hour of... judgment has come** (Revelation 14:7); **Babylon♦ is fallen** (Revelation 14:8). This is referring to the *religious* system of Babylon falling. Here, in the idolatrous religious system, those who "worship the beast" will be tormented "for ever" (Revelation 14:9-11). All **nations**—the whole world—are commanded to **fear God** and **give glory to Him** instead of the beast**
(Revelation 14:6-7).

[**Jeremiah 51:7** *Babylon was a gold cup in the LORD's hand; she made the whole earth drunk. The nations drank her wine; therefore they have now gone mad.* [KJV]]

♦**Babylon** represents apostate Judaism and apostate Christendom, which will be a vast religious and commercial conglomerate with headquarters in Rome. **All nations** will have become drunk with **the wine of the wrath of her fornication.**♦
Where the angel decries "*Babylon is fallen*" here in Revelation 14:8 it is referring to the religious system due to their idol worship. Revelation 17 provides the details of the religious system collapse and Revelation 18 will specifies the elements of the commercial system's destruction.

Please find at the end of this study guide a summary of **The Beginning of the Babylonian Religion.**

Chapter 14 Verses 6-8
References

Vv. 6-8
Matthew 24:14 *"And this gospel of the kingdom will be preached in all the world as a witness to all the nations, and then the end will come."*

Chapter 14 Verses 6-8
References Commentary

Vv. 6-8
Matthew 24:14 refers to the end of the world; not the same as Romans 11:25, the end of the Church Age. When the last member will be added to the Church, completing the Body of Christ, this will be when He will rapture His Church home to heaven. **The end** that **will come** at the Rapture will be **the end** of the Church Age which began 2,000 years ago at Pentecost. The subsequent context of Matthew 24 is about the Tribulation which occurs after the Rapture. **The end** of the Seven-year Tribulation period will come about when the Lord Jesus returns to the earth with His army of saints and ends the war of Armageddon (Revelation 19:11-17).

The chronological order of Revelation events is now beginning to be revealed, as we more clearly see Almighty God Lord Jesus Christ being revealed as the Star of past present and future.

Chapter 14 Verses 9-10

⁹Then a third angel followed them, saying with a loud voice, "If anyone worships the beast and his image, and receives *his* mark on his forehead or on his hand, ¹⁰he himself shall also drink of the wine of the wrath of God, which is poured out full strength into the cup of His indignation. He shall be tormented with fire and brimstone in the presence of the holy angels and in the presence of the Lamb.

Chapter 14 Verses 9-10
Commentary

14:9-10
A third angel informs us that unbelievers, beginning at mid-Tribulation [which is the same as the beginning of the Great Tribulation] who have received the **mark** of the **beast** [Antichrist] and **worshiped** him will all eventually receive God's eternal punishment in the lake of **fire** (Matthew 25:41; Revelation 20:15).

The wine of the wrath of God will make **all nations drunk (v. 8). God's righteous anger (Job 21:20; Psalm 75:8; Isaiah 51:17; Jeremiah 25:15-16♦) is **poured out** in full strength on those who reject Him.
The cup of His indignation *symbolizes* the place of God's punishment of sinners...all taking place **in the presence of** Christ and His **angels** making the punishment even more intense and shameful.**
Hādēs will only be a *foretaste* of the pangs of the eternal lake of fire. And the Savior, who died for us, took this wrath of God for each one of us!

Later, at the Great White Throne Judgment (Revelation 20:11-15) the unbelievers will pay that *eternal* price of having chosen Satan and evil over God's truth, love, and righteousness.

♦Jeremiah 25:15-38 details the wrath of the Lord from on high. (Definitely worth turning to and reading)

Chapter 14 Verses 9-10
References

Vv. 9-10
Matthew 25:41 "Then He will also say to those on the left hand, 'Depart from Me, you cursed, into the everlasting fire prepared for the devil and his angels:"

Job 21:20 His eyes shall see his destruction, and he shall drink of the wrath of the Almighty. [KJV]
Psalm 75:8 In the hand of the LORD is a cup full of foaming wine mixed with spices; he pours it out, and all the wicked of the earth drink it down to its very dregs. [NIV]
Isaiah 51:17 Awake, awake! Stand up, O Jerusalem, you who have drunk at the hand of the LORD the cup of His fury; you have drunk the dregs of the cup of trembling, *and* drained it out.
Jeremiah 25:15-16 ¹⁵This is what the LORD, the God of Israel, said to me: "Take from my hand this cup filled with the wine of my wrath and make all the nations, to whom I send you drink it. ¹⁶When they drink it, they will stagger and go mad because of the sword I will send among them." [NIV]

Revelation 20:11-15 ¹¹Then I saw a great white throne and Him who sat on it, from whose face the earth and the heaven fled away. And there was found no place for them. ¹²And I saw the dead, small and great, standing before God, and books were opened. And another book was opened, which is *the Book* of Life. And the dead were judged according to their works, by the things which were written in the books. ¹³The sea gave up the dead who were in it, and Death and Hādēs delivered up the dead who were in them. And they were judged, each one according to his works. ¹⁴Then Death and Hādēs were cast into the lake of fire. This is the second death. ¹⁵And anyone not found written in the Book of Life was cast into the lake of fire.

Chapter 14 Verses 9-10
References Commentary

Vv. 9-10
Matthew 25:41 quotes the Lord Jesus as He refers back to 25:33 so that we can understand whom those are that are on **the left hand**: He sets His true followers—the sheep—on His right, but the **cursed**—the goats—on **the left**. Furthermore, here in verse 41 He promises the unbelievers an eternal future **into the everlasting fire prepared for the devil and his angels**.

Job 21:20, Psalm 75:8, Isaiah 51:17, and Jeremiah 25:15-16 all speak of the **drink of the wrath of the Almighty**, or the **wine cup of His fury**. The **cup** here portrays the totality of God's divine judgment on the wicked (also in Psalm 75:8; Isaiah 51:17, Isaiah 51:22; Jeremiah 25:15-16; Jeremiah 49:12; Jeremiah 51:7; Ezekiel 23:31-34; Revelation 16:19; Revelation 17:4; and here in Revelation 14:10).
The cup can also represent blessings or salvation for a righteous person. (Psalm 16:5; Psalm 23:5; Psalm 116:13). Jesus voluntarily drank the cup of suffering (Matthew 20:22; 26:39, 42; Mark 10:38; 14:36; Luke 22:20; John 18:11).

In Revelation 20:11-15 **The **dead** are the *unbelieving* dead of all past ages—that is, the *rest of the dead* mentioned in Revelation 20:5a. They are **judged** from two sets of **books** containing the record of every unsaved person's life. Each person is judged in accordance with his **works** (Romans 2:6, 16; 3:23; 6:23). The **Book of Life** contains the name of every person who has received eternal life through faith in the Lord Jesus Christ. **Death and Hādēs** are the temporary holding places of unsaved bodies and souls (Luke 16:19-31). The **second death** is eternal punishment in the **lake of fire**.**

| Chapter 14 Verses 11-13 | Chapter 14 Verses 11-13 Commentary |

14:11

¹¹And the smoke of their torment will rise for ever and ever. There will be no rest day or night for those who worship the beast and its image, or for anyone who receives the mark of its name." [NIV]

Verse 11 reminds us that the eternal lake of fire consists of everlasting and conscious punishment. The **smoke of their torment will rise** perpetually—**no** relief **day or night**.

Daniel 12:2; John 5:29 give consequences for both the saved and unsaved. Verse 11 is in stark contrast to our eternal life that's already begun.

14:12-13

¹²This calls for patient endurance on the part of the people of God who keep his commands and remain faithful to Jesus. ¹³Then I heard a voice from heaven say, "Write this: Blessed are the dead who die in the Lord from now on." "Yes," says the Spirit, "they will rest from their labor, for their deeds will follow them." [NIV]

The Church—the Body of Christ—His Bride—will already have been raptured before the Tribulation Period (Revelation 4:1; 5:11; 15:2). The believers who have died or will die **in the Lord** from here on are Old Testament saints and Tribulation martyrs. Coming to Christ in the Tribulation Period, the Tribulation martyrs will endure extreme persecution including death (Revelation 7:9-14). During their suffering, **patience** will certainly be required. These saints will surely be leaning on the Lord Jesus Christ for His comfort. They will be called to endure the savagery of the beast and to obey **God** by refusing to worship man or idol, and to hold fast their confession of **faith in Jesus**. They will be **blessed** by being in the third and last part of the first resurrection and will reign with Christ and the other saints during the Millennium.

Chapter 14 Verses 11-13 References	Chapter 14 Verses 11-13 References Commentary
V. 11 **Daniel 12:2** Multitudes who sleep in the dust of the earth will awake: some to everlasting life, others to shame and everlasting contempt. [NIV] **John 5:29** *"and come out—those who have done good will rise to live, and those who have done evil will rise to be condemned."* [NIV]	**V. 11** **Eternal separation is now made between those who have **life** and those who have **death** (Daniel 12:2; John 5:28-29).**

Chapter 14 Verse 14	Chapter 14 Verse 14 Commentary
¹⁴Then I looked, and behold, a white cloud, and on the cloud sat *One* like the Son of Man, having on His head a golden crown, and in His hand a sharp sickle.	**14:14** ****The Son of Man** is Christ, the Messiah (Revelation 1:13; Daniel 7:13; Matthew 26:63-64). The **crown** pictures Him as the Ruler of the earth, and the **sickle** symbolizes judgment as an instrument of unbelievers harvest (John 5:27** "*and* [the Father] *has given Him authority to execute judgment also, because He is the Son of Man.*"). The **cloud** reminds us of Christ's ascension and relates to His soon Second Coming (Matthew 24:30; Acts 1:9-11).

Chapter 14 Verse 14 References	Chapter 14 Verse 14 References Commentary
V. 14	**V. 14**
Revelation 1:13 and in the midst of the seven lampstands *One* like the Son of Man, clothed with a garment down to the feet and girded about the chest with a golden band.	Revelation 1:13 describes John's vision of how **the Son of Man**—the Messiah—appeared when John saw Him in the vision of the prophecy.
Daniel 7:13 "I was watching in the night visions, and behold, *One* like the Son of Man, coming with the clouds of heaven! He came to the Ancient of Days, and they brought Him near before Him.	Daniel 7:13: **The Son of Man** in Daniel's prophecy also describes who Daniel saw in the vision—the Son of God approaching God the Father. Jesus took to referring to Himself as the Son of Man from Ezekiel and Daniel's writings.
Matthew 26:63-64 ⁶³But Jesus kept silent. And the high priest answered and said to Him, "I will put You under oath by the living God: Tell us if You are the Christ, the Son of God!" ⁶⁴Jesus said to him, "*It is as* you said. Nevertheless, I say to you, hereafter you will see the Son of Man sitting at the right hand of the Power, and coming on the clouds of heaven."	In Matthew 26:63-64 Jesus no longer remained silent as He did when the high priest had previously been questioning Him. He only answered now because the high priest **put** Him **under oath by the living God**. Jesus, being compelled to answer (since He is also God Himself), admits that He is **the Christ** (the Messiah—the Savior), **the Son of God**. This is in no way boasting. It is merely the truth. The rest of His answer refers to His Second Coming at the end of the Great Tribulation.
Matthew 24:30 "Then the sign of the Son of Man will appear in heaven, and then all the tribes of the earth will mourn, and they will see the Son of Man coming on the clouds of heaven with power and great glory."	In Matthew 24:30 Jesus is referring to His Second Coming at the end of the Seven-year Tribulation Period. He mentions the word **sign** of Himself, and "**then all the tribes of the earth will mourn.**" We believers have no way of knowing when He will come to rapture us (1 Thessalonians 4:16-17). We learn He will come in the air to take us up in the clouds at least seven years *before* the Tribulation.
Acts 1:9-11 ⁹Now when He had spoken these things, while they watched, He was taken up, and a cloud received Him out of their sight. ¹⁰And while they looked steadfastly toward heaven as He went up, behold, two men stood by them in white apparel, ¹¹who also said, "Men of Galilee, why do you stand gazing up into heaven? This *same* Jesus, who was taken up from you into heaven, will so come in like manner as you saw Him go into heaven."	The last sentence in Acts 1:9-11 says, **"This *same* Jesus, who was taken up from you into heaven, will so come in like manner as you saw Him go into heaven."**

Chapter 14 Verses 15-16

¹⁵And another angel came out of the temple, crying with a loud voice to Him who sat on the cloud, "Thrust in Your sickle and reap, for the time has come for You to reap for the harvest of the earth is ripe." ¹⁶So He who sat on the cloud thrust in His sickle on the earth, and the earth was reaped.

Chapter 14 Verses 15-16
Commentary

14:15-16
The fourth angel came out of the temple saying that **the time is come to finish the judgment of the **earth**.
The Second Coming of Christ includes more judgment.
The harvest of the earth is ripe meaning it is time for God's judgment of the earth right now!

To **reap** and harvest **the earth** means to judge and punish its people (Hosea 6:11; Matthew 13:30; Matthew 13:40-42).**

The sickle in verse 15 is the second of seven times the sickle we see in this Chapter.

Chapter 14 Verses 15-16 References	Chapter 14 Verses 15-16 References Commentary
Vv. 15-16	Vv. 15-16
Hosea 6:11 Also, O Judah, a harvest is appointed for you, when I return the captives of My people.	In Hosea 6:11 **The southern kingdom would fare no better than Ēphraim, but some 130 years later for the same reasons of idolatry, but by a different God-sent agent, **Babylon**.**
Matthew 13:40-42 ⁴⁰"Therefore as the tares are gathered and burned in the fire, so it will be at the end of this age. ⁴¹The Son of man will send out His angels, and they will gather out of His kingdom all things that offend, and those who practice lawlessness, ⁴²and will cast them into the furnace of fire. There will be wailing and gnashing of teeth."	Matthew 13:40-42 quoting T. Ernest Wilson's *God's Sacred Secrets*, p75, "The harvest is the ultimate test of that which is genuine wheat and that which is false and poisonous [grain]. One of Satan's chief weapons to undermine the work of God is imitation. Whenever God is working, the devil copies that work so cleverly that it is often difficult to distinguish the genuine [believers] from the counterfeit." The separation of tares from the wheat in Matthew 13:40-42 relates to the **gathering** of unbelievers from believers. (Revelation 14:15-16) *The reapers are angels who, at the Second Advent (Second Coming) will round up all evildoers and throw **them into the furnace of fire**, where they will weep and gnash their teeth.*

Chapter 14 Verses 17-20

¹⁷Another angel came out of the temple in heaven, and he too had a sharp sickle. ¹⁸Still another angel, who had charge of the fire, came from the altar and called in a loud voice to him who had the sharp sickle, "Take your sharp sickle and gather the clusters of grapes from the earth's vine, because its grapes are ripe." ¹⁹The angel swung his sickle on the earth, gathered its grapes and threw them into the great winepress of God's wrath. ²⁰They were trampled in the winepress outside the city, and blood flowed out of the press, rising as high as the horses' bridles, for a distance of 1,600 stadia. [NIV] [184 miles].

Chapter 14 Verses 17-20
Commentary

14:17-20
These next verses represent God's wrath. The fifth **angel came out of the temple** also having **a sharp sickle**. The sixth **angel came from the altar, who had charge of the fire** *which symbolizes even more judgment to follow. The mature grapes are gathered and thrown **into the great winepress of the wrath of God**. The trampling of grapes in the process of making wine is used here as a picture of *crushing* judgment.*
The **winepress was trampled outside the city** of Jerusalem, **and blood flowed out of the winepress** for one thousand six hundred **stadia.** One stadia, also a furlong equals 8.7 miles, so 1,600 furlongs equals 184 miles! This would reach **the full length of Palestine.** In short, the wrath of God—for the unbelievers rejecting Him and doing evil and worshiping an idol—is absolutely enormous!
The amount of blood that results from the winepress emphasizes the *severity* of the judgment.** The **great winepress of God's wrath** pictures the violence and intensity of God's coming judgment on the earth and the unbelievers (Revelation 19:15; Lamentations 1:15a, c; Joel 3:12-14; Isaiah 63:2-3a).

Perhaps the reference is to the coming Battle of Armageddon (Revelation 16:14-16; 19:11-16).

Chapter 14 Verses 17-20
References

Vv. 17-20
Revelation 19:15 Now out of His mouth goes a sharp sword, that with it He should strike the nations. And He Himself will rule them with a rod of iron. He Himself treads the winepress of the fierceness and wrath of Almighty God.
Lamentations 1:15a "The Lord has rejected all the warriors in my midst; ... [NIV]
Lamentations 1:15c In his winepress the Lord has trampled the Virgin Daughter of Judah. [NIV]
Joel 3:12-14 ¹²Let the heathen be wakened, and come up to the valley of Jehoshaphat: for there I will sit to judge all the heathen round about. ¹³Put ye in the sickle, for the harvest is ripe: come, get you down; for the press is full, the fats overflow; for their wickedness is great. ¹⁴Multitudes, multitudes in the valley of decision: for the day of the LORD is near in the valley of decision. [KJV]

Isaiah 63:2-3a ²Why *is* Your apparel red, and Your garments like one who treads in the winepress? ³ᵃ"I have trodden the winepress alone, and from the peoples no one *was* with Me, for I have trodden them in My anger, and trampled them in My fury;"

Chapter 14 Verses 17-20
References Commentary

Vv. 17-20
The three passages of Revelation 19:15, Lamentations 1:15a, c, and Joel 3:12-14 all speak of **the winepress of the fierceness and wrath of Almighty God**, because **their** [the unbelievers] **wickedness is great.**

Isaiah 63:2-3a describes how God's wrath will be felt by the unbelievers but the passage goes on to vs. 3b-6 telling that the reason for bringing an end to the age is because the year of His redeemed believers has come.

Chapter 15 Verses 1-4

Chapter 15 Verses 1-4
Commentary

Preparation for the Seven Golden Bowls of God's Wrath

¹Then I saw another sign in heaven, great and marvelous: seven angels having the seven last plagues, for in them the wrath of God is complete.

15:1
The **wrath of God began to be revealed in Chapter 6 with the seven seals, and will be finished with these **seven last plagues** which will be from the seven bowls.**
From this we know we are getting closer to the end of the Tribulation.

²And I saw *something* like a sea of glass mingled with fire, and those who have the victory over the beast, over his image and over his mark *and* over the number of his name, standing on the sea of glass, having harps of God. ³They sing the song of Moses, the servant of God, and the song of the Lamb, saying: "Great and marvelous *are* Your works, Lord God Almighty! Just and true *are* your ways, O King of the saints! ⁴Who shall not fear You, O Lord, and glorify Your name? For *You* alone *are* holy. For all nations shall come and worship before You, for Your judgments have been manifested."

15:2-4
Those who have victory will be those who refuse to worship **the beast** or **his** (A.I.?) **image**. Satan and his worldly ways will forever more be unable to deceive, influence or disturb them (Revelation 4:6).

The **victory over the beast is won by faith in Christ (1 John 2:15-16; 5:4-5) which provides strength to refuse submitting to the Antichrist.**

*Doubtless those who refused to take the **image** or **mark** will be martyred. But they will end up in heaven, singing **the song of Moses...and the song of the Lamb**, composed almost entirely of quotations from the Old Testament* **(Exodus 15:1-3, 11, 18; Deuteronomy 32:3-4).**

***The song of Moses** is about God's bringing His people out from slavery in Egypt. **The song of the Lamb** celebrates the final deliverance from Satan and all foes of spiritual life having belief in the One True Godhead.*
****All nations** will **come and worship** God in His Millennial kingdom.**
The Son of God is for the fourth time (Revelation 1:8; 4:8; 11:17; 15:3) referred to as **Almighty** reminding us of His equality with God the Father.

| Chapter 15 Verses 1-4 | Chapter 15 Verses 1-4 |
| References | References Commentary |

Vv. 2-4

Revelation 4:6 Before the throne *there was* a sea of glass, like crystal. And in the midst of the throne, and around the throne, *were* four living creatures full of eyes in front and in back.

Vv. 2-4

Revelation 4:6:   *The **sea of glass like crystal** tells us that the throne is located in a place that is undisturbed by the restless, wild tossings of this world, or by the opposition of the wicked, who are like a troubled sea.*

The **four living creatures** are probably cherubim.

1 John 2:15-16   ¹⁵Do not love the world or anything in the world. If anyone loves the world, the love of the Father is not in him. ¹⁶For everything in the world—the cravings of sinful man, the lust of his eyes and the boasting of what he has and does—comes not from the Father but from the world. [NIV]

1 John 2:15-16, much like Genesis 3:6a-d, which says *when the woman saw that the tree was good for food, and that it was pleasant to the eyes, and a tree to be desired to make one wise, she took of the fruit thereof, and did eat.* [KJV]

This indirectly points out that the world is being overrun with so many temptations such as drugs, alcohol, pornography, huge amounts of money, and attractive false teachings (2 Timothy 3:1-5). These things are all temporary, and people have become victims of such passing things.

1 John 5:4-5   ⁴for everyone born of God overcomes the world. This is the victory that has overcome the world, even our faith. ⁵Who is it, that overcomes the world? Only he who believes that Jesus is the Son of God.   [NIV]

1 John 5:4-5: *Only the man who is **born of God** really **overcomes the world**, because by **faith** he is able to rise above the perishing things of this world and to see things in their true, eternal perspective.* The simple believer, with guidance by the Holy Spirit realizes that the things which are seen are temporary and the things which are not seen are eternal. Nothing could be more valued than our loved ones' eternal futures.

(Jesus is the Son of God: Matthew 1:20-23; Luke 1:35)

Exodus 15:1-3, 11, 18;
Deuteronomy 32:3-4

-CONTINUED ON NEXT SET OF PAGES UNDER REFERENCES!-

-CONTINUED ON NEXT SET OF PAGES UNDER REFERENCES COMMENTARY!-

Chapter 15 Verses 2-4

Chapter 15 Verses 2-4 Commentary

-VERSES 2-4 REPEATED FROM PREVIOUS PAGE-

-PART OF COMMENTARY VERSES 2-4 REPEATED FROM PREVIOUS PAGE-

15:2-4

²And I saw *something* like a sea of glass mingled with fire, and those who have the victory over the beast, over his image and over his mark *and* over the number of his name, standing on the sea of glass, having harps of God. ³They sing the song of Moses, the servant of God, and the song of the Lamb, saying: "Great and marvelous *are* Your works, Lord God Almighty! Just and true *are* your ways, O King of the saints! ⁴Who shall not fear You, O Lord, and glorify Your name? For *You* alone *are* holy. For all nations shall come and worship before You, for Your judgments have been manifested."

John *recognizes them as those who refused to worship **the beast** or **his image** [or take the **mark**]. Doubtless they were martyred as a result. But they will end up in heaven, singing **the song of Moses...and the song of the Lamb**, composed almost entirely of quotations from the Old Testament* **(Exodus 15:1-3, 11, 18; Deuteronomy 32:3-4).**

***The song of Moses** is about God's bringing His people out from slavery in Egypt. **The song of the Lamb** celebrates the final deliverance from Satan and all foes of spiritual life having belief in the One True Godhead.*

All nations will **come and worship God in His Millennial kingdom.**

The Son of God is for the fourth time (Revelation 1:8; 4:8; 11:17; 15:3) referred to as **Almighty** reminding us of His equality with God the Father.

Chapter 15 Verses 2-4 References	Chapter 15 Verses 2-4 References Commentary
-CONTINUED FROM PREVIOUS PAGE-	-CONTINUED FROM PREVIOUS PAGE-

Vv. 2-4

Vv. 2-4

Exodus 15:1-3 ¹Then Moses and the children of Israel sang this song to the LORD, and spoke, saying: "I will sing to the LORD, for He has triumphed gloriously! The horse and its rider He has thrown into the sea! ²The LORD *is* my strength and song, and He has become my salvation; He *is* my God, and I will praise Him; my father's God, and I will exalt Him. ³The LORD is a man of war; the LORD *is* His name."
Exodus 15:11 "Who *is* like You, O LORD, among the gods? Who *is* like You, glorious in holiness, fearful in praises, doing wonders?"
Exodus 15:18 "The LORD will reign for ever and ever." [NIV]

Exodus 15:1-3: 15:11; 15:18 is described by Matthew Henry: *"It is the most ancient song we know of; it is a holy song, consecrated to the honor of God, and intended to exalt His name and celebrate His praise, and His name only: It is a typical song [depicting] the triumphs of the gospel church, in the downfall of its enemies; and put together with this song of the Lamb here in Revelation 15:2-3, they are said to be sung upon a **sea of glass**,* as this in Exodus 15 *was upon the Red **Sea**."*
Exodus 14:26-29 compares our salvation to the Israelites being saved crossing the Red Sea.

Deuteronomy 32:3-4 ³"For I proclaim the name of the LORD: ascribe greatness to our God. ⁴*He is* the Rock, His work *is* perfect; for all His ways *are* justice, a God of truth and without injustice; righteous and upright *is* He."

In Deuteronomy 32:3-4 *Moses speaks of attributing **greatness to God**. The song reveals God's **greatness** in the context of His historical dealings with His people.*

Chapter 15 Verses 5-8

⁵After this I looked, and I saw in heaven the temple — that is, the tabernacle of the covenant law — and it was opened. ⁶Out of the temple came the seven angels with the seven plagues. They were dressed in clean, shining linen and wore golden sashes around their chests. ⁷Then one of the four living creatures gave to the seven angels seven golden bowls filled with the wrath of God, who lives for ever and ever. ⁸And the temple was filled with smoke from the glory of God and from his power, and no one could enter the temple until the seven plagues of the seven angels were completed. [NIV]

Chapter 15 Verses 5-8 Commentary

15:5-8
Next John saw the Most Holy place in **the temple of the tabernacle opened** (**the temple represents the presence of God Himself**) and **out came** *the bright, pure, linen clothed **seven angels** who have the last **seven plagues**. The **golden bands** around their **chests** declare they are equipped to execute righteous judgment by which God will be glorified.*

The **seven golden bowls** are bowls (also called *vials* in the KJV) and they are **filled with the wrath of God who lives for ever and ever**.

The **smoke** is **from the glory of God and from his power**.

The immediate verse that follows Moses' relaying that God Himself would *come down upon Mount Sinai in the sight of all the people* (Exodus 19:11-15) made the people tremble (Exodus 19:16), and the cloud of smoke covered their meeting place (Exodus 19:18, 24; 40:34).

(The next Chapter of Exodus, Chapter 20, is where God first gives the Ten Commandments on Mount Sinai.)

Until the seven plagues are finished, no one is able to enter the temple. The time for any priestly intercession is past; God's judgment will now be completed.

Intercession is the act of intervening or mediating between differing parties, particularly the act of praying to God on behalf of another person. Since **no one** is **able to enter the temple** to pray to God, there is absolutely no hope left for any unbeliever left on the earth. However, at the end of the Tribulation Period, newly converted believers will be blessed during the Battle of Armageddon by the Lord Jesus as we will see in Revelation 16:15-16.

Chapter 15 Verses 5-8
References

Vv. 5-8

Exodus 19:16 On the morning of the third day there was thunder and lightning, with a thick cloud over the mountain, and a very loud trumpet blast. Everyone in the camp trembled. [NIV]

Exodus 19:18 Mount Sinai was covered with smoke, because the LORD descended on it in fire. The smoke billowed up from it like smoke from a furnace, the whole mountain trembled violently. [NIV]

Exodus 40:34 Then the cloud covered the Tent of Meeting, and the glory of the LORD filled the tabernacle. [NIV]

Chapter 15 Verses 5-8
References Commentary

Vv. 5-8

All the things spoken of in Exodus 19:16, 18 and Exodus 40:34—**thunder and lightning, a thick cloud over the mountain**; the **loud trumpet**, seeing each other trembling; a cloud of **smoke covered the Tent of Meeting, in fire** and **smoke, because the LORD** was coming down to meet with the people; **the whole mountain trembled violently**— *the Israelites probably spoke among themselves of the terrors of meeting God, especially on the basis of law-keeping. They all had been taught that Mount Sinai was a forbidden place. Only Moses and Aaron were allowed to ascend the **mountain**. Neither mankind nor animal were to touch it on penalty of death* (Exodus 19:13).

No wonder they trembled.

Chapter 16 Verse 1	**Chapter 16 Verse 1** **Commentary**
	The Seven Bowl Judgments of God's Wrath
¹Then I heard a loud voice from the temple saying to the seven angels, "Go, pour out the seven bowls of God's wrath on the earth." [NIV]	**16:1** Then John heard a loud voice telling **the seven angels** to complete God's **wrath on the earth**. ****The bowls of the wrath of God** represent the climax of God's punishment of [unbelieving] sinners during the Tribulation Period.** There is no more offer to allow for repentance. The seven bowls are emptied rapidly in a short period of time. **The judgments are somewhat parallel to the ten plagues on Egypt (Exodus 7-12, 7:17-18; 8:4, 8:17, 8:24; 9:3, 9:6a) and to [those of] the trumpets (Revelation Chapters 8, 9, and 11:15). The bowls are more total and universal in their effects than were the trumpets, and generally affect people more directly.** The effects of each bowl are described in verses 2-13.

Chapter 16 Verse 1 References	Chapter 16 Verse 1 References Commentary
V. 1 **Exodus Ten Plagues:** **Exodus 7:17-18** ¹⁷'This is what the LORD says: By this you will know that I am the LORD: With the staff that is in my hand I will strike the water of the Nile, and it will be changed into blood. ¹⁸The fish in the Nile will die, and the river will stink; the Egyptians will not be able to drink its water.' " [NIV] **Exodus 8:4** 'The frogs will go up on you and your people and on all your officials.' " [NIV] **Exodus 8:17** They did this, and when Aaron stretched out his hand with the staff and struck the dust of the ground, gnats came upon men and animals. All the dust throughout all the land of Egypt became gnats. [NIV] **Exodus 8:24; 9:3, 6a**	**V. 1** Exodus 7:17-18: The effects of this first plague (the **fish** died and the **river** stank, and, in verse 21, it was not drinkable) **seem to prove that the **blood** was real, as it shall be also under the second trumpet of Revelation 8:8-9 and the second and third bowls of Revelation 16:3-4.** Exodus 8:4: In verse 8:7 *the magicians were able to produce **frogs** also—as if there were not enough already! They probably did this by demonic power, but they dared not destroy the **frogs** because the frog was worshiped as the god of fertility!* (**The goddess Heket, the spouse of the ram-god Khnum, was depicted in the form of a woman with a frog's head.**) Can you imagine kissing that??? Our true God used the situation to show what He thinks of other gods before Himself. *When the **frogs** died the next day, there was a tremendous stench from their dead bodies, but **Pharaoh** once again **hardened his heart**.* In Exodus 8:17 the third plague, like the sixth and ninth ending cycles, concludes a cycle and comes unannounced as a special judgment: **the dust of the earth** turned into **lice**. *This time the magicians, unable to produce **lice**, warned Pharaoh that a power greater than theirs* (**the finger of God** *verse 19) was at work, but the king was inflexible. The more he hardened his own **heart**, the more God hardened it.*

-CONTINUED ON NEXT SET OF PAGES UNDER REFERENCES!-   **-CONTINUED ON NEXT SET OF PAGES UNDER REFERENCES COMMENTARY!-**

Chapter 16 Verse 1

Chapter 16 Verse 1
Commentary

-VERSE 1 REPEATED FROM PREVIOUS PAGE-

-VERSE 1 COMMENTARY REPEATED FROM PREVIOUS PAGE-

¹Then I heard a loud voice from the temple saying to the seven angels, "Go, pour out the seven bowls of God's wrath on the earth." [NIV]

16:1
Then John heard a loud voice telling **the seven angels** to complete God's **wrath on the earth**.

The bowls of the wrath of God represent the climax of God's punishment of [unbelieving] sinners during the Tribulation Period.

There is no more offer to allow for repentance. The seven bowls are emptied rapidly in a short period of time.

**The judgments are somewhat parallel to the ten plagues on Egypt (Exodus 7-12, 7:17-18; 8:4, 8:17, 8:24; 9:3, 9:6a) and to [those of] the trumpets (Revelation Chapters 8, 9, and 11:15).

The bowls are more total and universal in their effects than were the trumpets, and generally affect people more directly.** The effects of each bowl are described in verses 2-13.

Chapter 16 Verse 1 References	Chapter 16 Verse 1 References Commentary

-CONTINUED FROM PREVIOUS PAGE-

-CONTINUED FROM PREVIOUS PAGE-

V. 1

V. 1

Exodus Ten Plagues continued:

Exodus 8:24 And the LORD did this. Dense swarms of flies poured into Pharaoh's palace and into the houses of his officials, and throughout Egypt the land was ruined by the flies. [NIV]

Exodus 8:24: **Each of the plagues in a new cycle (the first, fourth, and seventh) proceeds with a warning from Moses to Pharaoh.**
*In the NKJV the italicized *flies* may in Hebrew probably, literally, mean **swarms** of a mixture of many species. Since most or all of the plagues were aimed at the false gods of Egypt (the "sacred" Nile, and virtually every creature was a deity in Egypt) this could have been an attack by God against Khepri, the god of the sacred beetle.*

Exodus 9:3 "the hand of the LORD will bring a terrible plague on your livestock in the field—on your horses and donkeys and camels and on your cattle and sheep and goats. [NIV]
Exodus 9:6a And the next day the LORD did it: All the livestock of the Egyptians died, [NIV]

Exodus 9:3, 9:6a: *The discriminating judgment by God to **kill the Egyptian livestock**, but not the Israelites' animals cannot be explained by natural phenomena. The Egyptians worshiped various animals such as the bull-gods Apis and Mnevis, the cow-god Hathor, and the ram-god Khnum.*
(See also Deuteronomy 28:18)

Chapter 16 Verse 2

²The first angel went and poured out his bowl on the land, and ugly, festering sores broke out on the people who had the mark of the beast and worshiped its image. [NIV]

Chapter 16 Verse 2
Commentary

16:2
The **first bowl** causes **ugly and festering sores** to break out on **those who worshiped the mark of the beast and its image**. (**Parallels Egypt's sixth plague; Exodus 9:9-10;**

The seventh to tenth plagues are listed in Exodus respectively; Exodus 9:24; 10:4, 10:22; 12:29; Romans 9:17)

Chapter 16 Verse 2
References

V. 2

Exodus 9:9-10 ⁹"It will become fine dust over the whole land of Egypt, and festering boils will break out on men and animals throughout the land." ¹⁰So they took soot from a furnace and stood before Pharaoh. Moses tossed it into the air, and festering boils broke out on men and animals. [NIV]

Exodus 9:24 hail fell and lightning flashed back and forth. It was the worst storm in all the land of Egypt since it had become a nation. [NIV]

Exodus 10:4 'Or else, if you refuse to let My people go, behold, tomorrow I will bring locusts into your territory.'

Exodus 10:22 So Moses stretched out his hand toward the sky, and total darkness covered all Egypt for three days. [NIV]

Exodus 12:29 At midnight the LORD struck down all the firstborn in Egypt, from the firstborn of Pharaoh, who sat on the throne, to the firstborn of the prisoner, who was in the dungeon, and the firstborn of all the livestock as well. [NIV]

Romans 9:17 For the Scripture says to the Pharaoh, *"For this very purpose I have raised you up, that I may show My power in you, and that My name may be declared in all the earth."*

Chapter 16 Verse 2
References Commentary

V. 2

In Exodus 9:9-10 *even the magicians were affected by the **boils**.*
(See also Deuteronomy 28:24, 27)

We see **hail** in Exodus 9:24, in Revelation 8:7; 11:19, and we will see it again here in Revelation 16:21.

In Exodus 10:4 *the Egyptian god Serapis was powerless to protect from **locusts**.*
The locusts were previewed at the sound of the fifth trumpet in Revelation 9:1-3.

In Exodus 10:22 *the **darkness** humbled one of the greatest Egyptian gods, the sun god Ra.*
(See also Deuteronomy 28:29)

In Exodus 12:29 God's unstoppable power brought Pharaoh to yield. Two verses later, in 12:31, *the Israelites were at last permitted to leave Egypt.*

Paul quotes Exodus 9:16 in Romans 9:17 as God gives His purpose for using **Pharaoh** for this kind of judgment.

Chapter 16 Verses 3-11

³Then the second angel poured out his bowl on the sea, and it became blood as of a dead *man*; and every living creature in the sea died. ⁴Then the third angel poured out his bowl on the rivers and springs of water, and they became blood. ⁵And I heard the angel of the waters saying; "You are righteous, O Lord, the One who is and who was and who is to be, because You have judged these things. ⁶For they have shed the blood of saints and prophets, and You have given them blood to drink. For it is their just due. ⁷And I heard another from the altar saying, "Even so, Lord God Almighty, true and righteous *are* Your judgments."

⁸Then the fourth angel poured out his bowl on the sun, and power was given to him to scorch men with fire. ⁹And men were scorched with great heat, and they blasphemed the name of God who has power over these plagues; and they did not repent and give Him glory.

¹⁰The fifth angel poured out his bowl on the throne of the beast, and its kingdom was plunged into darkness. People gnawed their tongues in agony ¹¹and cursed the God of heaven because of their pains and their sores, but they refused to repent of what they had done. [NIV]

Chapter 16 Verses 3-11
Commentary

16:3-7
The **second bowl** turns the entire **sea** to **blood** and kills **every living creature in the sea**. The **third bowl** turns all the **rivers and springs** to **blood**. *At this point **the angel of the waters** defends the justice of God's judgments. Men who had **shed** others' **blood** in large quantities are rewarded with **blood to drink** instead of water.* **It is their just due**. In 16:7 the Lord Jesus is for the fifth time referred to as **Lord God Almighty**.

16:8-9
*The **fourth bowl** causes men to suffer severe sunburn or solar radiation. This does **not**, however, cause them to **repent**. Instead, they curse God for this scorching heat on them.*

16:10-11
The **fifth bowl** causes **darkness** on the **kingdom** of **the beast** (Antichrist). His followers suffer **pain**, *but it does not soften their hearts. They only become more settled in their hatred of God.*

Chapter 16 Verses 3-11
References

Chapter 16 Verses 3-11
References Commentary

Chapter 16 Verses 12-15

¹²The sixth angel poured out his bowl on the great river Eūphrātēs, and its water was dried up to prepare the way for the kings from the East. ¹³Then I saw three impure spirits that looked like frogs; they came out of the mouth of the dragon, out of the mouth of the beast and out of the mouth of the false prophet. ¹⁴They are demonic spirits that perform signs, and they go out to the kings of the whole world, to gather them for the battle on the great day of God Almighty. ¹⁵*"Look, I come like a thief! Blessed is the one who stays awake and remains clothed, so as not to go naked and be shamefully exposed."* [NIV]

Chapter 16 Verses 12-15 Commentary

16:12-15
The **sixth bowl** dries up the **river Eūphrātēs** allowing armies **from the East** to come toward Israel. *Then John sees **three frog**-like **spirits** issuing from **the mouth of the dragon** (Satan), **the beast** (Antichrist), **and the mouth of the false prophet**—the **spirits are of demons, performing** miracles (2 Thessalonians 2:9-12) to deceive the world's rulers, and to lure them to a climactic **battle** on the **great day of God Almighty**.* The war of Armageddon begins!

Believers of the Church Age are so very blessed to be omitted from God's furious wrath! 1Thessalonians 4:13-18 explains how He will first come in the air to rapture the Church which will save believers in Jesus Christ from His wrath (1 Thessalonians 5:9; Romans 5:9; John 3:36).

The Church saints aren't the only ones blessed:
In 16:15, immediately prior to the battle of **Armageddon**, the Lord Jesus Christ is quoted, **"Behold, I am coming as a thief. Blessed *is* he who watches; and keeps his garments, lest he walk naked and they see his shame."** *This is His special blessing on the Tribulation saints, those who are watching for His Return—His Second Coming, and have kept themselves pure from the idolatrous worship of that day. He will come to the unsaved as a **thief*** (1 Thessalonians 5:1-4).
In 2 Thessalonians 2:1-2, 2:3-4, 2:6-8a the saints were being so severely persecuted that they thought that the Tribulation Period had already begun. Paul corrects their understanding in these verses.
Revelation 16:14 refers to the Lord Jesus Christ as God Almighty for the sixth time.

Chapter 16 Verses 12-15
References

Vv. 12-15
2 Thessalonians 2:9-12 ⁹The coming of the lawless one will be in accordance with the work of Satan displayed in all kinds of counterfeit miracles, signs and wonders, ¹⁰and in every sort of evil that deceives those who are perishing. They perish because they refused to love the truth and so be saved. ¹¹For this reason God sends them a powerful delusion so that they will believe the lie ¹²and so that all will be condemned who have not believed the truth but have delighted in wickedness. [NIV]

1 Thessalonians 4:13-18 ¹³But I do not want you to be ignorant, brethren, concerning those who have fallen asleep, lest you sorrow as others who have no hope. ¹⁴For if we believe that Jesus died and rose again, even so God will bring with Him those who sleep in Jesus. ¹⁵For this we say to you by the word of the Lord, that we who are alive *and* remain until the coming of the Lord will by no means precede those who are asleep. ¹⁶For the Lord Himself will descend from heaven with a shout, with the voice of an archangel, and with the trumpet of God. And the dead in Christ will rise first. ¹⁷Then we who are alive and remain shall be caught up together with them in the clouds to meet the Lord in the air. And thus we shall always be with the Lord. ¹⁸Therefore comfort one another with these words.

1 Thessalonians 5:9 For God did not appoint us to suffer wrath but to receive salvation through our Lord Jesus Christ. [NIV]

1 Thessalonians 5:1-4;
2 Thessalonians 2:1-2, 2:3-4, 2:6-8a

-CONTINUED ON NEXT SET OF PAGES UNDER REFERENCES!-

Chapter 16 Verses 12-15
References Commentary

Vv. 12-15
2 Thessalonians 2:9-12: The unbelievers who've actually heard the Gospel message and yet adopted the lies about the truth; will most likely not be raptured. It leaves one wondering whether they can be redeemed during the Tribulation. Will God give these yet another chance after He has given His verdict of condemnation here in 2:12?

Hebrews 6:4-6: *⁴For it is impossible for those who were once enlightened, and have tasted the heavenly gift, and have become partakers of the Holy Spirit, ⁵and have tasted the good word of God and the powers of the age to come, ⁶if they fall away, to renew them again to repentance, since they crucify again for themselves the Son of God, and put Him to an open shame.*

Notice the word *taste* in this passage. They have only *tasted*; they have not *absorbed* the indwelling Holy Spirit who *seals* a true believer.

The people who take that mark will be eternally condemned to the lake of fire (Revelation 20:14; 21:8).

1 Thessalonians 5:9 Since the Church saints will be raptured before the Tribulation can begin they will not suffer the wrath of God (Romans 5:9).

-CONTINUED ON NEXT SET OF PAGES UNDER REFERENCES COMMENTARY!-

Chapter 16 Verses 12-15

Chapter 16 Verses 12-15
Commentary

-VERSES 12-15 REPEATED FROM PREVIOUS PAGE-

-PART OF COMMENTARY VERSES 12-15 REPEATED FROM PREVIOUS PAGE-

16:12-15
The Church saints aren't the only ones blessed:
In 16:15, immediately prior to the battle of **Armageddon**, the Lord Jesus Christ is quoted, **"Behold, I am coming as a thief. Blessed *is* he who watches; and keeps his garments, lest he walk naked and they see his shame."** *This is His special blessing on the Tribulation saints, those who are watching for His Return—His Second Coming, and have kept themselves pure from the idolatrous worship of that day. He will come to the unsaved as a **thief*** (1 Thessalonians 5:1-4).

¹²The sixth angel poured out his bowl on the great river Eūphrātēs, and its water was dried up to prepare the way for the kings from the East. ¹³Then I saw three impure spirits that looked like frogs; they came out of the mouth of the dragon, out of the mouth of the beast and out of the mouth of the false prophet. ¹⁴They are demonic spirits that perform signs, and they go out to the kings of the whole world, to gather them for the battle on the great day of God Almighty. ¹⁵"Look, I come like a thief! Blessed is the one who stays awake and remains clothed, so as not to go naked and be shamefully exposed." [NIV]

In 2 Thessalonians 2:1-2, 2:3-4, 2:6-8a the saints were being so severely persecuted that they thought that the Tribulation Period had already begun. Paul corrects their understanding in these verses.

Revelation 16:14 refers to the Lord Jesus Christ as God Almighty for the sixth time.

Chapter 16 Verses 12-15
References

-CONTINUED FROM PREVIOUS PAGE-

Vv. 12-15
1 Thessalonians 5:1-4   ¹But concerning the times and the seasons, brethren, you have no need that I should write to you. ²For you yourselves know perfectly that the day of the Lord so comes as a thief in the night. ³For when they say, "Peace and safety!" then sudden destruction comes upon them, as labor pains upon a pregnant woman. And they shall not escape. ⁴But you, brethren, are not in darkness, so that this Day should overtake you as a thief.

2 Thessalonians 2:1-2   ¹Now, brethren, concerning the coming of our Lord Jesus Christ and our gathering together to Him, we ask you, ²not to be soon shaken in mind or troubled, either by spirit or by word or by letter, as if from us, as though the day of Christ had come.

2 Thessalonians 2:3-4   ³Let no one deceive you by any means; for that Day will not come unless the falling away comes first, and the man of sin is revealed, the son of perdition, ⁴who opposes and exalts himself above all that is called God or that is worshiped, so that he sits as God in the temple of God, showing himself that he is God.

2 Thessalonians 2:6-8a   ⁶And now you know what is restraining, that he may be revealed in his own time. ⁷For the mystery of the lawlessness is already at work; only He who now restrains will do so until He is taken out of the way. ⁸ªAnd then the lawless one will be revealed...

Chapter 16 Verses 12-15
References Commentary

-CONTINUED FROM PREVIOUS PAGE-

Vv. 12-15
1 Thessalonians 5:1-4   *The Chapter break is appropriate. Paul begins a new subject. He leaves his discussion of the Rapture and turns [briefly] to the Day of the Lord. ….. Paul felt **no need** to **write** to the Thessalonians about **the times and the seasons**. For one thing, the saints would not be affected by them; they would be taken to heaven before both the Tribulation and Christ's Second advent. Also, **the times and the seasons** and the Day of the Lord are subjects that are found in the Old Testament. The Rapture was a mystery (1 Cor. 15:51), never revealed until the time of the apostles.*

In 1 Thessalonians 5:2-3 **day of the Lord** refers to Christ's Coming at the end of the Tribulation. [Christ will come back again like a thief at the end of the Tribulation Period for His Second Coming to earth (1 Thessalonians 5:1-3.]

Then in 2 Thessalonians 2:1-2 Paul reminds them that the Rapture has not yet happened. In verse 2, the NIV, NLT, ESV, *instead* of day of **Christ**, have d*ay of the Lord*, which refers to God's wrath in the Tribulation Period and the Second Advent.

2 Thessalonians 2:3-4   In today's world we see many churches are falling away. The falling away has to happen before the Antichrist (**the man of sin**) will be revealed; but the Rapture *must also* take place before the Antichrist is revealed (2:6-8):

2 Thessalonians 2:6-8a   The Antichrist (**lawless one**) will no longer be restrained after the Church, with the indwelling Holy Spirit, is raptured. At some time after the believers and Spirit are gone, the Antichrist will be revealed and the Seven-year Tribulation Period will begin.

Chapter 16 Verse 16	Chapter 16 Verse 16 Commentary
¹⁶Then they gathered the kings together to the place that in Hebrew is called Armageddon. [NIV]	**16:16** So the warriors were **gathered to the place in Hebrew, Armageddon**. In Hebrew, *Har Megiddon*, or Mount Megiddō in Northern Israel—about 6 miles (10 km) SW of Nazareth, 21 miles (35 km) SW of the Sea of Galilee, and 15 miles (25 km) east of the Mediterranean coast (the sight of battles in Judges 5:19-21; 2 Kings 23:29). The war of Armageddon will be the final battle where the Lord Jesus, at His Second Coming, will be victorious without human means (Daniel 8:25). The previously raptured believers will follow Him on white horses and be there with the King of kings, but He will win the battle solely with His own power (Revelation 19:14-16).

Chapter 16 Verse 16
References

V. 16

Judges 5:19-21 ¹⁹"The kings came and fought, then fought the kings of Cānaan in Tāanach, by the waters of Megiddō; they took no gain of money. ²⁰They fought from the heaven; the stars in their courses fought against Sisera. ²¹The river of Kishon swept them away, that ancient river, the river Kishon. O my soul, thou hast trodden down strength. [KJV]

2 Kings 23:29 While Jōsīah was king, Pharaoh Nēcho king of Egypt went up to the Eūphrātēs River to help the king of Assyria. King Jōsīah marched out to meet him in battle, but Nēcho faced him and killed him at Megiddō. [NIV]

Daniel 8:25 "Through his cunning He shall cause deceit to prosper under his rule; and he shall exalt himself in his heart. He shall destroy many in their prosperity. He shall even rise against the Prince of princes; But he shall be broken without human means.

Chapter 16 Verse 16
References Commentary

V. 16

Judges 5:19-20: **Soggy ground and God's well-timed cloudburst immobilized Sisera's military chariots.**

2 Kings 23:29: Judah's King Jōsīah was killed at the battle of Megiddō. But the Egyptians were defeated by the Babylonians at the Eūphrātēs River (2 Kings 24:7). It is interesting to note that Megiddō is near the predicted battle ground of Armageddon.

Daniel 8:25: We will read the details of the Antichrist's defeat in Revelation 19:13-17.

Chapter 16 Verses 17-18

¹⁷Then the seventh angel poured out his bowl into the air, and out of the temple came a loud voice from the throne, saying, "It is done!" ¹⁸Then there came flashes of lightning, rumblings, peals of thunder and a severe earthquake. No earthquake like it has ever occurred since mankind has been on earth, so tremendous was the quake. [NIV]

Chapter 16 Verses 17-18
Commentary

Battle of Armageddon

The Seventh and Final Bowl of Wrath Finishes the Tribulation

16:17-18
In this, the seventh and final bowl, judgment is given by **a loud voice from the throne: "It is done!"** **With this **seventh bowl** and the return of Christ Himself, the judgments of the Tribulation Period are now finished.** *The wrath of God is over as far as the Tribulation Period is concerned.* The unbelievers who have taken the mark are condemned (Revelation 14:9-11).

When the **seventh angel** poured out his bowl into the air, **there were noises and thunderings and lightnings; and** there was **a severe earthquake** bigger than any **earthquake** that had ever occurred **since** the beginning of mankind (Ezekiel 38:18-22).

Revelation 14:8 marked the breakdown of Babylon's religious system and here we see the disintegration of its commercial structure. The details of the religious system's falling are given in the next Chapter Revelation 17. Then Revelation 18 describes the collapse of the commercial structure.

Chapter 16 Verses 17-18
References

Chapter 16 Verses 17-18
References Commentary

Vv. 17-18
Revelation 14:9-11 ⁹Then a third angel followed them, saying with a loud voice, "If anyone worships the beast and his image, and receives his mark on his forehead or on his hand, ¹⁰"he himself shall also drink of the wine of the wrath of God, which is poured out full strength into the cup of His indignation. ¹¹And the smoke of their torment ascends forever and ever; and they have no rest day or night, who worship the beast and his image, and whoever receives the mark of his name."

Vv. 17-18
Revelation 14:9-11: The **wine of the wrath of God** will make **all nations** drunk. God's righteous anger (Job 21:20; Psalm 75:8; Isaiah 51:17; Jeremiah 25:15-38) is **poured out** in full strength on those who reject Him.
The **cup of His indignation *symbolizes* the place of God's punishment of sinners...all taking place **in the presence of** Christ and His **angels** making the punishment even more intense and shameful.**
This will only be a *foretaste* of the pangs of the eternal lake of fire. And the Savior, who died for us, took more than this wrath of God for each one of us! Later, at the Great White Throne Judgment (Revelation 20:11-15) **the unbelievers will pay that *eternal* price of having chosen Satan and evil over God and righteousness.**

Ezekiel 38:18-22 ¹⁸"And it will come to pass at the same time, when Gog comes against the land of Israel," says the Lord GOD, "*that* My fury will show in My face. ¹⁹For in My jealousy *and* in the fire of My wrath I have spoken: 'Surely in that day there shall be a great earthquake in the land of Israel, ²⁰so that the fish of the sea, the birds of the heavens, the beasts of the field, all creeping things that creep on the earth, and all men who *are* on the face of the earth shall shake at My presence. The mountains shall be thrown down, the steep places shall fall, and every wall shall fall to the ground.' ²¹I will call for a sword against Gog throughout all My mountains," says the Lord GOD. "Every man's sword will be against his brother. ²²And I will bring him to judgment with pestilence and bloodshed; I will rain down on him, on his troops, and on the many peoples who *are* with him, flooding rain, great hailstones, fire, and brimstone.'"

Ezekiel 38:18-22: Looking back at the first three-and-a-half years of the Tribulation, we see remarkable similarities: *The forces of **Gog** will swarm over the land. But they will meet the blazing **wrath** and **jealousy** of God. The **land** will be terribly shaken by **a great earthquake**; Gog's men will be terrified by **pestilence, bloodshed, flooding rain, hailstones**, fire, and **brimstone**. The destruction of the enemies of God's people reminds us of the Lord's promise in Isaiah 54:17: *"No weapon formed against you shall prosper...This is the heritage of the servants of the LORD."**
Also, in Joshua 10:11, the discriminating **hailstones** affected only the enemy—as also here in Ezekiel, those against God are the ones being shaken and terrified.

Chapter 16 Verses 19-20   **Chapter 16 Verses 19-20**
                                                                    Commentary

16:19

¹⁹Now the great city was divided into three parts, and the cities of the nations fell. And great Babylon was remembered before God, to give her the cup of the wine of the fierceness of His wrath.

16:19
The great city of **Babylon, divided into three parts** by the huge earthquake, drinks **the cup** which symbolizes God's wrath (Revelation 14:10-11),**

God's anger and fury. *He has not forgotten her unremorseful idolatry, cruelty, and religious confusion. The **cities of the nations** are laid flat.* **The great city, Babylon** is further described and identified in Chapters 17 and 18 as possibly Rome or perhaps all of the Antichrist's evil world.
The seventh vial is the last of the seven plagues (15:6-8), and also completes both the seventh trumpet (11:15) and the seventh seal (8:1).

16:20

²⁰Every island fled away and the mountains could not be found. [NIV]

16:20
*Every island** and **the mountains** disappear as God's earthquake flattens the earth.*
Ezekiel 38:20b also mentions mountains being thrown down during the first half of the Seven-year Tribulation.

Chapter 16 Verses 19-20
References

Chapter 16 Verses 19-20
References Commentary

V. 19
Revelation 14:10-11 ¹⁰"he himself shall also drink of the wine of the wrath of God, which is poured out full strength into the cup of His indignation. He shall be tormented with fire and brimstone in the presence of the holy angels and in the presence of the Lamb. ¹¹And the smoke of their torment ascends forever and ever; and they have no rest day or night, who worship the beast and his image, and whoever receives the mark of his name."

V. 20
Ezekiel 38:20b 'The mountains shall be thrown down, the steep places shall fall, and every wall shall fall to the ground.'

Chapter 16 Verse 21

²¹From the sky huge hailstones, each weighing about a hundred pounds, fell on people. And they cursed God on account of the plague of hail, because the plague was so terrible. [NIV]

Chapter 16 Verse 21
Commentary

16:21
The *large* **hail weighing about a hundred pounds (Think of that!) may help to destroy the cities (Joshua 10:11; Ezekiel 38:22).

But unbelieving mankind still blasphemes **God** and has no opportunity for repentance. Not only is the seventh bowl the last of the seven plagues (Revelation 15:6-8), but also it completes the previews of both the seventh seal (Revelation 8:1) and the seventh trumpet (Revelation 11:15).**

Chapter 16 Verse 21
References

V. 21

Joshua 10:11 And it came to pass, as they fled from before Israel, and were in the going down to Bethhoron, that the LORD cast down great stones from heaven upon them unto Azēkah, and they died: they were more which died with hailstones than they whom the children of Israel slew with the sword. [KJV]

Ezekiel 38:22 And I will bring him to judgment with pestilence and bloodshed; I will rain down on him, on his troops, and on the many peoples who are with him, flooding rain, great hailstones, fire, and brimstone.

Revelation 15:6-8 ⁶Out of the temple came the seven angels with the seven plagues. They were dressed in clean, shining linen and wore golden sashes around their chests. ⁷Then one of the four living creatures gave to the seven angels seven golden bowls filled with the wrath of God, who lives for ever and ever. ⁸And the temple was filled with smoke from the glory of God and from his power, and no one could enter the temple until the seven plagues of the seven angels were completed. [NIV]

Revelation 8:1 When He opened the seventh seal, there was silence in heaven for about half an hour.

Revelation 11:15

-CONTINUED ON NEXT SET OF PAGES UNDER REFERENCES!-

Chapter 16 Verse 21
References Commentary

V. 21

In Joshua 10:11 and Ezekiel 38:22 God used hailstones for judgment against His enemies; *note that the *discriminating* hail killed *only* the enemy.*

Revelation 15:6-8: ***Out came** the bright, pure, linen clothed **seven angels** who have the last **seven plagues**. The **golden bands** around their **chests** declare they are equipped to execute righteous judgment by which God will be glorified.*

The **seven golden bowls** are called *vials* in the KJV, and they are **full of the wrath of God who lives for ever and ever**. The **smoke is from the glory of God and from His power**. Since **no one is able to enter the temple** to pray to God, there is absolutely no hope left for any unbeliever left on the earth.

Revelation 8:1: ****The **seventh seal** probably contains the **seven trumpets**.****

The Lamb opens the seventh seal, and then silence is held for about half an hour to indicate the beginning of these further series of judgments. Following the **silence** the first four trumpets were blasted in Revelation 8, the fifth and sixth in Revelation 9:1, 9:13. The seventh trumpet sounded in Revelation 11:15.

-CONTINUED ON NEXT SET OF PAGES UNDER REFERENCES COMMENTARY!-

Chapter 16 Verse 21	Chapter 16 Verse 21 Commentary
-VERSE 21 REPEATED FROM PREVIOUS PAGE -	**-PART OF COMMENTARY VERSE 21 REPEATED FROM PREVIOUS PAGE-**

16:21

²¹From the sky huge hailstones, each weighing about a hundred pounds, fell on people. And they cursed God on account of the plague of hail, because the plague was so terrible. [NIV]

But unbelieving mankind still blasphemes **God and has no opportunity for repentance. Not only is the seventh bowl the last of the seven plagues (Revelation 15:6-8), but also it completes both the seventh seal (Revelation 8:1) and the seventh trumpet (Revelation 11:15).**

Chapter 16 Verse 21
References

Chapter 16 Verse 21
References Commentary

-CONTINUED FROM PREVIOUS PAGE-

-CONTINUED FROM PREVIOUS PAGE-

V. 21

V. 21

Revelation 11:15 Then the seventh angel sounded: And there were loud voices in heaven, saying, "The kingdoms of this world have become *the kingdoms* of our Lord and of His Christ, and he shall reign forever and ever!"

Revelation 11:15: **The **seventh** trumpet results in the millennial kingdom of Christ. The seven vials or bowls (Revelation 16:1) are probably contained in the judgment of the seventh trumpet. They will occur in a very brief period of time at the end of the Great Tribulation. The Second Coming of Christ, while a great blessing for believers, will be God's most severe judgment of the earth. The **kingdoms of this world** will be completely overthrown by the coming kingdom of Christ (Revelation 19:11; 19:20-21; Daniel 2:34-35a, 2:44), who will **reign for ever and ever** (Daniel 7:13-14, 7:27).**

{**Chapters **17** and **18** picture the judgment of God on a system, empire, or city called **Babylon the Great** (Revelation 17:5)**. Chapter 17 gives a more detailed description of the failure of the idolatrous religious system; then Chapter 18 describes the ruin of the commercial structure. The great city is probably Rome.
Religion in Jerusalem certainly includes Islamic Muslim sects (Ezekiel 8:15-16) and apostate Christendom, both Protestant and Catholic.
*According to MacDonald it may include the ecumenical (habitable world—"universal") so-called *church*.*
Specifically concerning the Muslims or idol worship, Ezekiel 8:15-16 offers interesting insight to the practice of facing the east while praying.
Revelation 17:5: *And on her forehead a name was written: MYSTERY, BABYLON THE GREAT, THE MOTHER OF HARLOTS AND OF THE ABOMINATIONS OF THE EARTH is printed here only as an appetizing preview for the mystery of Babylon.*}

Chapter 17 Verses 1-2

¹One of the seven angels who had the seven bowls came and said to me, "Come, I will show you the punishment of the great prostitute, who sits on many waters. ²With her the kings of the earth committed adultery, and the inhabitants of the earth were intoxicated with the wine of her adulteries." [NIV]

Chapter 17 Verses 1-2
Commentary

The Fall of Babylon's Religious System

17:1-2
One of the seven angels** invites John to witness **the judgment of the great harlot (*whore* in KJV). *The **harlot** "*church*" (called **harlot** because of not being faithful to Almighty God, but worshiping idols instead) **sits on many waters**, controlling great areas of the Gentile world.*
The **waters represent the various peoples and nations of the earth (Revelation 17:15).**

To better understand the reason our Lord God Creator has so long been angered by the Babylonian practices we need to look back at the way it all began and then spread world-wide: This chapter of the last Book of the Bible describes the *end of Babylonian Religion*. Please find **The Beginning of Babylonian Religion** at the end of this study guide. This addendum gives a vivid description of how a disgusting harlot religious idolatry spread like wildfire throughout the world.

In verse 1, the great harlot, who is in other verses known as Babylon, refers to a literal large city which is very likely to be Rome. It is composed of both a religious structure and a commercial system. The commercial segment is similar to Wall Street which is an actual street as well as a distinct commercial organization. The immoral religious culture of Babylon being destroyed is described here in Chapter 17, and the collapse of the commercial side is detailed in Chapter 18. To understand the power of God to destroy all of Babylon, the prophecy in Jeremiah 51:7, 11-14 gives a vivid warning. The adultery of Babylon in the Old Testament prophesies the Babylon here in Revelation.

Chapter 17 Verses 1-2
References

Vv. 1-2
Revelation 17:15   Then the angel said to me, "The waters you saw, where the prostitute sits, are peoples, multitudes, nations, and languages. [NIV]

Jeremiah 51:7   ⁷Babylon was a gold cup in the LORD's hand; she made the whole earth drunk. The nations drank her wine; therefore they have now gone mad. [NIV]

Jeremiah 51:11-14   ¹¹"Make arrows bright! Gather the shields! The LORD has raised up the spirit of the kings of the Mēdes, for His plan *is* against Babylon to destroy it, because it *is* the vengeance of the LORD, the vengeance for His temple. ¹²Set up the standard on the walls of Babylon; make the guard strong, set up the watchmen, prepare the ambushes. For the LORD has both devised and done what He spoke against the inhabitants of Babylon. ¹³O you who dwell by many waters, abundant in many treasures, your end has come, the measure of your covetousness. ¹⁴The LORD of hosts has sworn by Himself: "Surely I will fill you with men, as with locusts, and they shall lift up a shout against you."

Chapter 17 Verses 1-2
References Commentary

Vv. 1-2
Revelation 17:15:   ****The waters** where the **prostitute sits, are peoples, multitudes, nations,** and **languages** indicating the worldwide influence and authority of the harlot.**

Jeremiah 51:11-14:   Where the Lord urged the Mēdes to set up watchmen, He also made Ezekiel a watchman for the house of Israel (Ezekiel 33:7). As it pertains to us today, we need to be the watchmen for the lost so that they will not die in their sin (Ezekiel 33:8). Those who will miss the Rapture need us to get this vital information to them so they can come to a knowledge of God's truth if they are caught in the Tribulation Period.

2 Corinthians 5:18:
And all things are of God. who hath reconciled us to himself by Jesus Christ, and hath given us the ministry of reconciliation, [KJV]

Chapter 17 Verse 3

³The angel carried me away in the Spirit into a wilderness. There I saw a woman sitting on a scarlet beast that was covered with blasphemous names and had seven heads and ten horns. [NIV]

Chapter 17 Verse 3
Commentary

17:3
In verse 3 the woman is the idolatress church harlot of Babylon.
***The kings of the earth** have **committed fornication** with her; she has seduced political leaders with her compromise and intrigue. **The inhabitants of the earth** have become **drunk with the wine of her fornication**; vast numbers have come under her evil influence and have been reduced to staggering wretchedness.* (Jeremiah 3:6-9; Ezekiel 20:3-9, 30)

The future nations under Babylon authority will commit the same adultery as the nation of Israel did in Jeremiah and Ezekiel. They will follow an example of being Antichrist-like.

*The apostate, **harlot** *church* is seen **sitting on a scarlet beast**.*

As we have seen in Revelation 13:1-2; and will see in 17:9, 10, this red, devilish **beast** is probably the revived Roman Empire.

*The beast is **full of** blasphemous **names** and has **seven heads and ten horns**.* The **seven heads** could be the seven kings, or rulers, *or* seven mountains on which the city of Babylon is built (Revelation 17:9). There were previously ten kings, but the Antichrist subdued three of them (Daniel 7:20; 11:42-43).

The **ten horns** were predicted by Daniel 7:24 to be a ten-kingdom form.

Chapter 17 Verse 3 References	Chapter 17 Verse 3 References Commentary
V. 3	**V. 3**
Revelation 13:1-2 ¹Then I stood on the sand of the sea. And I saw a beast rising up out of the sea, having seven heads and ten horns, and on his horns ten crowns, and on his heads a blasphemous name. ²Now the beast which I saw was like a leopard, his feet were like *the feet* of a bear, and his mouth like the mouth of a lion. The dragon gave him his power, his throne, and great authority.	Revelation 13:1-2: The first **beast**, Antichrist, who, although not known yet, will already be *among* the Church before the Rapture (1 John 4:3; 2 Thessalonians 2:3-4). He is the Gentile head of a revived Roman Empire, which will be a ten-kingdom form. **The **sea** here is the Gentile nations of the world, from one of which the Antichrist comes.**
Revelation 17:9 "This calls for a mind with wisdom. The seven heads are seven hills on which the woman sits. [NIV]	Revelation 17:9: *The angel says that this calls for a **mind** with **wisdom**. **The seven heads are seven mountains on which the woman sits**. A traditional interpretation is that the harlot has her headquarters in Rome, which is built on seven hills.*
Revelation 17:10 "They are also seven kings. Five have fallen, one is, the other has not yet come; but when he does come, he must remain for a little while. [NIV]	Revelation 17:10: **The **seven kings** are likely the seven kingdoms or empires which throughout history have ruled over Israel and much of the back-then-known world:** **Five have fallen**: Egypt, Assyria, Babylon, Persia, and Greece. Rome was the sixth, and will possibly be revived as the seventh future Roman Empire (Daniel 2:41-44; 7:7, 7:20, 7:24).
Daniel 7:24 "'The ten horns are ten kings who will come from this kingdom. After them another king will arise, different from the earlier ones, he will subdue three kings. [NIV]	The **ten horns** were predicted by Daniel 7:24 to be ten kingdoms. In Revelation 13:1-2 above, **Ten crowns on his horns** speak of the power to rule, from a **throne** with **great authority**, given to him by the **dragon**. Satan is attempting to duplicate how the Father gives all authority to the Son. A possible interpretation is that the first **beast**—Antichrist—will rule over the three previous **subdued** empires to the ancient Roman Empire of which Daniel's prophesies were fulfilled: Greek: **leopard**; Medo-Persia: **bear**; Babylon: **lion**. *In short, the revived empire combines all the evil features of the preceding world empires. The new empire and its ruler receive supernatural strength from Satan.* (All of Daniel's prophecies so far have been fulfilled.)

Chapter 17 Verses 4-6

⁴The woman was arrayed in purple and scarlet, and adorned with gold and precious stones and pearls, having in her hand a golden cup full of abominations and the filthiness of her fornication. ⁵And on her forehead a name was written: MYSTERY, BABYLON THE GREAT, THE MOTHER OF HARLOTS AND OF THE ABOMINATIONS OF THE EARTH. ⁶I saw the woman, drunk with the blood of the saints and with the blood of the martyrs of Jesus. And when I saw her, I marveled with great amazement.

Chapter 17 Verses 4-6
Commentary

17:4-6
The elegant clothing and jewelry of the woman show her wealth and attractiveness, but her activities (such as probable emperor [Antichrist A.I.] and idol worship) **are filthy and abominable to God. Her mysterious, hidden truth name is BABYLON THE GREAT.**

The harlot will do what literal Babylon did in the past:
1. oppress God's people; and
2. propagate a false religious system

—much of the world's idolatry can be traced back to historical Babylon in Mesopotāmia (Genesis 11:7-9), including the mother-child cult of Sumerian-Tammūz (Jeremiah 44:18-19; Ezekiel 8:13-14), which entered other cultures as Ashtaroth-Bāal, Aphrodite-Eros, Venus-Cupid, and even Madonna-Child. As the fountainhead of idolatry, Babylon the harlot is the **MOTHER OF HARLOTS AND ABOMINATIONS OF THE EARTH**. The harlot has convinced terrorists to shed the blood of Christian martyrs down through the centuries, and will still be doing it here during the Tribulation Period.**

She is drunk with their blood.

- -

[This **MYSTERY of BABYLON THE GREAT, THE MOTHER OF HARLOTS AND OF THE ABOMINATIONS OF THE EARTH** has now been possibly revealed enough to be partially solved. We cannot say with absolute certainty, but we can conclude that the whore of Babylon is an evil world system, controlled by the Antichrist during the last days before the Savior's return to earth. The Babylon beast is the center of attention in an ungodly, end-times, huge *religious* craze—and the Antichrist is also called a beast. The Antichrist beast and his beast of an empire are together, possibly, BABYLON THE GREAT, THE MOTHER OF HARLOTS AND THE ABOMINATIONS OF THE EARTH. In Revelation 19:20 we will see the vindictive Antichrist, along with the False Prophet, hurled into the lake of fire burning with brimstone.]

Chapter 17 Verses 4-6 References	Chapter 17 Verses 4-6 References Commentary
Vv. 4-6	**Vv. 4-6**
Genesis 11:7-9 ⁷"Come, let Us go down and there confuse their language, that they may not understand one another's speech." ⁸So the LORD scattered them abroad from there over the face of all the earth, and they ceased building the city. ⁹Therefore its name is called Bābel, because there the LORD confused the language of all the earth; and from there the LORD scattered them abroad over the face of all the earth.	Genesis 11:7-9: The founder of Bābel was Nimrod, father of Tammūz. God confused the different peoples in Bābel by making them babble to one another in different languages. *Babel means *confusion*, the inevitable result if God is left out or if things aren't in accordance with— or—according to God.*
Jeremiah 44:18-19 ¹⁸"But ever since we stopped burning incense to the Queen of Heaven and pouring out drink offerings to her, we have had nothing and have been perishing by the sword and famine." ¹⁹The women added, "When we burned incense to the Queen of Heaven and poured out drink offerings to her, did not our husbands know that we were making cakes like her image and pouring out drink offerings to her?" [NIV]	Jeremiah 44:18-19: *The people served the goddess queen of heaven.* Our Lord God reminds them in Jeremiah 44:25 that the Israelite men and their wives that they had made vows "*to the queen of heaven*" (likely a reference to Ashtoreth) and "*will surely keep your vows and perform your vows!*"
Ezekiel 8:13-14 ¹³And He said to me, "Turn again, *and* you will see greater abominations that they are doing." ¹⁴So He brought me to the door of the north gate of the LORD'S house; and to my dismay, women were sitting there weeping for Tammūz	In Ezekiel 8:13-14 **worship of Tammūz was one of many fertility cults of the Assyrian deity. Weeping for Tammūz was an act intended to bring *him* back from "*a lower world*."** This Assyrian deity is the Greek god Adonis.
Revelation 19:20 Then the beast was captured, and with him the false prophet who worked signs in his presence, by which he deceived those who received the mark of the beast and those who worshiped his image. These two were cast alive into the lake of fire burning with brimstone.	Revelation 19:20: Again, **his image** could be his look-alike, sound-alike *artificial intelligent* robot. Both the Antichrist **beast and the false prophet** will be **captured** and hurled **alive into the lake of fire burning with brimstone**.

Chapter 17 Verses 7-9

⁷But the angel said to me, "Why did you marvel? I will tell you the mystery of the woman and of the beast that carries her, which has the seven heads and the ten horns. ⁸The beast that you saw was, and is not, and will ascend out of the bottomless pit and go to perdition. And those who dwell on the earth will marvel, whose names are not written in the Book of Life from the foundation of the world, when they see the beast that was, and is not, and yet is."

⁹"This calls for a mind with wisdom. The seven heads are seven hills on which the woman sits. [NIV]

Chapter 17 Verses 7-9
Commentary

Reasoning for Babylon Possibly being the Revived Roman Empire

17:7-8
The **beast as an empire goes through four stages:
1. It **was**, that is, it existed in the form of the ancient Roman Empire at the time of Christ's crucifixion.
2. It **is not**, that is, it has not existed as an empire since the fifth century and will not exist again until the Antichrist appears during the Tribulation.
3. Satan **will ascend out of the bottomless pit** and raise up the mortally wounded Antichrist as the emperor/false messiah (Revelation11:7; 13:3-4).
4. The Roman Empire will possibly be back to life (**yet is**), but not for long, as Revelation 19:21 tells us there is a reservation for **perdition**** (destruction) —immediate and then eternal suffering for her followers. These verses describing the empire, that existed, make it clearer that the Roman Empire of the past is the Babylon of the future.

17:9
The mind which has **wisdom** will understand the mystery. **The seven heads are seven hills on which the woman sits.**
The city of Rome, perhaps the location of the harlot's headquarters, was known throughout the ancient world as a city built on seven hills or **mountains** from where the Vatican in Rome has given much worldwide influence—and is still doing so to this day.

Chapter 17 Verses 7-9
References

Vv. 7-8
Revelation 11:7 Now when they have finished their testimony, the beast that comes up from the Abyss will attack them, and overpower and kill them. [NIV]

Revelation 13:3-4 ³And I saw one of his heads as if it had been mortally wounded, and his deadly wound was healed. And all the world marveled and followed the beast. ⁴So they worshiped the dragon who gave authority to the beast; and they worshiped the beast, saying, "Who *is* like the beast? Who is able to make war with him?"

Chapter 17 Verses 7-9
References Commentary

Vv. 7-8
Revelation 11:7: **The **beast** is the Antichrist (Revelation 13:1, 8) or false messiah under the control of Satan. At the end of three-and-a-half years of preaching, the witnesses (the two witnesses of Revelation 11:3 are possibly Moses and Elijah) will be **killed** by the **beast** in the great city (Jerusalem; *where also our Lord was crucified*** {just outside the wall of Jerusalem} John 19:20; Hebrews 13:12).

Revelation 13:3-4: **One of the beast's seven heads** receives a **deadly wound**, and **all the world marveled** as the **wound was healed**. The Antichrist was possibly **wounded** and lived (Revelation 13:14). Or—the thing that ceased—or was deceased—was the imperial form of government. Saying that the **wound** is **healed** could mean the empire is revived—with an emperor—namely, the **beast**—the Antichrist.

Chapter 17 Verses 10-11

¹⁰They are also seven kings. Five have fallen, one is, the other has not yet come; but when he does come, he must remain for only a little while. ¹¹The beast who once was, and now is not, is an eighth king. He belongs to the seven and is going to his destruction. [NIV]

Chapter 17 Verses 10-11 Commentary

17:10-11
The **seven kings are likely the seven kingdoms or empires which throughout history have ruled over Israel and much of the back-then-known world: **Five have fallen**: Egypt, Assyria, Babylon, Persia, and Greece. Rome was the sixth, and the future revived Roman Empire would be the seventh (Daniel 2:41-44; 7:7, 7:20, 7:24). Therefore, when the Antichrist is revealed, he will be the eighth king of the empire. The rule will be for a **short** time.**

In verse 11, **of the seven** means: the Antichrist is similar to the seven wicked, idolatrous kings ruling over ten nations from Revelation 12:3. The **eighth beast** that **was**, and **is not**—is the future world kingdom ruled by the Antichrist, and is himself similar to the seven, **that he is the culmination of all the previous, pagan, idolatrous empires** **and is going to his destruction** or perdition (lake of fire, entire loss or ruin; utter destruction. **Perdition** can be applied to a *place* or a *soul*).

Quoting J M Mason:
"If we reject the truth, we seal our own perdition."

The Antichrist will be allowed to continue his authority for forty-two months (Revelation 13:5); the last half of the Tribulation Period.
Ron Rhodes, in his book, *Forty Days Through Revelation*, pg. 213, writes:
"The Antichrist is the seventh king prior to his mortal wound, and the eighth king after his so-called resurrection. This eighth king goes to destruction."

Chapter 17 Verses 10-11
References

Vv. 10-11
Daniel 2:41-44 ⁴¹"Just as you saw the feet and toes were partly of baked clay and partly of iron, so this will be a divided kingdom; yet it will have some of the strength of iron in it, even as you saw iron mixed clay. ⁴²As the toes were partly iron and partly clay, so this kingdom will be partly strong and partly brittle. ⁴³"And just as you saw the iron mixed with baked clay, so the people will be a mixture and will not remain united, any more than iron mixes with clay. ⁴⁴In the time of those kings, the God of heaven will set up a kingdom that will never be destroyed, nor will it be left to another people. It will crush all those kingdoms and bring them to an end, but it will itself endure forever." [NIV]

Daniel 7:7 "After that, in my vision at night I looked, and there before me was a fourth beast- terrifying and frightening and very powerful. It had large iron teeth; it crushed and devoured its victims and trampled underfoot whatever was left. It was different from all the former beasts, and it had ten horns. [NIV]

Daniel 7:20 I also wanted to know about the ten horns on its head and about the other horn that came up, before which three of them fell—the horn that looked more imposing that the others and that had eyes and a mouth that spoke boastfully. [NIV]
Daniel 7:24 The ten horns are ten kings who will come from this kingdom. After them another king will arise, different from the earlier ones; he will subdue three kings. [NIV]

Chapter 17 Verses 10-11
References Commentary

Vv. 10-11
Daniel 2:41-44: *The **feet** of **iron** and **ceramic clay** (baked clay) depict a weakened Roman Empire.
(In Daniel 2:38 the **head of gold** is the absolute monarch of Babylon, Nebuchadnezzar. Persia was the **arms of silver**, one arm representing Media and the other Persia. Greece, the third kingdom, was the **belly and thighs of bronze*** {Daniel 2:32}.

Daniel 7:7: *The **fourth beast** (Roman Empire), following the Grecian Empire, would cease, and then, after considerable time, would be revived. The **ten horns are ten kings** in the revived empire.*
(In Daniel 7:8 the little horn is the Antichrist—head of the Revived Roman Empire.)

Daniel 7:20 and 7:24: *Daniel saw the little horn...making war with the saints* (Daniel 7:21; Revelation 13:7) *of the [Great] Tribulation Period until the Ancient of Days (God the Father) came, ended their sufferings, and gave them the kingdom (Daniel 7:22). The future **pompous** little horn (Antichrist) will blaspheme the Most High, persecute the saints, and intend to change the Jewish calendar for three-and-a-half years* (Daniel 7:25). (This *three-and-a-half years* is the Great Tribulation referred to by the Lord Jesus in Matthew 24:21.)
But the Antichrist will be stripped of his power and the glorious, everlasting kingdom of our Lord will begin (Daniel 7:27). The **three kings** he will subdue, are named in Daniel 11:42-43.

Chapter 17 Verses 12-14

**Chapter 17 Verses 12-14
Commentary**

¹²"The ten horns you saw are ten kings who have not yet received a kingdom, but who for one hour will receive authority as kings along with the beast. ¹³They have one purpose and will give their power and authority to the beast. ¹⁴They will wage war against the Lamb, but the Lamb will triumph over them because he is Lord of lords and King of kings — and with him will be his called, chosen and faithful followers." [NIV]

17:12-14
*Sure enough, **the ten horns** symbolizing the future **kings** who will serve under the Roman **beast**, will rule for only **one hour** in the fall of the Babylon's religious realm. (The short time of one hour in Revelation 17:12 also appears during the defeat of the commercial element. (Revelation 18:10, 17, 19). The ten kings unanimously yield **their power and authority** to the Roman **beast** for him to have worldwide control (one government). This ten-kingdom empire futilely goes to war against the Lord Jesus when He returns for His **Second Coming** at the **end of the Tribulation*** (**Revelation 16:14; 19:19**).
When we read of the short time and *one hour* it denotes chaos. In Revelation 17:16 the kings, with the interceding of God, will come to hate the Antichrist.

*They will meet their demise in this *Battle of Armageddon*, because the **Lamb** is **Lord of lords and King of kings**.*
Those who follow Christ during the Church Age He will Rapture; and they will be His wife who will continue to follow Him even when He returns to earth to end the Great Tribulation by winning the Battler of Armageddon. (Revelation 19:7-8, 19:14).

Chapter 17 Verses 12-14
References

Vv. 12-14
Revelation 16:14   They are spirits of demons performing miraculous signs, and they go out to the kings of the whole world, to gather them for the battle on the great day of God Almighty. [NIV]

Revelation 19:19   And I saw the beast, the kings of the earth, and their armies, gathered together to make war against Him who sat on the horse and against His army."

Revelation 19:7-8   ⁷"Let us be glad and rejoice and give Him glory, for the marriage of the Lamb has come, and His wife has made herself ready." ⁸And to her it was granted to be arrayed in fine linen, clean and bright, for the fine linen is the righteous acts of the saints.

Revelation 19:14   And the armies in heaven, clothed in fine linen, white and clean, followed Him on white horses.

Chapter 17 Verses 12-14
References Commentary

Vv. 12-14
Revelation 16:14:   *The **spirits** are **of demons, performing** miracles to deceive the world's rulers, and to lure them to a climactic **battle** on the **great day of God Almighty**.*

Revelation 19:19:   the **beast** is the Antichrist who gathers **together the kings of the earth**—a bogus one world government—**to make war against** the Lord Jesus **and against His army**.

Revelation 19:7-8:   **The **wife** or the bride of Christ is the Church. The **fine linen, clean and bright**, represents the **righteous**ness of the Church, which has now been judged and purified at the judgment seat of Christ.**
The judgment seat will probably take place right after the Rapture and prior to the Antichrist being revealed (Revelation 4:4, 10; Revelation 5:11).

Revelation 19:14:   *Riding white horses and **clothed in white linen** depicting their righteousness, **the armies** may be made up of heavenly Jerusalem angels, the raptured Church, and spirits of the Old Testament. But it is noteworthy that they are not required to fight.*
(2 Chronicles 20:23: *For the children of Ammon and Moab stood up against the inhabitants of mount Seir, utterly to slay and destroy them: and when they had made an end of the inhabitants of Seir, every one helped to destroy one another.* [KJV]). *The Lord Jesus defeats His foes unaided.*

234

Chapter 17 Verses 15-18

¹⁵Then the angel said to me, "The waters which you saw, where the prostitute sits, are peoples, multitudes, nations and languages. ¹⁶The beast and the ten horns you saw will hate the prostitute. They will bring her to ruin and leave her naked; they will eat her flesh and burn her with fire. ¹⁷For God has put it into their hearts to accomplish his purpose by agreeing to hand over to the beast their royal authority, until God's words are fulfilled. ¹⁸The woman you saw is the great city that rules over the kings of the earth." [NIV]

NOTE
[Definition, purpose, history and possible future of the "Holy Roman Empire": Nations outside the empire are called kingdoms. The purpose of becoming an empire was globalization: giving supreme dominion, sovereignty, and imperial power to the emperor. The "Roman Empire" existed from 31 BC till AD 476, but the "*Holy* Roman Empire" began in AD 962 and lasted until Martin Luther's time in mid AD 1500. For those 600 years, the Popes claimed

Chapter 17 Verses 15-18 Commentary

17:15-18
The waters on which the **prostitute** [harlot] **sits, are peoples, multitudes, nations, and languages** indicates the harlot *church's* worldwide influence and authority. But the *ten horns*—that is, the new Roman Empire which included the ten kings in verse 12 who ruled for one hour, realize they have been deceived by the influence of the harlot church. **The ten kings, only by the **will** of God (verses 16-17), strip the **harlot**, consume her, and **burn her with fire**. After overthrowing the harlot *church*, the kings will turn their total devotion and worship to the **beast** himself (Revelation 13:12; 17:13; Daniel 11:36-37).

The ten kings will be God's instrument to destroy the harlot Babylon (Revelation 16:19; 18:5-6; 19:2b).**

Looking at verse 17, the reason for all the kings and their nations destroying the *great city* is because **God has put it into their hearts to accomplish his purpose** just as He controlled Pharaoh's heart (Exodus 9:12; 10:1, 20)

It is this compiler's opinion that God controls the hearts of all the nation's leaders in today's world. I believe this is the reason we are seeing the efforts made for globalization and digital currency leading to the mark of the beast.

------

the right to install the most powerful rulers on the European Continent. Today, we are seeing once again his powerful influence. His Headquarters is the Vatican in Rome. Although the Reformation of the church has had great influence, the papacy's power, at times, seems to be regaining strength. The coming prophesied empire could have different political and military Headquarters than for the *religious* control center.]

Chapter 17 Verses 15-18
References

Vv. 15-18

Revelation 13:12 He exercised all the authority of the first beast on his behalf, and made the earth and its inhabitants worship the first beast, whose fatal wound had been healed. [NIV]

Revelation 17:13 "They have one purpose and will give their power and authority to the beast. [NIV]

Daniel 11:36-37 ³⁶"The king will do as he pleases. He will exalt and magnify himself above every god and will say unheard-of things against the God of gods. He will be successful until the time of wrath is completed, for what has been determined must take place. ³⁷He will show no regard for the gods of his fathers or for the one desired by women, nor will he regard any god, but will exalt himself above them all." [NIV]

Revelation 16:19 Now the great city was divided into three parts, and the cities of the nations fell. And great Babylon was remembered before God, to give her the cup of the wine of the fierceness of His wrath.
Revelation 18:5-6 ⁵"for her sins are piled up to heaven, and God has remembered her crimes. ⁶Give back to her as she given; pay her back double for what she has done. Mix her a double portion from her own cup." [NIV]
Revelation 19:2b "He has avenged the blood of His servants *shed* by her."

Chapter 17 Verses 15-18
References Commentary

Vv. 15-18

Revelation 13:12:   The False Prophet works closely with the Antichrist, organizing an international campaign for the worship of the Antichrist, and making an image(s) (huge idol illustrations; A.I.'s?) of the Antichrist to show the Antichrist was wounded—and lived.

Revelation 17:13:   *The ten kings unanimously yield *their* **power and authority** to the Roman **beast** for him to have worldwide control* (one world government and digital currency).

Daniel 11:36-37:   *The Antichrist will **prosper** till God's **wrath** against Israel is **accomplished**.* Verse 37 could be giving us a glimpse of the reason for the world's recent insisting on "politically correct" enforcement of sexual and gender orientation indoctrination. However, God is in control, and His plan will prevail, come what may.

Revelation 16:19, 18:5-6 and 19:2b:
The pronoun **her** is referencing the harlot.
The capitol of *Babylon* is possibly Rome or Roman Empire nations, whose sins God will no longer put up with, because His judgments of **her** harlotry are righteous...and vengeance is His. (Deuteronomy 32:35; Romans 12:19)

- -

Chapter 18 reveals the destruction of the *woman*, or harlot, pictured as a celebrated downfall of a *great city*. Chapter 18 describes, perhaps the greatest commercial establishment in the world; apparently, temporarily controlling the world market.

Chapter 18 Verses 1-3

¹After this I saw another angel coming down from heaven. He had great authority, and the earth was illuminated by his splendor. ²With a mighty voice he shouted:
"Fallen! Fallen is Babylon the Great! She has become a dwelling for demons and a haunt for every impure spirit, a haunt for every unclean bird, a haunt for every unclean and detestable animal. ³For all the nations have drunk the maddening wine of her adulteries. The kings of the earth committed adultery with her, and the merchants of the earth grew rich from her excessive luxuries." [NIV]

Chapter 18 Verses 1-3
Commentary

The Political/Commercial Babylon Falls

*Chapter 18 is [a prophesy prediction that is also] *like a funeral song for the death of a great commercial city.* In Chapter 17, *Babylon refers to the harlot *church* which is not only a vast religious system but* also, here in Chapter 18 Babylon is *perhaps the greatest commercial establishment in the world. It apparently will control the world market.*

18:1-3
In verse 1, **the earth was illuminated by his splendor**, reminds us of how Moses' face reflected the light of his recent visit with God, Exodus 34:29-30.

The nations committed **adultery** [fornication] not only against God, but also against the Antichrist false messiah; it is of absolute vital importance to note what this **adultery** [fornication] means: they have worshiped those idols instead of our only one true God—having a relationship of devotion and adoration to created objects instead of their Creator. The seven kings would finally realize their people here in the Tribulation Period were being deceived to worship idols instead of the Antichrist, so they would then wipe out the harlot *church*. The harlot system, having been destroyed brings down an **angel from heaven** to earth who loudly makes the announcement **Babylon the great is fallen** (Isaiah 13:1, 13:9, 13:19; 21:9b; Isaiah 13:19-21; 21:9; Jeremiah 50:35-46; 51:6-10; 51:24-26; 51:33-37; Revelation 17:1-2), and describes the total destruction including **demons** and **every foul spirit** being imprisoned.

The entire Chapter of Isaiah 13 is Isaiah's prophecy of the fall of Babylon.
The **merchants of the earth had become wealthy through the apostate, idolatrous system, possibly centered in Rome.**

Chapter 18 Verses 1-3 References	Chapter 18 Verses 1-3 References Commentary
Vv. 1-3 **Exodus 34:29-30** ²⁹When Moses came down from Mount Sinai with the two tablets of the Testimony in his hands, he was not aware that his face was radiant because he had spoken with the LORD. ³⁰When Aaron and all the Israelites saw Moses, his face was radiant, and they were afraid to come near him. [NIV]	**Vv. 1-3** Exodus 34:29-30 May we the children of God also reflect His light to the lost. When **Moses came down from Mount Sinai the two tablets of the Testimony** (The Ten Commandments) *were* **in his hand**s.
Isaiah 13:1 The burden of Babylon, which Isāiah the son of Āmoz did see. [KJV] **Isaiah 13:9** Behold, the day of the LORD comes, cruel, with both wrath and fierce anger, to lay the land desolate; and He will destroy its sinners from it. **Isaiah 13:19** Babylon, the jewel of kingdoms, the glory of the Babylonians' pride, will be overthrown by God like Sodom and Gomorrah. [NIV]	Isaiah 13:1, 13:9, 13:19: *Chapter 13 of Isaiah is the first of eleven Chapters containing prophecies against Gentile nations. The first is **Babylon**, the world power that crushed Assyria* —the nation that had exiled the northern kingdom, Israel. *The Babylonians defeated the Assyrians in about 609 B.C.* The Babylonians later exiled the southern Jewish kingdom of Judah. But here in Chapter 13 we learn the *Babylonians were subsequently conquered by the Medes and Persians (in 539 B.C.) However, some of the [burden] prophecies look beyond that event to the final destruction of **Babylon** at the close of the Great Tribulation as we have seen beginning in Revelation 17 and now see here ending in Chapter 18.* **The day of the LORD comes** to **destroy** the whole **land** and its **sinners** in Isaiah 13:9.
Isaiah 21:9b "Babylon is fallen, is fallen! And all the carved images of her gods He has broken to the ground."	Isaiah 21:9b: A prophecy that was made about two hundred years before the ancient Babylon's fall.
Revelation 17:1-2 ¹One of the seven angels who had the seven bowls came and said to me, "Come, I will show you the punishment of the great prostitute, who sits on many waters. ²With her the kings of the earth committed adultery and the inhabitants of the earth were intoxicated with the wine of her adulteries." [NIV]	Revelation 17:1-2: **Babylon** in Chapter 18 will offend God not only by their fornication of idol worship, but also with their becoming rich, most probably, by high-priced selling of their manmade idols for worship, and living in luxury and drunkenness. This is the same as the whore or harlot in Chapter 17, and the summary of God's judgment is the same. **Many waters** represents many peoples and religions of idol worship.

Chapter 18 Verses 4-8

⁴Then I heard another voice from heaven say: "Come out of her, my people, so that you will not share in her sins, so that you will not receive any of her plagues; ⁵for her sins are piled up to heaven, and God has remembered her crimes. ⁶Give back to her as she has given; pay her back double for what she has done. Pour her a double portion from her own cup. ⁷Give her as much torment and grief as the glory and luxury she gave herself. In her heart she boasts, 'I sit enthroned as queen. I am not a widow, I will never mourn.' ⁸Therefore in one day her plagues will overtake her: death, mourning and famine. She will be consumed by fire, for mighty is the Lord God who judges her." [NIV]

Chapter 18 Verses 4-8 Commentary

18:4-8
The newly sanctified believers must be separate from the harlot system of sin, or else they could receive some of **her plagues.** ***Another voice from heaven** warns God's people to **come out of** the doomed system on the eve of its Armageddon destruction.*

In Isaiah 48:20 we read that God told His people of Israel to get out of Babylon.
The connection with the ancient city of Babylon is given in verse 5: **her sins** *have piled up* **to heaven**. Babylon will be destroyed. But God's chosen people Israel will be saved and brought back to their homeland.

The **double judgment emphasizes full punishment (Jeremiah 16:14-18; 17:17-18; 50:29-32).

Arrogantly she sees herself as **queen and** not a **widow** and thinks she is safe from **sorrow**. As she exalts herself she will be quickly humbled** (Matthew 23:12; Luke 14:11; 18:14) with **death, mourning and famine**, and the **Lord God** *will punish her **with fire***.

In Ezekiel 28:2-8 the prince of Tyre (Lebanon) is a "type" or picture of the Antichrist calling himself a god. God tells Ezekiel, whom He refers to as "Son of man", to say to the prince of Tyre that he will be *thrown into the Pit* in verse 8. God will first tell Ezekiel to mock the prince of Tyre in verses 3-5.

Chapter 18 Verses 4-8
References

Vv. 4-8
Isaiah 48:20 "Go forth from Babylon! Flee from the Chaldēans! With a voice of singing, declare, proclaim this, utter it to the end of the earth; say, "The LORD has redeemed His servant Jacob!"

Jeremiah 16:14-18 ¹⁴"Therefore behold, the days are coming," says the LORD, "that it shall no more be said, 'The LORD lives who brought up the children of Israel from the land of Egypt,' ¹⁵"but, 'The LORD lives who brought up the children of Israel from the land of the north and from all the lands where He had driven them.' For I will bring them back into their land which I gave to their fathers. ¹⁶Behold, I will send for many fishermen," says the LORD, "and they shall fish them; and afterward I will send for many hunters, and they shall hunt them from every mountain and every hill, and out of the holes of the rocks. ¹⁷For My eyes *are* on all their ways; they are not hidden from My face, nor is their iniquity hidden from My eyes. ¹⁸And first I will repay double for their iniquity and their sin, because they have defiled My land; they have filled My inheritance with the carcasses of their detestable and abominable idols."

Jeremiah 17:17-18; 50:29-32; Matthew 23:12; Luke 14:11; Ezekiel 28:2-8

-CONTINUED ON NEXT SET OF PAGES UNDER REFERENCES!-

Chapter 18 Verses 4-8
References Commentary

Vv. 4-8
Isaiah 48:20: Compared to **Jacob** (Israel) in the past, Israel's responsibility in the future is to declare the works and power of the Lord Jesus Christ. The two witnesses and the 144,000 are commissioned to proclaim the saving Gospel message which will result in some souls to be blessed with eternal life during the Tribulation (Romans 16:20; Revelation 7:14; 12:11). The 144,000 will be spreading the Gospel message in the near future. Today, while we are still here amongst so many lost souls, God the Savior gives more than plentiful warnings for people to get away from Satan and come to Him.
Romans 10:14c: and h*ow shall they hear without a preacher*? [KJV]
How will they hear if I don't tell them? We all need to serve God and help at every opportunity.

Jeremiah 16:14-18: **God includes a reassuring hope to Jeremiah. After Judah has paid for its sins and the divine purposes have been realized, God will re-gather His people to the land in a deliverance from the nations that surpasses that of Israel's redemption from **Egypt**. Nevertheless, Judah must first be judged (vv. 16-17).**

-CONTINUED ON NEXT SET OF PAGES UNDER REFERENCES COMMENTARY!-

Chapter 18 Verses 4-8	Chapter 18 Verses 4-8 Commentary

-VERSES 4-8 REPEATED FROM PREVIOUS PAGE -

-PART OF COMMENTARY VERSES 4-8 REPEATED FROM PREVIOUS PAGE-

18:4-8

⁴Then I heard another voice from heaven say: "Come out of her, my people, so that you will not share in her sins, so that you will not receive any of her plagues; ⁵for her sins are piled up to heaven, and God has remembered her crimes. ⁶Give back to her as she has given; pay her back double for what she has done. Pour her a double portion from her own cup. ⁷Give her as much torment and grief as the glory and luxury she gave herself. In her heart she boasts, 'I sit enthroned as queen. I am not a widow, I will never mourn.' ⁸Therefore in one day her plagues will overtake her: death, mourning and famine. She will be consumed by fire, for mighty is the Lord God who judges her." [NIV]

The **double judgment emphasizes full punishment (Jeremiah 16:14-18; 17:17-18; 50:29-32)**.

Arrogantly **she sees herself as **queen and** not a **widow** and thinks she is safe from **sorrow**. As she exalts herself she will be quickly humbled** (Matthew 23:12; Luke 14:11; 18:14) with **death, mourning and famine**, and the **Lord God** *will punish her **with fire**.*

In Ezekiel 28:2-8 the prince of Tyre (Lebanon) is a "type" or picture of the Antichrist calling himself a god. God tells Ezekiel, whom He refers to as "Son of man", to say to the prince of Tyre that he will be *thrown into the Pit* in verse 8. God will first tell Ezekiel to mock the prince of Tyre in verses 3-5.

Chapter 18 Verses 4-8 References	Chapter 18 Verses 4-8 References Commentary
-CONTINUED FROM PREVIOUS PAGE-	-CONTINUED FROM PREVIOUS PAGE-

Vv. 4-8

Jeremiah 17:17-18 ¹⁷Do not be a terror to me; You are my hope in the day of doom. ¹⁸Let them be ashamed who persecute me, but do not let me be put to shame; let them be dismayed, but do not let me be dismayed. Bring on them the day of doom, and destroy them with double destruction!

Jeremiah 50:29-32 ²⁹Summon archers against Babylon, all those who draw the bow. Encamp all around her; let no one escape. Repay her for her deeds; do to her as she has done. For she has defied the LORD, the Holy One of Israel. ³⁰Therefore her young men will fall in the streets; all her soldiers will be silenced in that day," declares the LORD. ³¹"See, I *am* against you, O arrogant one," declares the Lord, the LORD Almighty, "for your day has come, the time for you to be punished. ³²The arrogant one will stumble and fall and no one will help her up; I will kindle a fire in her towns, that will consume all who are around her." [NIV]

Matthew 23:12a
Luke 14:11
Luke 18:14b
Ezekiel 28:2-8

Vv. 4-8

Jeremiah 17:17-18: **Jeremiah pleas for vindication and help. He prays not to be rescued from the persecution but to be delivered through it (James 1:2-4; 1 Peter 1:3-7; 1 Peter 4:12-19).** He also prays for **double** punishment for his and God's enemies as we also read of in Revelation 18:6.

In Jeremiah 50:29-32 We should compare God's wrath against Babylon of the past to that of the near future. Our God is a jealous God; He does not change; He is the One who takes vengeance.

-CONTINUED ON NEXT SET OF PAGES UNDER REFERENCES!-   -CONTINUED ON NEXT SET OF PAGES UNDER REFERENCES COMMENTARY!-

Chapter 18 Verses 4-8

Chapter 18 Verses 4-8
Commentary

-VERSES 4-8 REPEATED FROM PREVIOUS PAGE -

-PART OF COMMENTARY VERSES 4-8 REPEATED FROM PREVIOUS PAGE-

18:4-8

⁴Then I heard another voice from heaven say: "Come out of her, my people, so that you will not share in her sins, so that you will not receive any of her plagues; ⁵for her sins are piled up to heaven, and God has remembered her crimes. ⁶Give back to her as she has given; pay her back double for what she has done. Pour her a double portion from her own cup. ⁷Give her as much torment and grief as the glory and luxury she gave herself. In her heart she boasts, 'I sit enthroned as queen. I am not a widow, I will never mourn.' ⁸Therefore in one day her plagues will overtake her: death, mourning and famine. She will be consumed by fire, for mighty is the Lord God who judges her." [NIV]

Arrogantly **she sees herself as **queen and** not a **widow** and thinks she is safe from **sorrow**. As she exalts herself she will be quickly humbled** (Matthew 23:12; Luke 14:11; 18:14) with **death, mourning and famine**, and the **Lord God** *will punish her **with fire**.*

In Ezekiel 28:2-8 the prince of Tyre (Lebanon) is a "type" or picture of the Antichrist calling himself a god. God tells Ezekiel, whom He refers to as "Son of man", to say to the prince of Tyre that he will be *thrown into the Pit* in verse 8. God will first tell Ezekiel to mock the prince of Tyre in verses 3-5.

Chapter 18 Verses 4-8 References	Chapter 18 Verses 4-8 References Commentary

-CONTINUED FROM PREVIOUS PAGE-   -CONTINUED FROM PREVIOUS PAGE-

Vv. 4-8

Vv. 4-8

Matthew 23:12a *For whoever exalts himself will be humbled,* [NIV]
Luke 14:11 *"For everyone who exalts himself will be humbled, and he who humbles himself will be exalted.* [NIV]
Luke 18:14b *For everyone who exalts himself will be humbled,* [NIV]

The **haughty one** will be humbled in Matthew 23:12 Luke 14:11; 18:14b. Some of today's churches have those in leadership positions who cause their flock to look up to them as though they were not part of the flock themselves. We have *all* sinned and fallen short of the glory of God. *Jesus taught that it is better to be advanced to a place of honor than to grasp that place and later have to relinquish it. He Himself is the living example of self-renunciation (Philippians 2:5-9). He humbled Himself and God exalted Him.* *Whoever exalts himself will be humbled* by God.

Ezekiel 28:2-8 ²"Son of man, say to the ruler of Tyre, 'This is what the Sovereign LORD says: In the pride of your heart you say, 'I am a god; I sit on the throne of a god in the heart of the seas.' But you are a man and not a god, though you think you are as wise as a god. ³Are you wiser than Daniel? Is no secret hidden from you? ⁴By your wisdom and your understanding you have gained wealth for yourself and amassed gold and silver into your treasuries. ⁵By your great skill in trading you have increased your wealth, and because of your wealth your heart has grown proud. ⁶'Therefore this is what the Sovereign LORD says: "Because you think you are wise, as wise as a god, ⁷I am going to bring foreigners against you, the most ruthless of nations; they will draw their swords against your beauty and wisdom and pierce your shinning splendor. ⁸They will bring you down to the pit, and you will die a violent death in the heart of the seas.'" [NIV]

Ezekiel 28:2-8: Notice how in Ezekiel 28:7-8 God will even **bring foreigners** to throw the prince of Tyre into **the pit**, mirroring the end of the Antichrist in Revelation 19:20. (**Foreigners** like Gog and Māgog in Ezekiel 38 to break the Antichrist's promise of peace.)
In 2 Thessalonians 2:4 the Antichrist will seat himself in the temple as God, exalting himself after the pattern of the prince of Tyre. God has been trying to tell the lost, but they have ears and cannot hear.

Chapter 18 Verses 9-16

⁹"When the kings of the earth who committed adultery with her and shared her luxury see the smoke of her burning, they will weep and mourn over her. ¹⁰Terrified at her torment, they will stand far off and cry: " ' Woe! Woe to you, great city, you mighty city of Babylon! In one hour your doom has come!' ¹¹The merchants of the earth will weep and mourn over her because no one buys their cargoes anymore — ¹²cargoes of gold, silver, precious stones and pearls, fine linen, purple, silk and scarlet cloth; every sort of citron wood, and articles of every kind made of ivory, costly wood, bronze, iron and marble; ¹³cargoes of cinnamon and spice, of incense, myrrh and frankincense, of wine and olive oil, of fine flour and wheat; cattle and sheep; horses and carriages; and human beings sold as slaves. [NIV]

¹⁴"They will say, 'The fruit you longed for is gone from you. All your luxury and splendor have vanished, never to be recovered.' ¹⁵The merchants who sold these things and gained their wealth from her will stand far off, terrified at her torment. They will weep and mourn ¹⁶and cry out: "Woe! Woe to you, great city, dressed in fine linen, purple and scarlet, and glittering with gold, precious stones and pearls!" [NIV]

Chapter 18 Verses 9-16
Commentary

18:9-13
The **kings**, **merchants** and sailors lament over the fallen city, because *of the loss of pleasure and luxury. **Standing at a distance**, they marvel at the extent of **her torment** and the suddenness of her end. Their hope of gain is gone, the trafficking in the **souls of men** and all the worldwide products are gone.*
Now all that wealth has suddenly come to nothing.

18:14-16
The kings and merchants shall never again find the riches for which their souls so deeply longed. They will simply continue to weep and lament until their final judgment. The words **woe, woe** [or "alas" in the NKJV] are used back-to-back on three occasions, in verses 10, 16, and 19. This means the people who are left are about to experience immeasurable grief; the worst type of *woe*. This *doubled woe*—**woe, woe**—is an exclamation of exceedingly terrible, dreadful grief, sorrow, misery, and heavy calamity.

Chapter 18 Verses 9-16
References

Chapter 18 Verses 9-16
References Commentary

Chapter 18 Verses 17-19

Chapter 18 Verses 17-19
Commentary

¹⁷In one hour such great wealth has been brought to ruin!' "Every sea captain, and all who travel by ship, the sailors, and all who earn their living from the sea, will stand far off. ¹⁸When they see the smoke of her burning, they will exclaim, 'Was there ever a city like this great city?' ¹⁹They will throw dust on their heads, and with weeping and mourning cry out: 'Woe! Woe to you, great city, where all who had ships on the sea became rich through her wealth! In one hour she has been brought to ruin!' " [NIV]

18:17-19
Ezekiel prophesied details that match these verses (Ezekiel 27:29-36).

Jeremiah also compares the lamenting (Lamentations 2:10).

Either Ezekiel or Jeremiah was a probable writer of 1ˢᵗ and 2ⁿᵈ Kings.
The LORD was provoked to wrath by King Manasseh of Judah (2 Kings 21:10-13).

In Revelation 17:12 the ten kings received authority for one hour. Here in Revelation 18:17-19, we read that after that one hour, their authority, along with their great riches will be **made desolate**.

247

Chapter 18 Verses 17-19	Chapter 18 Verses 17-19
References	References Commentary

Vv. 17-19
Ezekiel 27:29-36 ²⁹"All who handle the oars will abandon their ships; the mariners and all the seamen will stand on the shore. ³⁰They will raise their voice and cry bitterly over you; they will sprinkle dust on their heads and roll in ashes. ³¹They will shave their heads because of you and will put on sackcloth. They will weep over you with anguish of soul and with bitter mourning. ³²As they wail and mourn over you, they will take up a lament concerning you: "Who was ever silenced like Tyre, surrounded by the sea?" ³³When your merchants went out on the seas, you satisfied many nations; with your great wealth and your wares you enriched the kings of the earth. ³⁴Now you are shattered by the sea in the depths of the waters; your wares and all your company have gone down with you. ³⁵All who live in the coastlands are appalled at you; their kings shudder with horror and their faces are distorted with fear. ³⁶The merchants among the nations hiss at you; you have come to a horrible end and will be no more.' " [NIV]

Lamentations 2:10 The elders of the daughter of Zion sit upon the ground, and keep silence: they have cast dust upon their heads; they have girded themselves with sackcloth: the virgins of Jerusalem hang down their heads to the ground. [KJV]

2 Kings 21:10-13

Vv. 17-19
Ezekiel 27:29-36: The city of **Tyre** is on the Mediterranean coast in today's southern Lebanon, about 70 km south of Beirut and on the edge of Israel's northern coastal border.
Ezekiel 27 *verses 10-11 inform us that Tyre's army, includes soldiers from Persia, Lydia, and Libya. Then verses 12-27 describe the vastness of Tyre's commerce in luxury goods. But it was to be wrecked by an east wind (the Babylonians). The other nations would be seriously shaken by the fall of the city.*
This compares to the fall of the great city Babylon in the future Battle of Armageddon.

Lamentations 2:10: **All of these actions express the depths of grief (cf. 2 Kings 19:1:**
When King Hezekiah heard this, he tore his clothes and put on sackcloth, and went into the temple of the LORD. [NIV]
The bad news that was given to Hezekiah came from the chief of the household, the scribe and the recorder—*all three men with their clothes torn* (2 Kings 18:37).
Job 2:8 ⁸*And he took for himself a potsherd with which to scrape himself while he sat in the midst of the ashes.*
A potsherd is a fragment of a broken, baked, clay pot that Job used to scrape the sores covering his body.

-CONTINUED ON NEXT SET OF PAGES UNDER REFERENCES!-

-CONTINUED ON NEXT SET OF PAGES UNDER REFERENCES COMMENTARY!-

Chapter 18 Verses 17-19

-VERSES 17-19 REPEATED FROM PREVIOUS PAGE -

¹⁷In one hour such great wealth has been brought to ruin!' "Every sea captain, and all who travel by ship, the sailors, and all who earn their living from the sea, will stand far off. ¹⁸When they see the smoke of her burning, they will exclaim, 'Was there ever a city like this great city?' ¹⁹They will throw dust on their heads, and with weeping and mourning cry out: " 'Woe! Woe to you, great city, where all who had ships on the sea became rich through her wealth! In one hour she has been brought to ruin!' [NIV]

Chapter 18 Verses 17-19
Commentary

-VERSES 17-19 COMMENTARY REPEATED FROM PREVIOUS PAGE-

18:17-19
Ezekiel prophesied details that match these verses (Ezekiel 27:29-36).

Jeremiah also compares the lamenting (Lamentations 2:10).

Either Ezekiel or Jeremiah was a probable writer of 1ˢᵗ and 2ⁿᵈ Kings.

The LORD was provoked to wrath by King Manasseh of Judah (2 Kings 21:10-13).

In Revelation 17:12 the ten kings received authority for one hour. Here in Revelation 18:17-19, we read that after that one hour, their authority, along with their great riches will be **made desolate**.

Chapter 18 Verses 17-19 References	Chapter 18 Verses 17-19 References Commentary
-CONTINUED FROM PREVIOUS PAGE-	-CONTINUED FROM PREVIOUS PAGE-
2 Kings 21:10-13 [10]And the LORD spoke by His servants the prophets, saying, [11]"Because Manasseh king of Judah has done these abominations [12]therefore thus says the LORD God of Israel: 'Behold, *I* am bringing *such* calamity upon Jerusalem and Judah, that whoever hears of it, both his ears will tingle.[13]And I will stretch over Jerusalem the measuring line of Samaria and the plummet of the house of Āhab; I will wipe Jerusalem as *one* wipes a dish, wiping *it* and turning *it* upside down.'"	2 Kings 21:10-13: This passage gives evidence that the LORD God does not put up with sin. ***Manasseh** had led the people into such terrible **abominations** that God stretched **the measuring line** and used **the plummet**, both of which symbolize judgment. His people would be led off into captivity in Babylon because they had provoked the LORD so grievously.* **Manasseh's abominations** were more wicked than all the Amorītes who *were* before him, and has also made Judah sin with his idols. We still cannot say with absolute certainty exactly what city or region the great Babylon will be in the end times. But Babylon possibly consists of more than just one city; it could also even include nations. No matter what, the prophecy will be fulfilled.

- -

[The center of Rome is about 20 km {about 12 miles} off the Mediterranean coast of western Italy. The edge of the metropolis city then stretches nearly to the coast. If Rome were to be destroyed by all that has been prophesied, the smoke rising up would be easily visible by the sailors on the sea.]

Chapter 18 Verses 20-24

²⁰"Rejoice over her, you heavens! Rejoice, you people of God! Rejoice, apostles and prophets! For God has judged her with the judgment she imposed on you." ²¹Then a mighty angel picked up a boulder the size of a large millstone and threw it into the sea, and said: "With such violence the great city of Babylon will be thrown down, never to be found again. ²²The music of harpists and musicians, pipers and trumpeters, will never be heard in you again. No worker of any trade will ever be found in you again. The sound of a millstone will never be heard in you again. ²³The light of a lamp will never shine in you again. The voice of bridegroom and bride will never be heard in you again. Your merchants were the world's important people. ²⁴In her was found the blood of prophets and of God's holy people, of all who have been slaughtered on the earth."
[NIV]

Chapter 18 Verses 20-24
Commentary

18:20-24
But while all the godless tears are being shed on earth, there is great rejoicing in **heaven**. The **stone** cast **into the sea** in verse 21 depicts the total end of **the great city Babylon**. At last **God has avenged** His *saints* (verse 20 NKJ Bible reference), and your holy **apostles** and **prophets**.

**Three main reasons are given for her destruction:
1. arrogance,
2. deception of the nations, and
3. persecution and martyrdom of God's people. **

There will be no more merriment in the great city, for by her "sorcery, all the nations were deceived. **In her was found the blood of prophets and saints, and of all who were slaughtered on the earth.**" In these verses is the *sixfold* repetition of the phrase **never to be found again**; with the likes of **shall be found no more at all** in the KJV; emphasizes God's wrath to the point of total annihilation Isaiah 13:19-20.

The Babylonian system began in Genesis 10 [with Cush's son Nimrod—and his son Tammuz], and has continued uninterrupted in one form or another to the present day. But one day it will suddenly "sink," never to return.
However, the eternal suffering for those who have rejected the righteous Judge who loves them will have just begun.

Chapter 18 Verses 20-24
References

Chapter 18 Verses 20-24
References Commentary

Isaiah 13:19-20 ¹⁹"Babylon, the jewel of kingdoms, the glory of the Babylonians' pride, will be overthrown by God like Sodom and Gomorrah. ²⁰She will never be inhabited, or lived in through all generations; no Arab will pitch his tent there, no shepherd will rest his flocks there. [NIV]

Isaiah 13:19-20 God keeps His promises, and He has never told a lie. Titus 1:2 *In hope of eternal life, which God, that cannot lie, promised before the world began*; [KJV]
God does *not change*. (Malachi 3:6)

Chapter 19 Verses 1-5

¹After these things I heard a loud voice of a great multitude in heaven, saying, "Alleluia! Salvation and glory and honor and power *belong* to the Lord our God! ²For true and righteous *are* His judgments, because He has judged the great harlot who corrupted the earth with her fornication; and He has avenged on her the blood of His servants *shed* by her." ³Again they said, "Alleluia! Her smoke rises up forever and ever!" ⁴And the twenty-four elders and the four living creatures fell down and worshiped God who sat on the throne, saying, "Amen! Alleluia!" ⁵Then a voice came from the throne, saying, "Praise our God, all you His servants and those who fear Him, both small and great!"

Chapter 19 Verses 1-5 Commentary

The Church Age Saints are Called the *Wife* of the Lamb {Revelation 19:7}

More on the Second Coming of Christ, His Victory in the Battle of Armageddon, and His Millennial Kingdom

19:1-20:9
begin the climax of the Book of Revelation. But first, the first five verses of Chapter 19 which show the heaven's response to the judgment of the harlot.

19:1-5
****After these things a great multitude in heaven** praises the Lord for His righteous punishment of the great harlot and avenging the **blood** of martyrs. The word **Alleluia** is the Greek equivalent of *hallelujah*, and means "Praise Yahweh" or "Praise the Lord"**

(Psalm 106:1, 106:48d; 111:1; 112:1; 113:1, 113:9c; 117:1, 117:2c; 135:1a, 135:21c; Psalm 146-150).

The eternal **smoke symbolizes the permanence of Babylon's destruction. **Amen** derives from a Hebrew word meaning "to be firm," and may be translated "truly" or "so be it."**

253

| Chapter 19 Verses 1-5 References | Chapter 19 Verses 1-5 References Commentary |

Vv. 1-5

Psalm 106:1 PRAISE the LORD! Oh, give thanks to the LORD, for *He is* good! For His mercy *endures* forever.
Psalm 106:48d Praise be to the LORD, [NIV]
Psalm 111:1 Praise the LORD. I will extol [praise] the LORD with all my heart in the council of the upright and in the assembly. [NIV]
Psalm 112:1 PRAISE the LORD! Blessed *is* the man *who* fears the LORD, *who* delights greatly in His commandments.
Psalm 113:1 Praise the LORD. Praise, O servants of the LORD, praise the name of the LORD. [NIV]
Psalm 113:9b Praise the LORD. [NIV]
Psalm 117:1 PRAISE the LORD, all you Gentiles! Laud Him, all you peoples!
Psalm 117:2c Praise the LORD!
Psalm 135:1a PRAISE the LORD! Praise the name of the LORD; praise *Him*, O you servants of the LORD!
Psalm 135:21c Praise the LORD. [NIV]

Vv. 1-5

Psalm 106:1, 106:48d; 111:1; 112:1; 113:1, 113:9c; 117:1, 117:2c; 135:1a, 135:21c all say:

Praise the LORD!

And the last 5 Psalms, 146 to 150, all begin and end with **Praise the LORD!**

The word *alleluia* is the Greek equivalent of *hallelujah*, and means "Praise Yahweh," or "Praise Jehovah," or "Praise God Almighty," or "Praise the Lord."

Chapter 19 Verses 6-7

⁶And I heard, as it were, the voice of a great multitude, as the sound of many waters and as the sound of mighty thunderings, saying, "Alleluia! For the Lord God Omnipotent reigns! ⁷Let us be glad and rejoice and give Him glory for the marriage of the Lamb has come, and His wife has made herself ready."

Chapter 19 Verses 6-7
Commentary

19:6-7
*Another loud song breaks out of heaven with a great **Alleluia! For the Lord God Omnipotent reigns.*** ****God's power is endless!**** *The Tribulation is past. Babylon has been judged.* ****The marriage of the Lamb** takes place in heaven.**

Verse 7 says in past tense: **the marriage has come**. Additionally, the term *bride* has already been changed to **wife...has made herself ready**. Therefore, we believe the wedding will take place soon after the Rapture. It does not seem reasonable that the *bride* would be living with the Bridegroom before the marriage.

The **wife** or the bride of Christ is the Church (Matthew 22:2-3; 2 Corinthians 11:2; Ephesians 5:25-27, 30-32).

Revelation 21:9: *One of the seven angels who had the seven bowls full of the seven last plagues came and said to me, "Come, I will show you the bride, the wife of the Lamb."* [NIV]

The term *bride* here probably translates to *daughter-in-law* (of God the Father of the Bridegroom). In the same verse, the raptured Church is referred to as ***the Lamb's wife***.

The label of *bride* is used only one other time prior to this in the Book of Revelation, but it is in regards to the fall of Babylon:

Revelation 18:23b: *The voice of bridegroom and bride will never be heard in you again.*

(No more celebrating due to the total devastation of the *great city Babylon*.)

Chapter 19 Verses 6-7 References	Chapter 19 Verses 6-7 References Commentary
Vv. 6-7 **Matthew 22:2-3** ²"The kingdom of heaven is like a king who prepared a wedding banquet for his son. ³He sent his servants to those who had been invited to the banquet to tell them to come, but they refused to come." [NIV]	**Vv. 6-7** Matthew 22:2-3: **Rejection of the invitation to attend constitutes disloyalty to the King, as well as discourtesy to the Son, and accounts for the forthcoming severe treatment.**
2 Corinthians 11:2 For I am jealous over you with godly jealousy: for I have espoused you to one husband, that I may present you as a chaste virgin to Christ. [KJV]	2 Corinthians 11:2: *Paul undoubtedly felt a personal responsibility for the spiritual welfare of the Corinthian saints. His desire was that in a coming day—at the Rapture—he could present the bride to the Lord Jesus, uncorrupted by prevalent false teachings.*
Ephesians 5:25-27 ²⁵Husbands, love your wives, just as Christ also loved the church and gave Himself for her, ²⁶that He might sanctify and cleanse her with the washing of water by the word, ²⁷that He might present her to Himself a glorious church, not having spot or wrinkle or any such thing, but that she should be holy and without blemish.	Going to Ephesians 5:25-27, *it has been well said that no wife would mind being submissive to a husband who loves her as much as **Christ** loves **the church**. He demonstrated His love for **the church** by giving **Himself for her** in His sacrificial death on the cross. He paid the greatest price in order to purchase a bride for Himself.*
Ephesians 5:30-32 ³⁰For we are members of His body, of His flesh and of His bones. ³¹*"For this reason a man shall leave his father and mother and be joined to his wife, and the two shall become one flesh."* ³²This is a great mystery, but I speak concerning Christ and the church.	Ephesians 5:30-32 speaks volumes concerning His love for us. Whatever affects the members affects the Head also. It is unimaginable for Him to allow His precious *bride* to experience the deception attempts and the wrath of any part of the Seven-year Tribulation.

Chapter 19 Verse 8

⁸Fine linen, bright and clean, was given her to wear." (Fine linen stands for the righteous acts of God's holy people.) [NIV]

Chapter 19 Verse 8 Commentary

19:8
The **fine linen, clean and bright**, represents the **righteous acts** of the Church, which has already been judged and purified at the judgment seat of Christ (1 Corinthians 3:13-15; 2 Corinthians 5:10).**

Chapter 19 Verse 8 **References**	**Chapter 19 Verse 8** **References Commentary**
V. 8 **1 Corinthians 3:13-15** ¹³each one's work will become clear; for the Day will declare it, because it will be revealed by fire; and the fire will test each one's work, of what sort it is. ¹⁴If anyone's work which he has built on *it* endures, he will receive a reward. ¹⁵If anyone's work is burned, he will suffer loss; but he himself will be saved, yet so as through fire.	**V. 8** In 1 Corinthians 3:13-15 ***Day** refers to the judgment seat of Christ when all service for the Lord will be reviewed. Service that has brought glory to God and blessing to man, like gold, silver, and precious stones, will not be affected by the fire. On the other hand, that which has caused trouble among the people of God or failed to edify will nearly be consumed.*
2 Corinthians 5:10 For we must all appear before the judgment seat of Christ, that each one may receive what is due him for the things done while in the body, whether good or bad. [NIV]	In 2 Corinthians 5:10 *not only the *amount* of our service, but also its *quality*, and even the very *motives* that prompted it will be brought into review. It will not be a matter of whether we are saved or not; that is already an assured fact. But it is a matter of reward or loss of same.*

Chapter 19 Verses 9-10

⁹Then the angel said to me, "Write this: Blessed are those who are invited to the wedding supper of the Lamb!" And he added, "These are the true words of God." ¹⁰At this I fell at his feet to worship him. But he said to me, "Don't do that! I am a fellow servant with you and with your brothers and sisters who hold to the testimony of Jesus. Worship God! For it is the Spirit of prophecy who bears testimony to Jesus." [NIV]

Chapter 19 Verses 9-10
Commentary

19:9-10
The wedding supper of the Lamb **will take place on earth** when all believers are gathered for the Millennial Reign (verse 9). The souls whom will be resurrected at the end of the Tribulation will be blessed: the Old Testament saints along with the Tribulation martyrs. The Lord Jesus will return with His wife, the Church. Following Christ's return and victory the feast will take place.

The Jewish **marriage consisted of three major elements:
1. The betrothal (engagement) takes place on earth during the Church Age,
2. the wedding will take place in heaven following the Rapture (verse 7), and
3. the **marriage** feast will take place on earth following Christ's return with the Church (verses 9-11, 14). There will be rejoicing at the supper feast: Isaiah 62:5.

Called: Those who are invited to the **marriage supper** include Old Testament believers and the rest of the redeemed who will turn to Christ during the Tribulation (Revelation 7:14b♦; Jeremiah 31:31-34♦; Romans 11:25-27).**

♦These verses also speak of the Millennial Reign and the wedding supper.

Worship: *John falls before the angel's **feet**, but is forbidden. Only God is to be worshiped* (**Revelation 22:8-9; Acts 10:25-26**).

Spirit of prophecy: **The person and message of **Jesus** is the essence of all true **prophecy**.**
*The purpose of all true **prophecy** is to bear **testimony** to the Person and work of Jesus Christ.*

Chapter 19 Verses 9-10 References	Chapter 19 Verses 9-10 References Commentary
Vv. 9-10 **Isaiah 62:5** As a young man marries a maiden, so will your sons marry you; and as a bridegroom rejoices over his bride, so will your God rejoice over you. [NIV]	**Vv. 9-10** Isaiah 62:5: The Lord Jesus Christ will rejoice over His Church wife as will all those who are invited to the marriage supper—the resurrected Old Testament saints and the martyred, resurrected Tribulation saints. Providing an apologetic, some claim that Christ will be committing polygamy by seeming to have two wives—both Israel and His Church. However, we do not see this in the Scripture. We believe Israel will be the New Jerusalem's bride: Isaiah 65:17-19: *^{17}"For behold, I create new heavens and a new earth; and the former shall not be remembered or come to mind. ^{18}But be glad and rejoice forever in what I create; for behold, I create Jerusalem as a rejoicing, and her people a joy. ^{19}I will rejoice in Jerusalem, and joy in My people; the voice of weeping will no longer be heard in her, nor the voice of crying."* The woman Israel will deliver a nation. (Revelation 12:2)
Revelation 7:14b "These are the ones who come out of the great tribulation, and washed their robes and made them white in the blood of the Lamb."	In Revelation 5:11, tens of thousands who had already been raptured will witness a new **great multitude** in Revelation 7:14b arriving before the throne. The ones who have been raptured are able to see the many Jews and Gentiles who will be saved during the Tribulation.
Romans 11:25-27 ^{25}For I do not desire, brethren, that you should be ignorant of this mystery, lest you should be wise in your own opinion, that blindness in part has happened to Israel until the fullness of the Gentiles has come in. ^{26}And so all Israel will be saved, as it is written: *"The Deliverer will come out of Zion, and He will turn away ungodliness from Jacob; ^{27}For this is My covenant with them, when I take away their sins."*	In Romans 11:25-27 *Paul writes that the future restoration of Israel is an assured fact, but it has been a **mystery**. Some of Israel (**in part**) have been blinded (the unbelieving ones). The **blindness** is temporary. It will continue only **until** the Church has become full with the last believer from every nation. And then, the Rapture will happen! The *completed* Body of Christ will be taken home. Israel's judicial **blindness** will then be removed.*
Acts 10:25-26 ^{25}As Peter entered the house, Cornelius met him and fell at his feet in reverence. ^{26}But Peter made him get up. "Stand up," he said, "I am only a man myself." [NIV]	Acts 10:25-26: God desires we worship no one other than Himself—the One true God (Exodus 20:3, 20:5; Deuteronomy 5:7, 9; Hosea 13:4).

Chapter 19 Verses 11-12

**Chapter 19 Verses 11-12
Commentary**

¹¹Now I saw heaven opened, and behold, a white horse. And He who sat on him *was* called Faithful and True, and in righteousness He judges and makes war. ¹²His eyes *were* like a flame of fire, and on His head *were* many crowns. He had a name written that no one knew except Himself.

19:11-12
Verses 11-12 depict the Second Coming: the return of Christ to earth. (Matthew 25:1-13♦; Zechariah 13:9; 14:3-4; Luke 14:16, 14:18, 14:24; Revelation 20:4♦).

*When Christ is first seen back on earth He is riding a **white horse**—a war **horse**—since He is coming to conquer His enemies. He is **Faithful** to His promises **and True** to His own character. **His eyes** are **like a flame of fire**, suggesting the penetrating power of His **righteous judgment**. Only He wears the diadem (crown) of royalty and His mysteries will never be comprehended by any created being.*

♦These verses also speak of the wedding supper and point toward the Millennial Reign.

Chapter 19 Verses 11-12
References

Vv. 11-12
Zechariah 13:9 "I will bring *one*-third through the fire, will refine them as silver is refined, and test them as gold is tested. They will call on My name, and I will answer them. I will say, 'This *is* My people'; and each one will say, 'The LORD is my God.'"

Zechariah 14:3-4 ³Then the L0RD will go forth and fight against those nations, as He fights in the day of battle. ⁴And in that day His feet will stand on the Mount of Olives, which faces Jerusalem on the east. And the Mount of Olives shall be split in two, from east to west, making a very large valley; half of the mountain shall move toward the north and half of it toward the south.

Luke 14:16 Jesus replied: "A certain man was preparing a great banquet and invited many guests." [NIV]
Luke 14:18 But they all alike began to make excuses. The first said, 'I have just bought a field, and I must go and see it. Please excuse me.' [NIV]
Luke 14:24 "I tell you, not one of those men who were invited will get a taste of my banquet." [NIV]

Chapter 19 Verses 11-12
References Commentary

Vv. 11-12
In Zechariah 13:9 *although two-thirds of the nation of Israel will die during the Great Tribulation, **one-third** will be preserved. This remnant will be refined like **silver** and **gold**.*

In Zechariah 14:3-4 unlike the humble Triumphal Entry of Jesus riding in on a donkey, described in Matthew 21; in this, His Second Coming, the exalted and glorified Almighty Lord Jesus spectacularly, suddenly appears sitting on a white horse. His first priority upon return is to judge and to swiftly win the War of Armageddon against the evil antichrist and his followers.

In Luke 14:16, 14:18 and 14:24 *our Lord is saying that wonderful as it may be to eat bread in the kingdom of God, the sad fact is that many of those who are invited make all kinds of foolish excuses for their failure to accept His invitation. The one who had bought a piece of ground was putting material things ahead of the gracious invitation.*

Chapter 19 Verses 13

Chapter 19 Verse 13 Commentary

End of the Battle of Armageddon and the Great Tribulation

¹³He was clothed with a robe dipped in blood, and His name is called The Word of God.

19:13

***Clothed in a robe dipped in blood**, not the blood He shed on Calvary's cross, but the **blood** of His enemies whom He tramples in the winepress of the wrath of God* (Isaiah 63:3).

The name **Word of God expresses Christ as the revelation of God Himself (John 1:1, 1:14a; 1 John 1:1).

In His first advent, Jesus especially revealed the love and grace of God (John 1:17; Romans 5:8).

In His second advent, He will reveal the holiness, justice, and judgment of God (Hebrews 4:12).**

Giving one's word expresses truth. By Christ being the **Word**, *God has fully expressed Himself to man.*

Chapter 19 Verse 13	Chapter 19 Verse 13
References	References Commentary

V. 13

Isaiah 63:3 I have trodden the winepress alone, and from the peoples no one *was* with Me. For I have trodden them in My anger, and trampled them in My fury; their blood is sprinkled upon My garments, and I have stained all My robes.

John 1:1 In the beginning was the Word, and the Word was with God, and the Word was God.
John 1:14a The Word became flesh and made his dwelling among us. [NIV]

1 John 1:1 That which was from the beginning, which we have heard, which we have seen with our eyes, which we have looked at and our hands have touched—this we proclaim concerning the Word of life. [NIV]

John 1:17 For the law was given through Moses; grace and truth came through Jesus Christ. [NIV]

Romans 5:8 But God demonstrates His own love toward us, in that while we were still sinners, Christ died for us.

Hebrews 4:12 For the word of God is living and active. Sharper than any double-edged sword, it penetrates even to dividing soul and spirit, joints and marrow; it judges the thoughts and attitudes of the heart. [NIV]

V. 13

Isaiah 63:3: Instead of accepting the forgiveness by the shed blood of Jesus Christ, Isaiah prophesied that their stubbornness would result in their own blood staining the Lord's garment.

John 1:1, 1:14a: *This is the first of many clear statements in this Gospel that *Jesus Christ is God*.* He had always existed as God with the Father in heaven who now chose to send His Son into the world in a human body.

1 John 1:1: *The doctrinal foundation of all true fellowship is the Person of the Lord Jesus Christ. There can be no true fellowship with those who hold false views concerning Him.*

John 1:17: The **law** *was given to show men they were sinners, but it could not save them from their sins.* The punishment for sin is death. The Savior took that punishment for all, and all who believe so are saved. (2 Corinthians 3:17)

Romans 5:8: God showed us His marvelous **love** for sinners by dying for us. He **died for us** before we accepted His free offer to save us.

Hebrews 4:12: *This verse refers not to the Living Word, Jesus, but to the living, written word, the Bible. This **word of God is living**—constantly and actively alive. It is the **word** that judges us, not we who judge the **word**.*

Chapter 19 Verses 14-16

¹⁴And the armies in heaven, clothed in fine linen, white and clean, followed Him on white horses. ¹⁵Now out of His mouth goes a sharp sword, that with it He should strike the nations. And He Himself will rule them with a rod of iron. He Himself treads the winepress of the fierceness and wrath of Almighty God. ¹⁶And He has on *His* robe and on His thigh a name written:

KING OF KINGS AND LORD OF LORDS.

**Chapter 19 Verses 14-16
Commentary**

19:14-16

Riding white horses and **clothed in white linen** depicting their righteousness, **the armies** may be made up of the heavenly angels and the raptured Church. For sure the Old Testament believers will be resurrected (Hebrews 13:11-12), but it is not clear as to whether this will happen with the Rapture or whether it will happen with the resurrection of the Tribulation saints (Revelation 6:9-10; Hebrews 12: 22-24♦).

Verse 14 dismisses any notion that the saints who have already been in heaven and have already been **clothed in fine linen, white and clean**, would *still be waiting for the Second Coming to be raptured*. That the Rapture happens *after* the Tribulation is an example of false, deceiving teaching (2 Thessalonians 2:1-2a, c, 2:3-4a, 2:7, 2:11).

♦These verses also have to do with the subject matter.

But it is noteworthy that they are not required to fight (2 Chronicles 20:23).

The Lord Jesus defeats His foes unaided. There will be great confusion; the enemy will fight against themselves (1 Samuel 14:20). **The **sword** from His mouth depicts judgment through His spoken Word (Revelation 1:16; 2:12, 2:16, Isaiah 11:4♦)** *He will **rule** the nations **with a rod of iron** and tread **the winepress of fierceness and wrath of Almighty God**. Our Lord Jesus is the Supreme Ruler; all others must submit to His reign.* He is **KING OF KINGS AND LORD OF LORDS** (**Revelation 17:14a; Deuteronomy 10:17; Daniel 2:47a; 1 Timothy 6:14b-15**).

In verse 15 the Lord Jesus Christ is pointed out to be Almighty God for the seventh time in this Book.

♦These verses also have to do with the subject matter.

Chapter 19 Verses 14-16
References

Vv. 14-16

2 Thessalonians 2:1-2a, c ¹Now, brethren, concerning the coming of our Lord Jesus Christ and our gathering together to Him we ask you, ²ᵃnot to be soon shaken in mind or troubled, ²ᶜas though the day of Christ had come.

2 Thessalonians 2:3-4a ³Let no one deceive you by any means; for *that Day will not come* unless the falling away comes first, and the man of sin is revealed, the son of perdition, ⁴ᵃwho opposes and exalts himself above all that is called God or that is worshiped, so that he sits as God...

2 Thessalonians 2:7 For the mystery of lawlessness is already at work; only He who now restrains will do so until He is taken out of the way.

2 Thessalonians 2:11 For this reason God sends them a powerful delusion so that they will believe the lie [NIV]

2 Chronicles 20:23
Revelation 17:14a;
Deuteronomy 10:17;
Daniel 2:47a;
1 Timothy 6:14b-15

-CONTINUED ON NEXT SET OF PAGES UNDER REFERENCES!-

Chapter 19 Verses 14-16
References Commentary

Vv. 14-16

2 Thessalonians 2:1-2a, c; 2:3-4a; 2:7: Verse 1 focuses on the Rapture. The Thessalonians had mistakenly thought the Day of the Lord—the judgment in the Tribulation—had already begun. The saints had mistakenly reasoned, since they were suffering severe persecution, that the Tribulation Period had already begun. Paul is reminding them in verse 1 that the Rapture had to take place first. Furthermore, the Antichrist will not be revealed until two events take place: First the falling away—severe apostasy—and then the Rapture:

2 Thessalonians 2:8a *And then the lawless one will be revealed.*

This passage confirms that not only the falling away must happen, but also the Holy Spirit indwelled evangelizing Church must be taken up (**our gathering together to Him**) out of the way. *After the Church has been raptured, the Antichrist will be revealed, and he will continue his mad, seven-year career until Christ then returns to this earth.*

*The **lie** in 2 Thessalonians 2:11, is the Antichrist's claim to be God.*

-CONTINUED ON NEXT SET OF PAGES UNDER REFERENCES COMMENTARY!-

Chapter 19 Verses 14-16

-VERSES 14-16 REPEATED FROM PREVIOUS PAGE-

¹⁴And the armies in heaven, clothed in fine linen, white and clean, followed Him on white horses. ¹⁵Now out of His mouth goes a sharp sword, that with it He should strike the nations. And He Himself will rule them with a rod of iron. He Himself treads the winepress of the fierceness and wrath of Almighty God. ¹⁶And He has on *His* robe and on His thigh a name written:

KING OF KINGS AND LORD OF LORDS.

Chapter 19 Verses 14-16
Commentary

-PART OF COMMENTARY VERSES 14-16 REPEATED FROM PREVIOUS PAGE-

19:14-16
But it is noteworthy that they are not required to fight (2 Chronicles 20:23).

The Lord Jesus defeats His foes unaided. There will be great confusion; the enemy will fight against themselves (1 Samuel 14:20). **The **sword** from His mouth depicts judgment through His spoken Word (Revelation 1:16; 2:12, 2:16, Isaiah 11:4♦)** *He will **rule** the nations **with a rod of iron** and tread **the winepress of fierceness and wrath of Almighty God**. Our Lord Jesus is the Supreme Ruler; all others must submit to His reign.* He is **KING OF KINGS AND LORD OF LORDS** (**Revelation 17:14a; Deuteronomy 10:17; Daniel 2:47a; 1 Timothy 6:14b-15**).

In verse 15 the Lord Jesus Christ is pointed out to be Almighty God for the seventh time in this Book.

♦These verses also have to do with the subject matter.

Chapter 19 Verses 14-16 References	Chapter 19 Verses 14-16 References Commentary
-CONTINUED FROM PREVIOUS PAGE-	-CONTINUED FROM PREVIOUS PAGE-

Vv. 14-16

2 Chronicles 20:23 For the children of Ammon and Mōab stood up against the inhabitants of mount Sēir, utterly to slay and destroy them: and when they had made an end of the inhabitants of Sēir, every one helped to destroy one another. [KJV]

Revelation 17:14a "These will make war with the Lamb, and the Lamb will overcome them, for He is Lord of lords and King of kings;"

Deuteronomy 10:17 For the LORD your God is God of gods and Lord of lords, the great God, mighty and awesome, who shows no partiality and accepts no bribes. [NIV]

Daniel 2:47a The king said to Daniel, "Surely your God is the God of gods the Lord of kings" [NIV]

1 Timothy 6:14b-15 ¹⁴ᵇuntil our Lord Jesus Christ's appearing, ¹⁵which He will manifest in His own time, *He who is* the blessed and only Potentate, the King of kings and Lord of lords,

---

Vv. 14-16

2 Chronicles 20:23: *God confounded the enemy and stirred them up **to destroy one another**.*

Revelation 17:14a: The Antichrist and ten kingdoms will meet their demise in this *Battle of Armageddon*, because the **Lamb** is **Lord of lords and King of kings**. Those who follow Christ are called and chosen by Him, and are faithful to Him (Revelation 19:7-8, 19:14).

Deuteronomy 10:17: **In Mesopotamian literature, only kings showed concern for the welfare of widows and orphans, but God urged Israel to show kindness to such people** (Deuteronomy 10:18-19) because God shows no partiality (Romans 2:11).

Daniel 2:47a: *God gave Daniel the wisdom to impress King Nebuchadnezzar to the point that the king made Daniel ruler over the whole province of Babylon.*

1 Timothy 6:14b-15: When the Lord Jesus Christ comes back to reign on earth, men will realize **who is the blessed and only Potentate** (Sovereign King).

Chapter 19 Verses 17-21

¹⁷And I saw an angel standing in the sun, who cried in a loud voice to all the birds flying in midair, "Come, gather together for the great supper of God, ¹⁸so that you may eat the flesh of kings, generals, and the mighty, of horses and their riders, and the flesh of all people, free and slave, great and small." [NIV]

¹⁹And I saw the beast, the kings of the earth, and their armies, gathered together to make war against Him who sat on the horse and against His army. ²⁰Then the beast was captured, and with him the false prophet who worked signs in his presence, by which he deceived those who received the mark of the beast and those who worshiped his image. These two were cast alive into the lake of fire burning with brimstone. ²¹And the rest were killed with the sword which proceeded from the mouth of Him who sat on the horse. And all the birds were filled with their flesh.

Chapter 19 Verses 17-21
Commentary

19:17-18
The supper of the great God is different from the marriage supper of the Lamb (Revelation 19:9). Here, God calls **the birds—vultures—to gather to **eat the flesh** of all unbelievers who have died in the Battle of Armageddon (Revelation 16:14♦, Revelation 16:16♦; Revelation 19:21♦; Ezekiel 39:17a, 39:18a).**

19:19-21
The **beast** is the Antichrist who gathers **together the kings of the earth**—one world government's military—**to make war against** the Lord Jesus **and against His army**.
*But it is a futile attempt. Both the Antichrist **beast** and **the false prophet** will be **captured** and hurled **alive into the lake of fire burning with brimstone**. The rest of the unbelievers are **killed with the sword** of the Lord. The **sword** refers to the word of God (Ephesians 6:17♦; 2 Thessalonians 2:8; Hebrews 4:12a; Revelation 1:16a; 2:12, 2:16).*

The remaining unbelieving survivors of the Battle of Armageddon which ends the Tribulation Period will be judged by Christ and also sentenced to everlasting fire (Isaiah 66:24b; Jeremiah 7:20b; Ezekiel 20:47b, 20:48b; **Matthew 25:41, 46**♦; Mark 9:43-48♦; Jude 7b).
Christ's *Second Coming* was the theme of the Bible's first prophecy (Jude 14-15♦♦), and of the last message of our Lord Jesus Christ being quoted (Revelation 22:20♦♦).

♦These verses also have to do with the subject matter.
♦♦These verses reveal the first and last prophecies in all the Scriptures.

Chapter 19 Verses 17-21 References	Chapter 19 Verses 17-21 References Commentary
Vv. 17-18 **Ezekiel 39:17a** "Son of man" [Ezekiel], this is what the Sovereign LORD says: Call out to every kind of bird and all the wild animals: [NIV] **Ezekiel 39:18a** "You will eat the flesh of mighty men and drink the blood of the princes of the earth [NIV]	**Vv. 17-18** Ezekiel 39:17a, 39:18a: These verses are pointed out to show the similarities and repetition of God's unchanging ways. Ezekiel 38 and 39 will actually take place during the first half of the Tribulation. *The dead bodies of the horses and riders (Ezekiel 39:20) will provide a great feast for birds and beasts of prey.*
Vv. 19-21 **Hebrews 4:12a** For the word of God is living and active. Sharper than any double-edged sword, [NIV]	**Vv. 19-21** Hebrews 4:12: The Bible is alive, cutting like a sharp **double-edged sword**. God does not change (Malachi 3:6). He has no need to change—He is perfect.
Revelation 1:16a He had in His right hand seven stars, out of His mouth went a sharp two-edged sword,	Revelation 1:16a: The **seven stars** are the seven churches. At this point in Revelation this verse could be pointing out the difference between the faithful, universal raptured Church and the apostate disobedient churches.
Revelation 2:12 "And to the angel of the church in Pergamos write, 'These things says He who has the sharp two-edged sword:" **Revelation 2:16** "Repent, or else I will come to you quickly and will fight against them with the sword of My mouth."	Revelation 2:12, 2:16: **The Pergamos church is urged to **repent** of the toleration and sins from false teachers, before Christ judges them Himself. The church should discipline itself and not tolerate false teaching and immorality within.** (1 Corinthians 5:11-13)
Isaiah 66:24b "Nor will their fire be quenched," [NIV] **Jeremiah 7:20d** "and it will burn and not be quenched." [NIV] **Ezekiel 20:47d** "The blazing flame will not be quenched," [NIV] **Ezekiel 20:48b** "it will not be quenched." [NIV]	Isaiah 66:24b, Jeremiah 7:20b, Ezekiel 20:47b, 48b: These four verses all agree: **their fire is not quenched**. *God desires obedience, not rituals.* Disobedience is sin. *In Mark 9, Jesus uses Isaiah's solemn words three times!* " *'their worm does not die, and the fire is not quenched.'* " [NIV]
Jude 7b who suffer the punishment of eternal fire. [NIV]	In Jude 7b God's judgment on sexual sin and offensiveness to Christ's followers is severe: eternal fire.

Chapter 20 Verses 1-3

Chapter 20 Verses 1-3
Commentary

Millennial Reign

The Great White Throne

¹And I saw an angel coming down out of heaven, having the key to the Abyss and holding in his hand a great chain. ²He seized the dragon, that ancient serpent, who is the devil, or Satan, and bound him for a thousand years. ³He threw him into the Abyss, and locked and sealed it over him, to keep him from deceiving the nations anymore until the thousand years were ended. After that, he must be set free for a short time. [NIV]

20:1-3
The Devil, Satan, that is **the dragon, that serpent of old**, will not join the Antichrist and False Prophet in the lake of fire until after he is released from one-thousand years of being imprisoned in the **Abyss** [bottomless pit]. His "release" (Revelation 20:7-10) will be for only **a short time**.

Satan's demons—or fallen angels—are also in the pit with Satan (Isaiah 24:21-23).

Chapter 20 Verses 1-3 References	Chapter 20 Verses 1-3 References Commentary
Vv. 1-3 **Isaiah 24:21-23** [21]It shall come to pass in that day *that* the LORD will punish on high the host of exalted ones, and on the earth the kings of the earth. [22]They will be gathered together, *as* prisoners are gathered in the pit, and will be shut up in the prison; after many days they will be punished. [23]Then the moon will be disgraced and the sun ashamed; for the LORD of hosts will reign on Mount Zion and in Jerusalem and before His elders, gloriously.	**Vv. 1-3** Isaiah 24:21-23: **The LORD will punish the host on high of exalted ones** means above the earth (**Satanic powers**), and He will also punish **the kings on earth**. Warren Henderson explains in his Old Testament Commentary: *Sorrow and Comfort...A Devotional Study of Isaiah*: "Neither spiritual wickedness in high places (fallen angels), nor the political and military might below will be able to circumvent the righteous judgment of God on earth. Wicked people will be judged at the Second Advent of Christ and will be cast into the realm of torment (Hādēs) until their final judgment at the Great White Throne a thousand years later."

Chapter 20 Verses 4-6

⁴I saw thrones on which were seated those who had been given authority to judge. And I saw the souls of those who had been beheaded because of their testimony about Jesus and because of the word of God. They had not worshiped the beast or its image and had not received its mark on their foreheads or their hands. They came to life and reigned with Christ a thousand years. ⁵(The rest of the dead did not come to life until the thousand years were ended.) This is the first resurrection. ⁶Blessed and holy are those who share in the first resurrection. The second death has no power over them, but they will be priests of God and of Christ and will reign with him a thousand years. [NIV]

Chapter 20 Verses 4-6 Commentary

20:4-6
The saints of the Church Age, the Old Testament believers, and the martyrs who **had refused to take the mark of the beast...will be priests of God and of Christ** during His thousand-year reign. The Old Testament believers will be resurrected, but the Scripture is not clear to state whether it will be with the Church or that it will be after the Tribulation: Referring to the Old Testament believers, we get this assurance that they have most certainly been saved:
Hebrews 11:39-40: *³⁹These were all commended for their faith, yet none of them received what had been promised. ⁴⁰God had planned something better for us so that only together with us would they be made perfect.* [NIV]
They are included below, being listed in the third part with the martyred saints:

There are three parts to **the first resurrection:
1. Christ's resurrection—the first fruits (1 Corinthians 15:20, 23; Revelation 1:5)**
2. the Church's resurrection (John 14:2-3; Romans 11:25; 1 Thessalonians 4:16-17; 1 Corinthians 15:51-52; Revelation 4:1; 5:9, 11)
3. Old Testament believers' resurrection: (Hebrews 11:39-40; 12:23) and Tribulation martyred Jewish and Gentile saints' resurrection. These saints are the third part of the **first resurrection**. (Revelation 6:9b-10; 7:14b)

After the one-thousand year reign, the **rest of** ****the** *unbelieving* **dead** will be raised in the *second resurrection* and be sentenced to their second death and cast into the lake of fire (Revelation 20:13-15).** (Daniel 12:2)

Chapter 20 Verses 4-6
References

Vv. 4-6
1 Corinthians 15:20 But Christ has indeed been raised from the dead, the firstfruits of those who have fallen asleep. [NIV]
1 Corinthians 15:23 But each one in his own order: Christ the firstfruits, afterward those *who are* Christ's at His coming.

Revelation 1:5 and from Jesus Christ, the faithful witness, the firstborn from the dead, and the ruler over the kings of the earth. To Him who loved us and washed us from our sins in His own blood,

1 Thessalonians 4:16-17
Revelation 4:1; 5:11; 6:9b-10; 7:14b

-CONTINUED ON NEXT SET OF PAGES UNDER REFERENCES!-

Chapter 20 Verses 4-6
References Commentary

Vv. 4-6
1 Corinthians 15:20, 15:23: Where the verse ends with saying, **those who have fallen asleep** means they have died in Christ. The Lord Jesus Christ is the first to be raised from the dead to remain alive forever into eternity. His resurrection is the first part of what is called THE FIRST RESURRECTION. Believers of the Church Age (which we are now experiencing until the Rapture) will be the second part of "The First Resurrection." Old Testament believers will either be resurrected in the Second part with the Rapture of the Church—or—in the Third part of the First Resurrection with the Tribulation martyrs.

"The *Second Resurrection*" will consist of the masses of unbelievers who will face the Lord Jesus at the Great White Throne before experiencing their second death and the lake of fire (Revelation 20:13-15).

In Revelation 1:5 the Lord Jesus Christ **is the firstfruits of the first resurrection,** (the first to be raised and to remain alive forever) and the **ruler over the kings of the earth**. He **loved us, washed us from our sins in His own blood**, redeemed us, and even in the next verse (6) makes us kings and priests!

-CONTINUED ON NEXT SET OF PAGES UNDER REFERENCES COMMENTARY! -

Chapter 20 Verses 4-6

Chapter 20 Verses 4-6 Commentary

-VERSES 4-6 REPEATED FROM PREVIOUS PAGE -

-PART OF COMMENTARY VERSES 4-6 REPEATED FROM PREVIOUS PAGE-

20:4-6

⁴I saw thrones on which were seated those who had been given authority to judge. And I saw the souls of those who had been beheaded because of their testimony about Jesus and because of the word of God. They had not worshiped the beast or its image and had not received its mark on their foreheads or their hands. They came to life and reigned with Christ a thousand years. ⁵(The rest of the dead did not come to life until the thousand years were ended.) This is the first resurrection. ⁶Blessed and holy are those who share in the first resurrection. The second death has no power over them, but they will be priests of God and of Christ and will reign with him a thousand years. [NIV]

2. the Church's resurrection (John 14:2-3; Romans 11:25; 1 Thessalonians 4:16-17; 1 Corinthians 15:51-52; Revelation 4:1; 5:9, 11)

3. Old Testament believers' resurrection: (Hebrews 11:39-40; 12:23) and Tribulation martyred Jewish and Gentile saints' resurrection. These saints are the third **part** of the **first resurrection**.. (Revelation 6:9b-10; 7:14b)

After the one-thousand year reign, the **rest of** ****the** *unbelieving* **dead** will be raised in the *second resurrection* and be sentenced to their second death and cast into the lake of fire (Revelation 20:13-15).** (Daniel 12:2)

Chapter 20 Verses 4-6 References	Chapter 20 Verses 4-6 References Commentary

-CONTINUED FROM PREVIOUS PAGE-

Vv. 4-6

1 Thessalonians 4:16-17 ¹⁶For the Lord Himself will descend from heaven with a shout, with the voice of an archangel, and with the trumpet of God. And the dead in Christ will rise first. ¹⁷Then we who are alive *and* remain shall be caught up together with them in the clouds to meet the Lord in the air. And thus we shall always be with the Lord.

Revelation 4:1 After these things I looked, and behold, a door *standing* open in heaven. And the first voice which I heard *was* like a trumpet speaking with me, saying, "Come up here, and I will show you things which must take place after this."

Revelation 5:11 Then I looked, and I heard the voice of many angels around the throne, the living creatures, and the elders; and the number of them was ten thousand times ten thousand, and thousands of thousands,

Revelation 6:9b-10 ⁹ᵇI saw under the altar the souls of those who had been slain for the word of God and for the testimony which they held. ¹⁰And they cried with a loud voice, saying, "How long, O Lord, holy and true, until You judge and avenge our blood on those who dwell on the earth?"

Revelation 7:14b "These are the ones who come out of the great tribulation, and washed their robes and made them white in the blood of the Lamb.

Vv. 4-6

In 1 Thessalonians 4:16-17 *the exact order of events at Christ's coming to rapture His saints is given. **The trumpet of God** is the same as the **last trumpet** of 1 Corinthians 15:51-52:*
⁵¹*Listen, I tell you a mystery: We will not all sleep* [be previously dead], *but we will all be changed—*⁵²*in a flash, in the twinkling of an eye, at the last trumpet. For the trumpet will sound, the dead will be raised imperishable, and we will be changed.* [NIV]

Revelation 4:1 and 5:11 began the chronological order of events from the Rapture of the Church to the saints' [living creatures] voices praising the Lord Jesus Christ for having redeemed them by His blood (Revelation 5:10). Chapter 6 presented the appearance of the Antichrist coming in on his white horse and followed with the red, black, and pale horses which represent his seven-year career. Chapter 7 gives the arrival of the saved 144,000 Jews. All is in Scriptural agreement.

Revelation 6:9b-10 quotes what Old Testament prophet Zechariah said in Zechariah 1:12, thus, since John the writer of Revelation, seeing the souls of those Old Testament saints provides proof that they will indeed be raised. (Hebrews 11:39-40; 12:23)

Revelation 7:14 specifies that there will be those who become believers during the Tribulation. They will be in the third part of the First Resurrection. Only the Church will be married to the Lamb, but the Old Testament saints and Great Tribulation believers will attend the marriage supper (Revelation 19:7, 19:9).

Chapter 20 Verses 7-10

⁷When the thousand years are over, Satan will be released from his prison ⁸and will go out to deceive the nations in the four corners of the earth — Gog and Māgog — and to gather them for battle. In number they are like the sand on the seashore. ⁹They marched across the breadth of the earth and surrounded the camp of God's people, the city he loves. But fire came down from heaven and devoured them. ¹⁰And the devil, who deceived them, was thrown into the lake of burning sulfur, where the beast and the false prophet had been thrown. They will be tormented day and night for ever and ever. [NIV]

Chapter 20 Verses 7-10
Commentary

20:7-10
Unbelieving Tribulation survivors will enter the Millennium in [un-changed], natural bodies. At the end of the Millennium **Satan shall be released from his prison and **will go out to deceive** all **the nations** of the earth. **Gog and Māgog** here possibly refer to the nations of the world in general** and are not necessarily the same nations in Ezekiel 38 that comprised **Gog and Māgog** during the first three-and-a-half years of Tribulation. Here Gog and Māgog are the nations that will attack Jerusalem *after* the Millennium.

Gog and Māgog apparently added more nations and possibly had survivors who will return to their nations and eventually return at the end of the Millennial period to be, this time, totally defeated—and will be devoured in the lake of fire with Satan. *With the army of ungodly rebels, the devil marches against Jerusalem, **the beloved city**. But **fire** comes **down from God out of heaven** and consumes them*. The devil (Satan) himself is **cast into the lake of fire** to join **the beast** [Antichrist] **and the false prophet. And they will be tormented day and night forever and ever.**

Chapter 20 Verses 7-10
References

Chapter 20 Verses 7-10
References Commentary

Chapter 20 Verses 11-15

¹¹Then I saw a great white throne and Him who sat on it, from whose face the earth and the heaven fled away. And there was found no place for them. ¹²And I saw the dead, small and great, standing before God, and books were opened. And another book was opened, which is *the Book of Life*. And the dead were judged according to their works, by the things which were written in the books. ¹³The sea gave up the dead who were in it, and Death and Hādēs delivered up the dead who were in them. And they were judged, each one according to his works. ¹⁴Then Death and Hādēs were cast into the lake of fire. This is the second death. ¹⁵And anyone not found written in the Book of Life was cast into the lake of fire.

Chapter 20 Verses 11-15
Commentary

20:11-15
*The Lord Jesus is the Judge (John 5:22, 5:27) on the **great white throne**.

THE ETERNAL STATE BEGINS:
The expression **from whose face the earth and the heaven fled away** indicates that this judgment takes place *in eternity* after the destruction of the present earth and stars (2 Peter 3:10).

***Hādēs** (hell) will have given up the souls of all the rest of the dead who died in unbelief—bodies and souls will be reunited to be judged.* *Not one who appears at this judgment is registered in **the Book of Life**, but record of his evil **works** determines the degree of punishment. There would be no further need for **Death** or **Hādēs**, both **were cast into the lake of fire** with all the unsaved, since no one's name was **found written in the Book of Life**.

Believers are eternally blessed to have their name in the Book of Life. Halleluiah!!! Rejoice!!! (Philippians 4:3-4).

Chapter 20 Verses 11-15
References

Vv. 11-15
John 5:22 "For the Father judges no one, but has committed all judgment to the Son."...
John 5:27 "and has given Him authority to execute judgment also, because He is the Son of Man."

2 Peter 3:10 But the day of the Lord will come as a thief in the night, in which the heavens will pass away with a great noise, and the elements will melt with fervent heat; both the earth and the works that are in it will be burned up.

Philippians 4:3-4 ³And I urge you also, true companion, help these women who labored with me in the gospel, with Clement also, and the rest of my fellow workers, whose names are in the Book of Life. ⁴Rejoice in the Lord always. Again I will say, rejoice!

Chapter 20 Verses 11-15
References Commentary

Vv. 11-15
John 5:22, John 5:27: Since Christ is God with the Father, He is able *to judge by discerning the thoughts and motives of men's hearts.*

2 Peter 3:10: **The day of the Lord** *refers to any period when God acts in judgment* —in this case, judgment of all unbelievers at the Great White Throne.

Philippians 4:3-4   Believers' names are in the **Book of Life** and there are no words in any language that can express the degree of gratitude. Quoting Ironside from -*An Ironside Expository Commentary: REVELATION*, pg. 199-:
"Will any people be saved who stand before the Great White Throne? Not one, if we read the account aright because Death and Hādēs are to be '[emptied]' into the lake of fire."

Chapter 21 Verses 1-2

¹Then I saw "a new heaven and a new earth," for the first heaven and the first earth had passed away, and there was no longer any sea. ²I saw the Holy City, the new Jerusalem, coming out of heaven from God, prepared as a bride beautifully dressed for her husband. [NIV]

Chapter 21 Verses 1-2
Commentary

New Heaven and New Earth

Eternal State and Final Judgment Following the Millennium

21:1-2
Isaiah predicts the **new heaven and new earth** (Isaiah 65:17-19; [*eternal state is prophesied, but in 65:20-25, Millennial is still in view*] Isaiah 66:22 [the eternal state, comes after the Millennial]). These verses emphasize the consistent Word and intent of our unchanging God (Hebrews 6:17-18; 7:24; 1 Peter 1:23-25).

The **husband** of **New Jerusalem...prepared as a bride adorned for her husband** we believe is Israel. Isaiah 54 speaks a parable comparing Israel to be like a *wife* who honors and adores the Triune God. The passage is poetic and beautiful, but is not to be confused with the New Testament Church being the actual *wife* of the Lord Jesus Christ.

The first heaven and the first earth are replaced by a new heaven and a new earth because **the first earth had passed away**. The present universe will thus be cleansed from all the effects of sin (2 Peter 3:7, 2 Peter 3:11-12).

Anything that defiles, or causes an abomination or even **a lie** will be completely excluded from entering (Revelation 21:27).
The distinction between the Church as the Bride, the Lamb's wife (Revelation 21:9), Israel (Revelation 21:12), and the Gentile nations (Revelation 21:24), is maintained throughout.

Chapter 21 Verses 1-2
References

Vv. 1-2
Isaiah 65:17-19 ¹⁷"For behold, I create new heavens and a new earth; and the former shall not be remembered or come to mind. ¹⁸But be glad and rejoice forever in what I create; for behold, I create Jerusalem *as* a rejoicing, and her people a joy. ¹⁹I will rejoice in Jerusalem, and joy in My people; the voice of weeping shall no longer be heard in her, nor the voice of crying."

Isaiah 66:22 "For as the new heavens and the new earth which I will make shall remain before Me," says the LORD, "so shall your descendants and your name remain.

2 Peter 3:7 By the same word the present heavens and earth are reserved for fire, being kept for the day of judgment and destruction of ungodly men. [NIV]
2 Peter 3:11-12 ¹¹Therefore, since all these things will be dissolved, what manner *of persons* ought you to be in holy conduct and godliness, ¹²looking for and hastening the coming of the day of God, because of which the heavens will be dissolved, being on fire, and the elements will melt with fervent heat?

Chapter 21 Verses 1-2
References Commentary

Vv. 1-2
Isaiah 65:17-19:   There are actually three heavens:
1. The earth's atmosphere and blue sky,
2. the stars of the universe and the galaxies
3. the heaven of God's throne.

Since the earth and stars will be destroyed, God will replace them. Paul writes of God's heaven in 2 Corinthians 12:2b: *God knows—such a one as Paul was caught up to the third heaven*.

Isaiah 66:22: God will rejoice for our having joy in the new earth which will last for all eternity.

2 Peter 3:7, 3:11-12:   **Just as God once destroyed the world by water, so it is now **reserved for fire until the day of judgment.**
What kind of persons should we **be in holy conduct and godliness**, since our Savior shed His blood to forgive us and died for us to avoid undergoing eternal grief and suffering and, instead, to have this new eternal, joyful life?

Chapter 21 Verses 3-5

³And I heard a loud voice from heaven saying, "Behold, the tabernacle of God *is* with men, and He will dwell with them, and they shall be His people. God Himself will be with them *and be* their God. ⁴And God will wipe away every tear from their eyes; there shall be no more death, nor sorrow, nor crying. There shall be no more pain, for the former things have passed away." ⁵Then He who sat on the throne said, "Behold, I make all things new." And He said to me, "Write, for these words are true and faithful."

Chapter 21 Verses 3-5
Commentary

21:3-5
The tabernacle of God is with men means **God** will forever **dwell with** His people. We *will enjoy communion with Him closer than ever dreamed of.*

There shall be **no more** tears, **death, nor sorrow, nor crying,** nor **pain, for the former things have passed away.** When we are resurrected, God will **make all things new** including our bodies. (Philippians 3:20b-21a; John 1:3)

Chapter 21 Verses 3-5 **References**	**Chapter 21 Verses 3-5** **References Commentary**
Vv. 3-5 **Philippians 3:20b-21a** ²⁰ᵇeagerly wait for the Savior, the Lord Jesus Christ, ²¹ᵃwho will transform our lowly body that it may be conformed to His glorious body,	**Vv. 3-5** Philippians 3:20b-21a: God's Word promises us a new, glorious body. If believers should die before the Rapture, their souls and spirits will be with the Lord at the moment of death (2 Corinthians 5:8). Upon being resurrected we will be given a new, glorious body (Philippians 3:21).
John 1:3 All things were made through Him, and without Him nothing was made that was made.	In John 1:3 the Son, the Second Person of God, obeyed every desire of the Father. The Father is quoted speaking of His Son: Hebrews 1:10: *"You, LORD, in the beginning laid the foundation of the earth, and the heavens are the work of Your hands."*

Chapter 21 Verse 6	Chapter 21 Verse 6 Commentary
⁶And He said to me, "It is done! I am the Alpha and the Omega, the Beginning and the End. I will give of the fountain of the water of life freely to him who thirsts.	**21:6** **God's eternal purpose **is done**. He is the origin and source of all things (Isaiah 41:4; 44:6; 46:4a; 48:12)**. How could this not remind us of what the Son of God said on the cross? In John 19:30b the Savior *said, "It is finished!" And bowing His head, He gave up His spirit.* **He is also the goal or aim of all things** (John 18:6; **Romans 10:4**; 11:36). He is *the One who began creation and the One who finishes* (John 1:3: *All things were made through Him, and without Him nothing was made that was made.* Colossians 1:16-17: ¹⁶*For by Him all things were created that are in heaven and that are on earth, visible and invisible, whether thrones or dominions or principalities or powers. All things were created through Him and for Him.* ¹⁷*And He is before all things, and in Him all things consist.*) *He is the Eternal One. He is alive! It is He who gives **the water of life*** (John 4:14; salvation with eternal sustenance and provision) ***freely to** whoever **thirsts** for it* (Revelation 22:17). This is the last time that the Gospel invitation is seen in the Bible—it is for anyone who has not been reconciled to God and is reading this before it is too late. 2 Corinthians 6:2b: *behold, now is the accepted time; behold, now is the day of salvation.* [KJV]

Chapter 21 Verse 6
References

Chapter 21 Verse 6
References Commentary

V. 6

Isaiah 41:4 "Who has performed and done *it*, calling the generations from the beginning? 'I, the LORD, am the first; and with the last I *am* He.'"

Isaiah 44:6 "Thus says the LORD, the King of Israel, and his Redeemer, the LORD of hosts: 'I *am* the First and I *am* the Last; besides Me *there is* no God.'"

Isaiah 46:4a "Even to *your* old age, I *am* He,"

Isaiah 48:12 "Listen to Me, O Jacob, and Israel, My called: I *am* He, I *am* the First, I *am* also the Last."

V. 6

Isaiah 41:4; 44:6; 46:4a; 48:12: **The LORD, the King of Israel**, *challenges any so-called god to predict the future as He does. His people* (Israel back then; and all believers today) *need not fear any challenge to His supremacy.*

Revelation 1:8: *"I am the Alpha and the Omega, the Beginning and the End," says the Lord, "who is and who was and who is to come, the Almighty."*

John 18:6 Now when He said to them, "I am He," they drew back and fell to the ground.

In John 18:6 *for a brief moment, the Lord Jesus revealed Himself to them as **I *AM***, Almighty God. This was an overpowering statement!*

Romans 10:4 Christ is the end of the law so that there may be righteousness for everyone who believes. [NIV]

Romans 10:4: The Law convicts us; it does *not* save us. We obtain our righteousness (perfection) from Him by trusting and believing in Him (Christ Jesus).

Romans 11:36 For from him and through him and to him are all things. To him be the glory forever! Amen. [NIV]

Romans 11:36: *The Almighty is the Object for which everything has been created. Everything is designed to bring **glory** to Him.*

John 4:14 "but whoever drinks of the water that I shall give him will never thirst. But the water that I shall give him will become in him a fountain of water springing up into everlasting life."

John 4:14: *All that earth can provide is not sufficient to fill the human heart. The pleasures of this world are for a few short years, but the pleasures which Christ provides go on *into everlasting life.**

Revelation 22:17 The Spirit and the bride say, "Come!" And let him who hears say, "Come!" Whoever is thirsty, let him come; and whoever wishes, let him take the free gift of the water of life. [NIV]

In Revelation 22:17 **the water of life** refers to salvation. This verse can also refer to the believers' prayers for Christ to **Come**; for Him to return to the air, and later to the earth, to take us and keep us with Himself.

Chapter 21 Verses 7-17

⁷He who overcomes shall inherit all things, and I will be his God and he shall be My son.

⁸But the cowardly, the unbelieving, the vile, the murderers, the sexually immoral, those who practice magic arts, the idolaters and all liars — they will be consigned to the fiery lake of burning sulfur. This is the second death." [NIV]

⁹One of the seven angels who had the seven bowls full of the seven last plagues came and said to me, "Come, I will show you the bride, the wife of the Lamb." ¹⁰And he carried me away in the Spirit to a mountain great and high, and showed me the Holy City, Jerusalem, coming down out of heaven from God. ¹¹It shone with the glory of God, and its brilliance was like that of a very precious jewel, like a jasper, clear as crystal. ¹²It had a great, high wall with twelve gates, and with twelve angels at the gates. On the gates were written the names of the twelve tribes of Israel. ¹³There were three gates on the east, three on the north, three on the south and three on the west. ¹⁴The wall of the city had twelve foundations, and on them were the names of the twelve apostles of the Lamb. ¹⁵The angel who talked with me had a measuring rod of gold to measure the city, its gates and its walls. ¹⁶The city was laid out like a square, as long as it was wide. He measured the city with the rod and found it to be 12,000 stadia in length, and as wide and high as it is long. ¹⁷The angel measured the wall using human measurements, and it was 144 cubits thick. [NIV]

Chapter 21 Verses 7-17
Commentary

21:7
He who overcomes is he who has overcome man's way in the world and believes Jesus is the Son of God (1 John 5:4-5).
When speaking to His eleven after Judas Iscariot departed, the Lord Jesus had certainly set the example: John 16:33: *"These things I have spoken to you, that in Me you may have peace. In the world you will have tribulation; but be of good cheer, I have overcome the world."*.

21:8
But those who continue to reject Him by their lifestyle of sin, will feel their second death and be cast into the lake of fire (Revelation 20:13-15; Luke 16:19-31).

21:9-17
These verses describe the beauty and glory of the **holy Jerusalem. **The bride, the Lamb's wife** is perhaps a reference to the Church being the new city's principle inhabitant. Saved **Israel** is also present. The effect of the beautiful colors of precious stones is a magnificent city of brilliant gold adorned with gems of every color.**
The size will be **twelve thousand stadia** [furlongs]**,** length, breadth, and height all being equal. This is about 1,500 miles cubed.
The names of the twelve apostles of the Lamb will be on the **twelve foundations** of **the wall**.
The size of the wall is measured in cubits *according* to the **measure of a human**. A cubit, on average, is the length of a man's arm from the elbow to the extremity of the middle finger—about 18 inches. Converting **one hundred *and* forty-four cubits** to feet: the wall will be approximately 215 feet high.
In Revelation 21:9 **bride** is likely translated: *daughter-in-law* (of the Father). In the same verse, the Church is called **the Lamb's wife**.

Chapter 21 Verses 7-17 References	Chapter 21 Verses 7-17 References Commentary
V. 7 **1 John 5:4-5** ⁴for everyone born of God overcomes the world. This is the victory that has overcome the world, even our faith. ⁵Who is it who overcomes the world? Only he who believes that Jesus is the Son of God. [NIV]	**V. 7** 1 John 5:4-5: *The world system is a monstrous scheme of temptation, always trying to drag us away from God and from what is eternal, and seeking to occupy us with what is temporary and sensual. The believer is able to rise above the perishing things of this world and see things in their true, eternal perspective.*
V. 8 **Revelation 20:13-15** ¹³The sea gave up the dead who were in it, and Death and Hādēs delivered up the dead who were in them. And they were judged, each according to his works. ¹⁴Then Death and Hādēs were cast into the lake of fire. This is the second death. ¹⁵And anyone not found written in the Book of Life was cast into the lake of fire.	**V. 8** Revelation 20:13-15: ***Hādēs**, or hell, is a disembodied state of *conscious* punishment for unbelievers awaiting the Great White Throne*. The lake of fire (**the second death**) is the final, eternal prison of the unbeliever.

Chapter 21 Verses 18-21

Chapter 21 Verses 18-21
Commentary

The New Jerusalem's Brilliance

¹⁸The wall was mad of jasper, and the city of pure gold, as pure as glass. ¹⁹The foundations of the walls were decorated with every kind of precious stone. The first foundation was jasper, the second sapphire, the third agate, the fourth emerald, ²⁰the fifth onyx, the sixth ruby, the seventh chrysolite, the eighth beryl, the ninth topaz, the tenth turquoise, the eleventh jacinth, and the twelfth amethyst. [NIV]

21:18-20
*The **jasper** green **wall** and the **pure gold city** create an image of magnificence and brilliance. **The** twelve **foundations** adorned with twelve **precious stones** are similar to those of the breastplate of the high priest who represented the twelve tribes of Israel.*

Each **foundation** had its own special colored **precious stone**:
****jasper**-green, **sapphire**-blue, **chalcedony**-green, **emerald**-green, **sardonyx**-red and white, **sardius**-blood-red, **chrysolite**-yellow or gold, **beryl**-green, **topaz**-greenish gold or yellow, **chrysoprase**-green, **jacinth**-bluish purple, and **amethyst**-purple quartz.**

These precious stones closely resemble the high priest's breastplate of judgment which is described in Exodus 28:15-21.

²¹The twelve gates were twelve pearls, each gate made of a single pearl. The great street of the city was of gold, as pure as transparent glass. [NIV]

21:21
The twelve gates are twelve pearls, a reminder that the Church is the pearl of great price for which the Savior sold all that He had in order to have it (Matthew 13:45-46).

The street of the city *was* pure gold, like transparent glass.

(The number *twelve* is seen twenty-one times in this Book and seven times in this Chapter. It is commonly understood to stand for *governmental perfection*.)

| Chapter 21 Verses 18-21 | Chapter 21 Verses 18-21 |
| References | References Commentary |

Vv. 18-20

Exodus 28:15-21 ¹⁵"Fashion a breastpiece for making decisions—the work of a skilled craftsman. Make it like the ephod: of gold, and blue, purple and scarlet yarn, and of finely twisted linen. ¹⁶It is to be square—a span long and a span wide—folded double. ¹⁷Then mount four rows of precious stones on it. In the first row there shall be a ruby, a topaz and a beryl; ¹⁸in the second row a turquoise, a sapphire, and an emerald; ¹⁹in the third row a jacinth, an agate and an amethyst; ²⁰in the fourth row a chrysolite, an onyx and a jasper. Mount them in gold filigree settings. ²¹There are to be twelve stones, one for each of the names of the sons of Israel, each engraved like a seal with the name of one of the twelve tribes. [NIV]

Vv. 18-20

In Exodus 28:15-21 the stones on the high priest's breastplate are engraved with the names of Jacob's sons (the twelve tribes of Israel). These were very precious to Jacob, to Aaron and to God the Creator of everything—including these gems.

V. 21

Matthew 13:45-46 ⁴⁵"Again, the kingdom of heaven is like a merchant looking for fine pearls. ⁴⁶When he found one of great value, he went away and sold everything he had and bought it." [NIV]

V. 21

In Matthew 13:45-46 *the **merchant** is the Lord Jesus. The **pearl of great**, tremendous **price** is the Church. The Savior gave His all to purchase the Church.*

Chapter 21 Verses 22-23

²²I did not see a temple in the city, because the Lord God Almighty and the Lamb are its temple. ²³The city does not need the sun or the moon to shine in it, for the glory of God gives it light, and the Lamb is its lamp. [NIV]

Chapter 21 Verses 22-23
Commentary

21:22-23
****No temple** is necessary since both the Father and the Son will be present and revealed in their fullest.**
*There is **no sun** or **moon** because **the glory of God** illuminates it, and **the Lamb is** the lamp*
(**Exodus 3:3-4; 24:15-18; 33:14-16; Luke 2:9; 9:29; Hebrews 1:3**; John 8:12).

Revelation 21:22 speaks of the Lord God Almighty for the eighth time, but in this instance He is the Father God. This and the previous seven times were specifically saying that the Lord Jesus Christ is Almighty God with the Father and the Holy Spirit.
(Exodus 3:6, 3:13-14; 6:2-3; Philippians 2:6-8; Colossians 1:15-18; Hebrews 1:8-10).

Chapter 21 Verses 22-23
References

Vv. 22-23
Exodus 3:3-4 ³So Moses thought, "I will go over and see this strange sight—why the bush does not burn up." ⁴When the LORD saw that he had gone over to look, God called to him from within the bush, "Moses! Moses!" And Moses said, "Here I am." [NIV]

Exodus 24:15-18 ¹⁵When Moses went up on the mountain, the cloud covered it, ¹⁶And the glory of the LORD settled on Mount Sinai. For six days the cloud covered the mountain, and on the seventh day the LORD called to Moses from within the cloud. ¹⁷To the Israelites the glory of the LORD looked like a consuming fire on top of the mountain. ¹⁸Then Moses entered the cloud as he went on up the mountain. And he stayed on the mountain forty days and forty nights. [NIV]

Exodus 33:14-16 ¹⁴And He said, "My Presence will go *with you*, and I will give you rest." ¹⁵Then he said to Him, "If Your Presence does not go *with us*, do not bring us up from here. ¹⁶For how then will it be known that Your people and I have found grace in Your sight, except You go with us? So we shall be separate, Your people and I, from all the people who *are* upon the face of the earth."

Luke 2:9; 9:29;
Hebrews 1:3;
John 8:12

-CONTINUED ON NEXT SET OF PAGES UNDER REFERENCES!-

Chapter 21 Verses 22-23
References Commentary

Vv. 22-23
In Exodus 3:3-4 *the burning **bush** that is not consumed suggests the glory of God.* Moses turning to see the light of God can be compared to a sinner who is repenting: turning away from the world and turning toward God.

Exodus 24:15-18: Verse 18 *informs us that Moses was to remain on top of the mountain for forty days and forty nights. Forty is the number of testing or probation.*
In the eyes of **... Israel**, the sight...was **like a consuming fire**. Since Moses did not descend from the mountain for forty days, the Israelites gave up on him, saying in Exodus 32:1b: *"we don't know what has happened to him."* [NIV]
So, they talked Aaron into making a "golden calf" to worship! We need to listen to this example and be patient and wait upon the Lord (Psalm 27:14: *Wait on the LORD: be of good courage, and he shall strengthen thine heart: wait, I say, on the LORD.* [KJV]).

In Exodus 33:14-16 *Moses insisted that nothing short of God's **Presence** with them would do. Like Noah, Moses had **found grace in** the Lord's **sight** and received his request for God to **go with us**. "Safety does not consist in the absence of danger but in the **Presence** of God."*

-CONTINUED ON NEXT SET OF PAGES UNDER REFERENCES COMMENTARY!-

Chapter 21 Verses 22-23	Chapter 21 Verses 22-23 Commentary

-VERSES 22-23 REPEATED FROM PREVIOUS PAGE -

-VERSES 22-23 COMMENTARY REPEATED FROM PREVIOUS PAGE-

21:22-23
****No temple** is necessary since both the Father and the Son will be present and revealed in their fullest.**

²²I did not see a temple in the city, because the Lord God Almighty and the Lamb are its temple. ²³The city does not need the sun or the moon to shine in it, for the glory of God gives it light, and the Lamb is its lamp. [NIV]

*There is **no sun** or **moon** because **the glory of God** illuminates it, and **the Lamb is** the lamp* (**Exodus 3:3-4; 24:15-18; 33:14-16; Luke 2:9; 9:29; Hebrews 1:3**; John 8:12).

Revelation 21:22 speaks of the Lord God Almighty for the eighth time, but in this instance He is the Father God. This and the previous seven times were specifically saying that the Lord Jesus Christ is Almighty God with the Father and the Holy Spirit.
(Exodus 3:6, 3:13-14; 6:2-3; Philippians 2:6-8; Colossians 1:15-18; Hebrews 1:8-10).

Chapter 21 Verses 22-23
References

-CONTINUED
FROM PREVIOUS PAGE-

Vv. 22-23

Luke 2:9 An angel of the Lord appeared to them, and the glory of the Lord shone around them, and they were terrified. [NIV]

Luke 9:29 As He prayed, the appearance of His face was altered, and His robe *became* white *and* glistening.

Hebrews 1:3 who being the brightness of *His* glory and the express image of His person, and upholding all things by the word of His power, when He had by Himself purged our sins, sat down at the right hand of the Majesty on high,

John 8:12 Then Jesus spoke to them again, saying, "I am the light of the world. He who follows Me shall not walk in darkness, but have the light of life."

Chapter 21 Verses 22-23
References Commentary

-CONTINUED
FROM PREVIOUS PAGE-

Vv. 22-23

In Luke 2:9 at Christ's incarnate birth (God in flesh) **an angel of the Lord** *came to the shepherds, and a bright, glorious light **shone** all **around them**.* The glory of the Lord is never extinguished—not from His appearances in the Old Testament, not from His coming in the flesh, and not for forever in eternity future.

In Luke 9:29 In the Lord Jesus' Transfiguration, this bright radiance preceded the glory which will be His during His coming kingdom.

In Hebrews 1:3 *the Lord Jesus Christ is the outshining **of** God's **glory**. All the perfections found in God the Father are also found in His Son. Jesus Christ is the radiance **of His glory**. All the moral and spiritual glories of God Almighty are seen in Him.*

John 8:12: *Naturally speaking, **the world** is in the darkness of sin, ignorance, and aimlessness. **The light of the** world is Jesus. Apart from Him, there is no deliverance from the blackness of sin. Apart from Him, there is no guidance along the way of life, no knowledge as to the real meaning of life and the issues of eternity.*

Chapter 21 Verses 24-26	**Chapter 21 Verses 24-26** **Commentary**
²⁴The nations will walk by its light, and the kings of the earth will bring their splendor into it. ²⁵On no day will its gates ever be shut, for there will be no night there. ²⁶The glory and honor of the nations will be brought into it. [NIV]	**21:24-26** **Since the **glory of God** in the New Jerusalem will **light** the earth,** the Gentile **nations of those who are saved shall walk in its light, and the kings of the earth bring their glory and honor into it**. *The new Jerusalem has no closed **gates**, because there is perfect security and freedom of access* (Isaiah 60:11). *There is **no night**—no darkness—there. There is no sin present. It is a land of righteousness and fadeless day.* **The **nations**, ruled by various kings and levels of earthly authority, will honor the heavenly city as the dwelling place of God.**

Chapter 21 Verses 24-26
References

Vv. 24-26
Isaiah 60:11 "Your gates will always stand open, they will never be shut, day or night, so that men may bring you the wealth of the nations - their kings led in triumphal procession. [NIV]

Chapter 21 Verses 24-26
References Commentary

Vv. 24-26

Isaiah 60:11: *No need to lock the city **gates** because there is no danger. On the contrary, it is important to keep them **open** because **kings** and cart loads of **wealth** are arriving **day** and **night**.* (Revelation 21:25 and 22:5 say: *there shall be no night there* [Greek: *nux*: no absence of light]: The Greek word for *night*: nux, can metaphorically denote: that in darkness, a man can be alienated from God. Accordingly, there is continuous security with God and His light in our midst.

Repeating Revelation 21:23: *The city does not need the sun or the moon to shine on it, for the glory of God gives it light, and the Lamb is its lamp.* [NIV]

Chapter 21 Verse 27

²⁷But there shall by no means enter it anything that defiles, or causes an abomination or a lie, but only those who are written in the Lamb's Book of Life.

**Chapter 21 Verse 27
Commentary**

21:27
Only redeemed and glorified people will have access to or dwell in the New Jerusalem (Revelation 21:8; Revelation 22:15; Isaiah 52:1; Ezekiel 44:9; 1 Corinthians 6:9-11; 2 Peter 3:13b).

By no means shall anything that defiles, or causes an abomination or a lie, enter the city, but only those who are written in the Lamb's Book of Life.

The modern trends of LGBTQ+P etc., and the transgender **abominations** have misled a lot of people. However, God loves everyone. For many of those who've been deceived and persuaded to give any of this a try (Romans 1:18-32), it is not too late to repent. Turn around from following the world, and go toward God. Simply swallow the *pride*, (Proverbs 11:2; 13:10; 16:18) and with a sincere heart, ask God for forgiveness (Hebrews 8:12). When you love Him in return, He has a purpose for you (Romans 8:28; 2 Timothy 4:18; Titus 3:3-7).

Chapter 21 Verse 27
References

V. 27
Revelation 22:15 Outside are the dogs, those who practice magic arts, the sexually immoral, the murderers, the idolaters and everyone who loves and practices falsehood. [NIV]

Isaiah 52:1 Awake, awake, O Zion, clothe yourself with strength. Put on your garments of splendor, O Jerusalem, the holy city. The uncircumcised and defiled will not enter again. [NIV]

Ezekiel 44:9 Thus says the Lord GOD: "No foreigner, uncircumcised in heart or uncircumcised in flesh, shall enter My sanctuary, including any foreigner who *is* among the children of Israel."

1 Corinthians 6:9-11 ⁹Do you not know that the wicked will not inherit the kingdom of God? Do not be deceived: Neither the sexually immoral nor idolaters nor adulterers nor male prostitutes nor slanderers nor swindlers will inherit the kingdom of God. ¹¹And that is what some of you were. But you were washed, you were sanctified [separated from the world], you were justified [to be seen by God as being righteous] in the name of the Lord Jesus and by the Spirit of our God. [NIV]

2 Peter 3:13b we, according to His promise, look for new heavens and a new earth...

Chapter 21 Verse 27
References Commentary

V. 27
Revelation 22:15 tells us this: Forever excluded from heaven will be these wicked ones who perform abominations to God. ***Dogs** here may refer to male prostitutes (Deuteronomy 23:18), unclean Gentiles (Matthew 15:26), or Judaizers (Philippians 3:2).*

Isaiah 52:1: **The theme of God's deliverance for His people now reaches its greatest expression in the Servant of the Lord who will suffer for the sins of His people. The prophet foresees the Millennium, when Jerusalem will once again be **the holy city**, and the **uncircumcised and the unclean** (unrighteous) will no longer enter her gates.**

In Ezekiel 44:9 the use of any **foreigner** (unsaved ones today) in fellowshipping with the Lord is forbidden.

In 1 Corinthians 6:9-11 *People who *practice* such sins are not Christians*:
1 John 3:9: *Whosoever is born of God doth not commit [practice] sin, for his [God's] seed remaineth in him: and he cannot sin, because he is born of God.* [KJV]
The indwelling Holy Spirit within each and every true believer helps the believer to overcome such temptations.
1 Corinthians 10:13: *There hath no temptation taken you but such as is common to man: but God is faithful, who will not suffer you to be tempted above that ye are able; but will with the temptation also make a way to escape, that ye may be able to bear it.* [KJV]

In 2 Peter 3:13b God has never broken a promise and He cannot lie:
Titus 1:2: *In hope of eternal life, which God, that cannot lie, promised before the world began;* [KJV]

Chapter 22 Verses 1-3

Chapter 22 Verses 1-3
Commentary

Eternal Abundance of Life

¹Then the angel showed me the river of the water of life, as clear as crystal, flowing from the throne of God and of the Lamb ²down the middle of the great street of the city. On each side of the river stood the tree of life, bearing twelve crops of fruit, yielding its fruit every month. And the leaves of the tree are for the healing of the nations. [NIV]

22:1-2
***A pure river of water of life** [the ever fresh and fruitful influence of the Holy Spirit] flows **from the throne of God and of the Lamb** through **the middle of the street. On either side of the river** grows **the tree of life** with its **twelve** kinds of fruit, no longer forbidden.* Ezekiel prophesied the benefits of the tree (Ezekiel 47:12).

The leaves of the tree are **for the healing of the nations** *is a figurative way of saying they will enjoy perpetual health.*

³And there shall be no more curse, but the throne of God and of the Lamb shall be in it, and His servants shall serve Him.

22:3
The effects on Satan of the post-Edenic **curse (Genesis 3:14) will be totally gone forever.

God's saints will serve God (Revelation 7:15) and **reign** with Him **forever** (Daniel 7:18, 7:27).**

The throne of God and the Lamb shall be in it, meaning God is present in Person!

Chapter 22 Verses 1-3 References	Chapter 22 Verses 1-3 References Commentary
Vv. 1-2 **Ezekiel 47:12** "Fruit trees of all kinds will grow on both banks of the river. Their leaves will not wither, nor will their fruit fail. Every month they will bear fruit, because the water from the sanctuary flows to them. Their fruit will serve for food and their leaves for healing." [NIV]	**Vv. 1-2** Ezekiel 47:12: Abundant life and continuous provisions of the New Jerusalem is depicted.
V. 3 **Genesis 3:14** And the LORD God said unto the serpent, Because thou hast done this, thou art cursed above all cattle, and above every beast of the field; upon thy belly shalt thou go, and dust shalt thou eat all the days of thy life: [KJV]	**V. 3** Genesis 3:14: As a result of Adam and Eve's offense, all of creation was **cursed**, but the serpent was uniquely **cursed** by representing all that is detestable, disgusting and low. Reptiles are branded and avoided with fear. Reptiles, like lizards, turtles, snakes, etc. are branded and filled with fear, but have no respect for God.
Revelation 7:15 "Therefore they are before the throne of God, and serve Him day and night in His temple. And He who sits on the throne will dwell among them.	Revelation 7:15: **The principal activity of believers, who were redeemed back to God for eternity, will be to gladly **serve** God.** Here in Revelation 7:15 and in 7:14, these believers were saved during the Tribulation Period.
Daniel 7:18 'But the saints of the Most High will receive the kingdom and will possess the it forever—yes, for ever and ever.' [NIV] **Daniel 7:27** 'Then the kingdom and dominion, and the greatness of the kingdoms under the whole heaven, shall be given to the people, the saints of the Most High. His kingdom *is* an everlasting kingdom, and all dominions shall serve and obey Him.'	Daniel 7:18, 7:27: The word ***But*** begins the verse because Daniel foresees the four kingdoms nearer his time to eventually be succeeded by **the kingdom** of **the Most High** and of His **saints** who **shall serve and obey Him**. Where Daniel 7:27 speaks of *all dominions*, this is likely referring to all believers: Old Testament saints, Church Age believers, and the surviving and martyred Tribulation saints.

Chapter 22 Verses 4-5

⁴They shall see His face, and His name *shall be* on their foreheads. ⁵There shall be no night there: They need no lamp nor light of the sun, for the Lord God gives them light. And they shall reign forever and ever.

Chapter 22 Verses 4-5
Commentary

22:4-5
The greatest blessing of eternity is that **they shall see His face (Matthew 5:8; Hebrews 12:14).

Though seeing **His face** is now present day impossible for an unglorified human being (Exodus 33:20), it will occur in the eternal state.

The **name** of God **on their foreheads** shows constant focus on God, allegiance and devotion (Revelation 3:12; Exodus 28:38).

Since in the New Jerusalem God is always present, His glory makes all other sources of **light** unnecessary (Revelation 21:23; Isaiah 60:19).**

Chapter 22 Verses 4-5 References	Chapter 22 Verses 4-5 References Commentary
Vv. 4-5	Vv. 4-5
Matthew 5:8 "Blessed are the pure in heart, for they shall see God." [NIV]	Matthew 5:8: *A pure-hearted person is one whose motives are not mixed, whose thoughts are holy, whose conscience is clean.*
Hebrews 12:14 Make every effort to live in peace with all men and to be holy; without holiness no one will see the Lord. [NIV]	Hebrews 12:14: *Martin Luther said, "My holiness is in heaven." Christ is our holiness, that is, as far as our standing before God is concerned.* **Holiness** is one and the same as righteousness, perfection; which Jesus did for us, satisfying God's requirement to enter heaven (Romans 3:21-26). Believers are justified.
Exodus 33:20 But He said, "You cannot see My face; for no man shall see Me, and live."	Exodus 33:20: *No one can look upon the unveiled glory of God; He dwells "in unapproachable light" (1 Timothy 6:16).*
Revelation 3:12 "He who overcomes, I will make him a pillar in the temple of My God, and he shall go out no more. I will write on him the name of My God and the name of the city of My God, the New Jerusalem, which comes down out of heaven from My God. And *I will write on him* My new name."	Revelation 3:12: *That the believer will be **a pillar** certainly carries the thought of strength, honor, and permanent security. He shall never leave this place of safety and joy, and he will belong to **God, the New Jerusalem**, and the **new name** of the Lord Jesus.*
Exodus 28:38 "It will be on Aaron's forehead, and he will bear the guilt involved in the sacred gifts the Israelites consecrate, whatever their gifts may be. It will be on Aaron's forehead continually so that they will be acceptable to the LORD." [NIV]	Exodus 28:38: *The miter on Aaron's forehead served as a reminder for **the iniquity** (sins) **of the holy things**—a prompt that even our most sacred acts are stained with sin.*
Isaiah 60:19 "The sun will no more be your light by day, nor will the brightness of the moon shine o you, for the LORD will be your everlasting light, and your God will be your glory. [NIV]	Isaiah 60:19: *The light of **the sun** and **moon** will no longer be necessary in Jerusalem, since the glory of **the LORD will** provide all necessary **light**. Darkness will vanish and Israel's (and in Isaiah 60:20 *our*) **mourning shall be ended**.* Isaiah 60:3 says: *Nations will come to your light, and kings to the brightness of your dawn.* [NIV]

Chapter 22 Verses 6-7

⁶The angel said to me, "These words are trustworthy and true. The Lord the God who inspires the prophets, sent his angel to show his servants the things that must soon take place." ⁷"Look, I am coming soon! Blessed is the one who keeps the words of the prophecy written in this scroll." [NIV]

Chapter 22 Verses 6-7
Commentary

22:6-7
We are reminded by the interpreting angel that **the Lord God sent His angel to show us the many events that **must shortly take place (after the Rapture: Revelation 4:1). These **words** definitely refer to the entire Book of Revelation, but, perhaps also appropriately, to the *entire Bible*: Acts 20:27: *"For I have not hesitated to proclaim to you the whole will of God."* [NIV]
Soon here refers to the imminent return of Christ to rapture His Church (1 Thessalonians 4:16-17).

[Verse 6 and 7 take us back to present Church Age since the Lord tells us this is still a **prophecy**. The word **soon** can translate to quickly, swiftly, promptly, or suddenly. Therefore this can also be applied to Christ's Second Advent. Both events are prophesied.]

The Rapture can occur at any time. The blessing [reward] is for those who have been prepared by reading, absorbing, digesting, and applying the words of this Book (Revelation 1:3; Luke 11:28) and obeying the commands for repentance, faith, and perseverance.**

We can do this by living in the hope of His Coming to gather us together in the clouds and take us up to be with Him forever.

Chapter 22 Verses 6-7
References

Vv. 6-7
1 Thessalonians 4:16-17 ¹⁶For the Lord Himself will descend from heaven with a shout, with the voice of an archangel, and with the trumpet of God. And the dead in Christ will rise first ¹⁷Then we who are alive *and* remain shall be caught up together with them in the clouds to meet the Lord in the air. And thus we shall always be with the Lord.

Revelation 1:3 Blessed *is* he who reads and those who hear the words of this prophecy, and keep those things which are written in it; for the time *is* near.
Luke 11:28 But He said, *"More than that, blessed are those who hear the word of God and keep it!"*

Chapter 22 Verses 6-7
References Commentary

Vv. 6-7
1 Thessalonians 4:16-17: This passage gives a beautiful description of the instantaneous sequence of events of the Rapture.

Revelation 1:3; Luke 11:28: *It was obviously God's intention that this Book should be read in the assembly meeting because he promised a special blessing to the one **who reads** it aloud and to all **those** in the assembly **who hear** it and take it to heart. The reason: **The time** for the fulfillment of the prophecies is **near**.*
1 Timothy 2:4: *who* [God] *wants all men to be saved and to come to a knowledge of the truth.* [NIV]

304

Chapter 22 Verses 8-11

⁸I, John, am the one who heard and saw these things. And when I had heard and seen them, I fell down to worship at the feet of the angel, who had been showing them to me. ⁹But he said to me, "Don't do that! I am a fellow servant with you and with your fellow prophets and with all who keep the words of this scroll. Worship God!" ¹⁰Then he told me, "Do not seal up the words of the prophecy of this scroll, because the time is near. ¹¹Let the one who does wrong continue to do wrong; let the vile person continue to be vile; let the one who does right continue to do right; and let the holy person continue to be holy." [NIV]

Chapter 22 Verses 8-11
Commentary

22:8-11
*When John **fell down** at the angel's **feet**, he was forbidden to do so. The **angel** was only a created being; only God is to be worshiped* (Acts 5:29b; Revelation 19:10b).

Since the prophecies of this Book are not yet fulfilled, John is not to **seal** it up—and neither are we to seal it up. We need to open God's Word of truth and share it with others. The time is short, He is coming for us quickly! (Revelation 22:7, 12). The Book must be left for a little longer since the fulfillment is near.

**Daniel was told *to* "seal" up his Book since *the end* was still in the *distant* future (Daniel 12:4).

The time is at hand tells us His return is *imminent*. Verse 11 is a statement of fact and a warning. When the time of fulfillment comes—when Christ comes for us—the deliberate choice of each person will have fixed his eternal fate.** Whether **unjust** or **filthy**, the offer expires when the Lord returns in His Second Coming after the Seven-year Tribulation Period. The **righteous** and **holy** will continue. The offer allowing us to *avoid* the Tribulation or *wrath* expires at the Rapture (Romans 5:9; 1 Thessalonians 1:10; 5:9; 2 Thessalonians 2:9-12).

Chapter 22 Verses 8-11 References	Chapter 22 Verses 8-11 References Commentary
Vv. 8-11 **Acts 5:29b** "We must obey God rather than men!" [NIV]	**Vv. 8-11** Acts 5:29b: Those who do things man's way instead of God's way will find themselves on a slippery slope (Psalm 118:8-9). We need to follow God's prescription for His purpose—not ours (Acts 4:19). To avoid the slippery slope, Comply with Proverbs 3:6: *In all thy ways acknowledge him* [God], *and he shall direct your paths.* [KJV]
Revelation 19:10c "Worship God! For the testimony of Jesus is the spirit of prophecy." [NIV]	Revelation 19:10b The first three Commandments state the basic beginning of true, sincere worship: Deuteronomy 5:7: "*Thou shalt have no other gods before me* [God]." [KJV] The second Commandment is referring to idols: Deuteronomy 5:9a+b: "*Thou shalt not bow down thyself unto them: For, the LORD thy God am a jealous God,*" [KJV] And, worshiping with integrity instead of being disrespectful is the third Commandment: Deuteronomy 5:11: "*Thou shalt not take the name of the LORD thy God in vain: for the LORD will not hold him guiltless who taketh his name in vain.*" [KJV]
Daniel 12:4 "But you, Daniel, close up and seal the words of the scroll until the time of the end. Many will go here and there to increase knowledge." [NIV]	Daniel 12:4: **It was impossible to understand the significance of these prophecies in Daniel's own day, but God indicated that at **the time of the end; many** would seek to understand these predictions and be able to do so** —as we are now doing.

Chapter 22 Verse 12

¹²"And behold, I am coming quickly, and My reward *is* with Me, to give to every one according to his work."

Chapter 22 Verse 12 Commentary

22:12
Quickly as used in the original in this verse, translates to *as soon as possible—with all speed*. ****Reward** is always based on **work** (Jeremiah 17:10; Romans 2:5b-6; 1 Peter 1:17).

For believers, there is the Judgment Seat of Christ (2 Corinthians 5:10).

For Old Testament and Tribulation saints see Daniel 12:2.

For unbelievers there are various judgments culminating with the Great White Throne judgment (Revelation 20:11-15).
Matthew 25:31-35, 38, 40-41, 42-46** and Revelation 19:20 also point out the Lord's judgments.

Chapter 22 Verse 12 References	Chapter 22 Verse 12 References Commentary
V. 12	**V. 12**
Jeremiah 17:10 "I the LORD search the heart and examine the mind, to reward a man according to his conduct, according to what his deeds deserve." [NIV]	Jeremiah 17:10: **Man cannot trust his own heart, but must leave all to God who alone knows the heart and judges all men fairly.**
Romans 2:5b-6 ⁵ᵇfor the day of God's wrath, when his righteous judgment will be revealed. ⁶God *will give to each person according to what he has done.*" [NIV]	Romans 2:5b-6: **In the day of...judgment** at the Rapture and at the Great White Throne *the **judgment of God** will be seen to be absolutely **righteous**, without prejudice or injustice of any kind.*
1 Peter 1:17 Since you call on a Father who judges each man's work impartially, live your lives as strangers here in reverent fear. [NIV]	1 Peter 1:17: we should live with a respectful fear of displeasing the **Father**.
2 Corinthians 5:10 For we must all appear before the judgment seat of Christ, that each one may receive what is due him for the things done while in the body, whether good or bad. [NIV]	2 Corinthians 5:10: **The judgment seat of Christ** *will reveal our lives of service for Christ exactly as we have **done, whether good or bad**. Not only the *amount* of service, but also its *quality*, and the *motives* that prompted it will be revealed* when we appear **before...Christ** at His **judgment seat**...
Daniel 12:2 Multitudes who sleep in the dust of the earth will awake: some to everlasting life, others to shame and everlasting contempt. [NIV]	In Daniel 12:2 **after the Great Tribulation there will be two more resurrection events, one: of the righteous to **everlasting life** and another: of the unrighteous to **everlasting contempt**. These two resurrections are separated by Christ's one-thousand year reign** and more—back to His own resurrection, the Rapture of His Church prior to the Tribulation Period, and also resurrection of the Old Testament saints and surviving converts after the Tribulation. Then will come His Millennial Reign, and then, post-Millennial, the unsaved will be resurrected to bow their knees to Him at the Great White Throne.
Revelation 20:11-15 **Matthew 25:31-41** **Revelation 19:20**	
-CONTINUED ON NEXT SET OF PAGES UNDER REFERENCES!-	**-CONTINUED ON NEXT SET OF PAGES UNDER REFERENCES COMMENTARY!-**

Chapter 22 Verse 12

-VERSE 12 REPEATED FROM PREVIOUS PAGE-

¹²"And behold, I am coming quickly, and My reward *is* with Me, to give to every one according to his work."

Chapter 22 Verse 12 Commentary

-PART OF COMMENTARY VERSE 12 REPEATED FROM PREVIOUS PAGE-

22:12
**For unbelievers there are various judgments culminating with the Great White Throne judgment (Revelation 20:11-15) **.

Revelation 19:20 points out the Lord's judgments:
Revelation 19:20 *Then the beast was captured, and with him the false prophet who worked signs in his presence, by which he deceived those who received the mark of the beast and those who worshiped his image. These two were cast alive into the lake of fire burning with brimstone.*

see also Matthew 25:31-35, 38, 40-41, 42-46

Chapter 22 Verse 12
References

Chapter 22 Verse 12
References Commentary

**CONTINUED
FROM PREVIOUS PAGE**

**CONTINUED
FROM PREVIOUS PAGE**

V. 12
Revelation 20:11-15 ¹¹Then I saw a great white throne and Him who sat on it, from whose face the earth and the heaven fled away. And there was found no place for them. ¹²And I saw the dead, small and great, standing before God, and books were opened. And another book was opened, which is *the Book* of Life. And the dead were judged according to their works, by the things which were written in the books. ¹³The sea gave up the dead who were in it, and Death and Hādēs delivered up the dead who were in them. And they were judged, each one according to his works. ¹⁴Then Death and Hādēs were cast into the lake of fire. This is the second death. ¹⁵And anyone not found written in the Book of Life was cast into the lake of fire.

V. 12
In Revelation 20:11-15 *no one who appears at **the great white throne** judgment is registered in **the Book of Life**. The fact that his name is missing *condemns* him, but the record of his evil **works** determines the *degree* of punishment.*

Matthew 25:31-35 ³¹"When the Son of Man comes in His glory, and all the holy angels with Him, then He will sit on the throne of His glory. ³²All the nations will be gathered before Him, and He will separate them one from another, as a shepherd divides his sheep. ³³And He will set the sheep on His right hand, but the goats on the left. ³⁴Then the King will say to those on His right hand, 'Come, you blessed of My Father, inherit the kingdom prepared for you from the foundation of the world: ³⁵for I was hungry and you gave Me food; I was thirsty and you gave Me drink; I was a stranger and you took Me in;

Matthew 25:38 When did we see You a stranger and take You in, or naked and clothe You?

Matthew 25:40-41 ⁴⁰And the King will answer and say to them, 'Assuredly, I say to you, inasmuch as you did it to one of the least of these My brethren, you did it to Me.' ⁴¹Then He will also say to those on the left hand, 'Depart from Me, you cursed, into the everlasting fire prepared for the devil and his angels:"

Chapter 22 Verses 13-14

¹³"I am the Alpha and the Omega, *the* Beginning and *the* End, the First and the Last."

¹⁴Blessed *are* those who do His commandments, that they may have the right to the tree of life, and may enter through the gates into the city.

Chapter 22 Verses 13-14
Commentary

22:13
The three designations of verse 13 are virtually equivalent in meaning. By applying them to Himself, Christ claims unlimited, eternal equality with God (Revelation 1:8, 1:17; 2:8).

He is the uncreated Creator.
Philippians 2:6 agrees: [*Christ Jesus*] *Who, being in the form of God, thought it not robbery to be equal with God*: [KJV]

22:14
Verse 14 does not teach being saved by works, but rather teaches works as the fruit and proof of having been saved. The Lord Jesus Christ did the works to save us on the cross at Calvary (Romans 3:27-31: Ephesians 2:8-9; James 2:26).

Father God views all true believers as having the righteousness of God Himself by their having genuine faith in the Lord Jesus Christ. (Romans 3:21-22) **But **those who do His commandments** are believers now with Christ (Revelation 12:17; 14:12**; John 14:15, 21; 1 John 3:10; 5:3).

Only believers can have heavenly citizenship in the eternal dwelling place of God.

Chapter 22 Verses 13-14
References

V. 13

Revelation 1:8 "I am the Alpha and the Omega, *the* Beginning and *the* End," says the Lord, "who is and who was and who is to come, the Almighty."

Revelation 1:17 And when I saw Him, I fell at His feet as dead. But He laid His right hand on me, saying to me, "Do not be afraid; I am the First and the Last."

Revelation 2:8 "To the angel of the church in Smyrna write: These are the words of him who is the First and the Last, who died and came to life again." [NIV]

V. 14

Ephesians 2:8-9 ^{8}For it is by grace you have been saved, through faith – and this not from yourselves, it is the gift of God – ^{9}not by works, so that no one can boast. [NIV]

Revelation 12:17 Then the dragon was enraged at the woman and went off to make war against the rest of her offspring – those who obey God's commandments and hold to the testimony of Jesus. [NIV]

Revelation 14:12 This calls for patient endurance on the part of the saints who obey God's commandments and remain faithful to Jesus. [NIV]

John 14:15 "If you love Me keep My commandments."

John 14:21a "He who has My commandments and keeps them it is he who loves Me."

1 John 3:10 This is how we know who the children of God are and who the children of the devil are: Anyone who does not do what is right is not a child of God; nor is anyone who does not love his brother. [NIV]

1 John 5:3 For this is the love of God, that we keep His commandments. And His commandments are not burdensome.

Chapter 22 Verses 13-14
References Commentary

V. 13

Revelation 1:8; Revelation 1:17; Revelation 2:8: *The Lord Jesus reveals Himself as **the First and the Last**, a title of Jehovah, the One and only God (Isaiah 44:6; Isaiah 48:12).*

V. 14

Ephesians 2:8-9: We don't do good works to save *myself*. We do them because we *are saved*. Ephesians 2:10: *For we are his workmanship, created in Christ Jesus unto good works, which God hath before ordained that we should walk in them.* [KJV]

Revelation 12:17; Revelation 14:12: It outrages Satan so much when believers express their love and devotion to **God** by obeying His **commandments** that he wants **to make war with** us! We *practice* righteousness; we've stopped *practicing* unrighteousness—sin.

In John 14:15, 14:21; 1 John 3:10 and 5:3 *those who do not **practice righteousness** are **not of God**. There is no in-between ground. There are none who are half and half. God's children are known by their righteous lives.*

One should take note that the word **practice** is of utmost importance here. True believers practice righteousness and although God sees us as having His righteousness (Romans 3:21-22), we still have a sin nature. But the indwelling Spirit helps us to quickly recognize our faults so we can sincerely ask for forgiveness and turn back to doing things God's way.

Chapter 22 Verse 15	**Chapter 22 Verse 15** **Commentary**
¹⁵Outside are the dogs, those who practice magic arts, the sexually immoral, the murderers, the idolaters and everyone who loves and practices falsehood. [NIV]	**22:15** **All unbelievers are **outside**.** ***Dogs** here probably refers to male prostitutes (Deuteronomy 23:18), unclean Gentiles (Matthew 7:6a), or Judaizers (Philippians 3:2).* In this verse, and in the *Strong's Expanded Exhaustive concordance of the Bible*, "the word *dogs* is used metaphorically as it translates the Greek word *kuon* for dogs to mean these are "ungodly men with impure minds exercising immoral ways which will exclude them from the New Jerusalem".

Chapter 22 Verse 15
References

Chapter 22 Verse 15
References Commentary

V. 15
Deuteronomy 23:18 Thou shalt not bring the hire of a whore, or the price of a dog, into the house of the LORD thy God for any vow: for even both these are abomination unto the LORD thy God. [KJV]

V. 15
In Deuteronomy 23:18 a **whore**[(2)] is a harlot[(2)]—a female prostitute[(2)], **and **dog** in the sense used here** refers to the Hebrew word *keleb* which is a **male prostitute. God does not accept the wages that were taken by means of immorality—things that are an abomination—detestable to Him.**

Just to mention a few more abominations which God does not allow into His kingdom: witchcraft, soothsayers, or one who interprets omens, sorcerers, (Deuteronomy 18:10); magicians (Exodus 9:11); mediums (Leviticus 19:31); men laying with men (Leviticus 18:22; Romans 1:27; 1 Corinthians 6:9); women with women (Romans 1:26); drunkenness (Galatians 5:21); these things and many more. But do not lose hope. All of these can be forgiven with sincere repentance. Just ask. Salvation is free.

Romans 3:23: *for all have sinned and fall short of the glory of God,* [NIV]

All believers have repented and have come to believe. God's Word is truth:

Isaiah 65:24: *And it shall come to pass, that before they call, I will answer; and while they are yet speaking, I will hear.* [KJV]

Matthew 7:6a *"Do not give dogs what is sacred;"* [NIV]

In Matthew 7:6a just as God does not accept reprehensible gifts, He also does not approve of giving things that are holy to the people who are practicing shameful and disgraceful living. God separates all sin from Himself, and He retains all of those who have accepted His Truth.

Philippians 3:2 Watch out for those dogs, those men who do evil, those mutilators of the flesh. [NIV]

Philippians 3:2 tells us to beware of *dogs*.
*Here the term **dogs** refers to false teachers—**evil workers** who *profess* to be true believers. They attempt to gain admission into Christian fellowship in order to spread their false teachings. The result of their work can only be evil.*

The ones who practice unrighteousness and do not sincerely repent and seek forgiveness are not going to see their names found in the Book of Life.

Chapter 22 Verse 16

¹⁶"I, Jesus, have sent My angel to testify to you these things in the churches. I am the Root and the Offspring of David, the Bright and Morning Star."

Chapter 22 Verse 16 Commentary

22:16
*As to His deity, the Lord Jesus is David's *Creator*; as to His humanity, He is David's *Descendent** (**Isaiah 11:1-5; Romans 1:3**-4).

***The bright and morning star** appears before the sun rises. Christ will first come to the Church as **the Bright and Morning Star**, that is, at the Rapture of the **Church**.*
The **Church** has not been mentioned since the last word in Chapter 3; reason being: the **Church** was not present on earth during the Tribulation Period. Later marking the end of Tribulation, *He will come to the earth as the Sun of Righteousness to reign over the earth with healing of the nations in His wings (Malachi 4:2).*

Those who fear God's name will triumph over their foes (Malachi 4:3).

Chapter 22 Verse 16 References	Chapter 22 Verse 16 References Commentary
V. 16	**V. 16**
Isaiah 11:1-5 ¹There shall come forth a Rod from the stem of Jesse, and a Branch shall grow out of his roots. ²The Spirit of the LORD shall rest upon Him, the Spirit of wisdom and understanding, the Spirit of counsel and might, the Spirit of knowledge and of the fear of the LORD. ³His delight *is* in the fear of the LORD, and He shall not judge by the sight of His eyes, nor decide by the hearing of His ears; ⁴but with righteousness He shall judge the poor, and decide with equity for the meek of the earth; He shall strike the earth with the rod of his mouth, and with the breath of His lips He shall slay the wicked. ⁵Righteousness shall be the belt of His loins, and faithfulness the belt of His waist.	Isaiah 11:1-5: *Chapter 11 verse 4 of Isaiah carries us forward to the Second Coming of Christ.* After verse 5, Isaiah 11:6 takes us to the Millennial Kingdom which follows the Seven-year Tribulation. In verse 1 a **Rod** is a Shoot and **from the stem** means from a stock or trunk of Jesse. **Jesse** is David's earthly step-father, and the **Branch**, Jesus, **shall grow out of his**, Jesse's **roots**.
Romans 1:3-4 ³concerning His Son Jesus Christ our Lord, who was born of the seed of David according to the flesh, ⁴*and* declared *to be* the Son of God with power according to the Spirit of holiness, by the resurrection from the dead.	Romans 1:3-4: *The Gospel is the good news concerning God's **Son, Jesus Christ our Lord, who** is a descendant **of David according to the flesh** (that is, as far as His humanity is concerned;* Luke 3:23-31 informs us that David's son Nathan, leads from Adam to **Hēlī**—the father of Mary—the father-in-law of Joseph {Luke 3:23, like much of Scripture includes *in-laws* as parents}.) *The words **according to the flesh** imply that our Lord is more than a Man.* He is also fully **God**. Jesus is **declared to be...God**—that is, the Second Person of God—**the Son of God**—equally Almighty God—**with** the **power** ... of **God...by the resurrection from the dead. The Spirit of** holiness confirms the righteousness of the Lord Jesus—the righteousness that only God is capable of directly possessing.
Malachi 4:2 But to you who fear My name the Sun of Righteousness shall arise with healing in His wings; and you shall go out and grow fat like stall-fed calves.	Malachi 4:2: *Those **who**:* stand in awe with reverence and *fear God's name* will overcome the world and triumph over the worldly foes. These will be people who recognize the power and will of their Almighty God and Creator.

Chapter 22 Verse 17

¹⁷The Spirit and the bride say, "Come!" And let the one who hears say, "Come!" Let the one who is thirsty come; and let the one who wishes take the free gift of the water of life. [NIV]

Chapter 22 Verse 17
Commentary

22:17
Revelation 22:17 speaks of **the Holy **Spirit** who works through the Church to evangelize by taking the Gospel to the world. The **water of life** is eternal life, available freely by faith in Christ (Revelation 7:17; 21:6b; John 4:14; 7:37-38).**

In Revelation 22:17 the term **bride** most likely translates to *daughter-in-law*. The marriage had to take place over a millennium prior.

The time of the Rapture is imminent, and this is the last invitation for those who are reading this right now, either before the Rapture, or finding yourself already in the Tribulation and being coerced into taking the mark of the beast. Please hear God's Words of advice: *do not* take that mark. Proverbs 12:15 *a wise man listens to advice.* NIV.
The first quote of the Lord Jesus in the Gospel of Mark 1:15b: *"Repent and believe the good news!"* [NIV]

The world is noticing the Spirit in the bride—the Spirit indwelled Church—who is evangelizing and saying, "**Come!**" And the Antichrist is restrained from appearing until the Spirit with the Church is raptured and out of his way: (2 Thessalonians 2:7-8).

Chapter 22 Verse 17
References

V. 17

Revelation 7:17 For the Lamb at the center of the throne will be their shepherd; he will lead them to springs of living water. And God will wipe away every tear from their eyes." [NIV]

Revelation 21:6b "I will give of the fountain of the water of life freely to him who thirsts."

John 4:14 *"but whoever drinks of the water that I shall give him will never thirst. But the water that I shall give him will become in him a fountain of water springing up into everlasting life."*

John 7:37-38 *³⁷On the last day, that great* day *of the feast, Jesus stood and cried out, saying, "If anyone thirsts, let him come to Me and drink. ³⁸He who believes in Me, as the Scripture has said, out of his heart will flow rivers of living water."*

Chapter 22 Verse 17
References Commentary

V. 17

Revelation 7:17; 21:6b; John 4:14; 7:37-38: These verses are all in agreement that **water of life** is the free gift of God's grace, for all who believe, to save them from the punishment of their sins and save them from wrath and give them salvation—eternal life. "All that earth can provide is not sufficient to fill the human heart. The pleasures of this world are for a few short years, but the pleasures which Christ provides go on **into everlasting life**." **If anyone thirsts** means any person who realizes he is lost and needs spiritual influence to find his way to life. The Savior invited the thirsting soul to come to Him—not to the church, the preacher, the waters of baptism, or to the breaking of bread.

In John 7:37, Jesus said, *"Let him come to Me."* "No one or nothing else will do.
*To **drink** here means to accept Christ—to believe in Him—to know that He will save you. It means to take Him into our lives as we would take a drink of water into our bodies."*
Our body absorbs the water we drink. The Lord Jesus sends the Holy Spirit for our spirits to be indwelt by the Spirit (Ezekiel 36:26-27; John 14:17; 15:26). This only happens when we accept, trust, and believe the truth of Jesus being the Son of God who died for us. We need to absorb the Holy Spirit of God to indwell our spiritual being.

Ephesians 1:13: *In Him [Jesus] you also trusted, after you heard the word of truth, the gospel of your salvation; in whom also, having believed, you were sealed with the Holy Spirit of promise*

Ephesians 17-18: *that the God of our Lord Jesus Christ, the Father of glory, may give to you the spirit of wisdom and revelation in the knowledge of Him, the eyes of your understanding being enlightened; that you may know what is the hope of His calling, what are the riches of the glory of His inheritance in the saints,*

Chapter 22 Verses 18-19

¹⁸For I testify to everyone who hears the words of the prophecy of this book: If anyone adds to these things, God will add to him the plagues that are written in this book; ¹⁹and if anyone takes away from the words of the book of this prophecy, God shall take away his part from the Book of Life, from the holy city, and *from* the things which are written in this book.

Chapter 22 Verses 18-19
Commentary

22:18-19
*If anyone adds to the things written in **this book** of Revelation, they will suffer **the plagues** described in it. Since the subjects in this book are woven throughout the Bible, verse 18, in effect, condemns any tampering with God's Word* (**Deuteronomy 4:2; 12:32; Proverbs 30:6; Galatians 1:6-9**; Joshua 1:7; Ecclesiastes 3:14;).

In verse 19: *A similar judgment is pronounced on **anyone** who **takes away from the words of this prophecy**. This may not apply to minor differences of interpretation, but to an outright attack on the inspiration and completeness of the Bible.*

Revelation 22:18-19 effectively summarize not only the Book, *The Revelation of Jesus Christ*, but also the whole Bible and the entire counsel of God. What we have learned is that the Word of God just continues to reinforce His Truth each time we read and understand more. We have so much more to learn from our Lord's wisdom, and we should never stop hungering and thirsting. When we seek Him we not only find Him for our salvation, but we also find more wisdom from His absolute, flawless Truth.

Chapter 22 Verses 18-19
References

Vv. 18-19
Deuteronomy 4:2 Do not add to what I command you and do not subtract from it, but keep the commands of the LORD your God that I give you. [NIV]
Deuteronomy 12:32 See that you do all I command you; do not add to it or take away from it. [NIV]
Proverbs 30:6 Do not add to his words, or he will rebuke you and prove you a liar. [NIV]
Galatians 1:6-9 [6]I marvel that you are turning away so soon from Him who called you in the grace of Christ, to a different gospel, [7]which is not another; but there are some who trouble you and want to pervert the gospel of Christ. [8]But even if we, or an angel from heaven, preach any other gospel to you than what we have preached to you, let him be accursed. [9]As we have said before, so now I say again, if anyone preaches any other gospel to you than what you have received, let him be accursed.
Ecclesiastes 3:14 I know that everything God does will endure forever; nothing can be added to it and nothing taken from it. God does it so that men will revere him. [NIV]

Chapter 22 Verses 18-19
References Commentary

Vv. 18-19
Deuteronomy 4:2; 12:32; Proverbs 30:6; Galatians 1:6-9; Ecclesiastes 3:14: These verses are all in agreement that if anyone willfully changes God's Word in any way from His original intention they will be **accursed**.

Chapter 22 Verses 20-21

²⁰He which testifieth these things says, Surely I come quickly. Amen. Even so, come, Lord Jesus ²¹The grace of our Lord Jesus Christ *be* with you all. Amen. [KJV]

Chapter 22 Verses 20-21
Commentary

22:20-21
**The final promise of Christ in the Bible is our hope: that His return is imminent (Revelation 22:7; Revelation 22:12).

The answer to the problems of life is found in the return of the sovereign Son of God.

The benediction in verse 21** is best understood when the margin in the NKJ reference Bible is considered: **"The grace of our Lord Jesus Christ be *with all the saints*. Amen."**

Chapter 22 Verses 20-21
References

Chapter 22 Verses 20-21
References Commentary

Jesus Christ is Revealed;
He is Lord God Almighty
In this Book of *The Revelation of Jesus Christ* it must not go unnoticed that the Lord Jesus Christ is referred to as God Almighty or One of the Persons of Almighty God seven times.

1. Revelation 1:8 "who is and who was and who is to come, the Almighty"
2. Revelation 4:8 "Lord God Almighty, Who was and is and is to come!"
3. Revelation 11:17 "Lord God Almighty, the One who is and who was and who is to come"
4. Revelation 15:3 "Lord God Almighty!" ... "O King of the saints!"
5. Revelation 16:7 "Lord God Almighty, true and righteous *are* Your judgments."
6. Revelation 16:14 "the battle on the great day of God Almighty" [NIV]
7. Revelation 19:15 Speaks of His wrath being that of "Almighty God"

Also speaks of equality with the Trinity and exhibits unity.

DANIEL'S PROPHECY TIMELINE

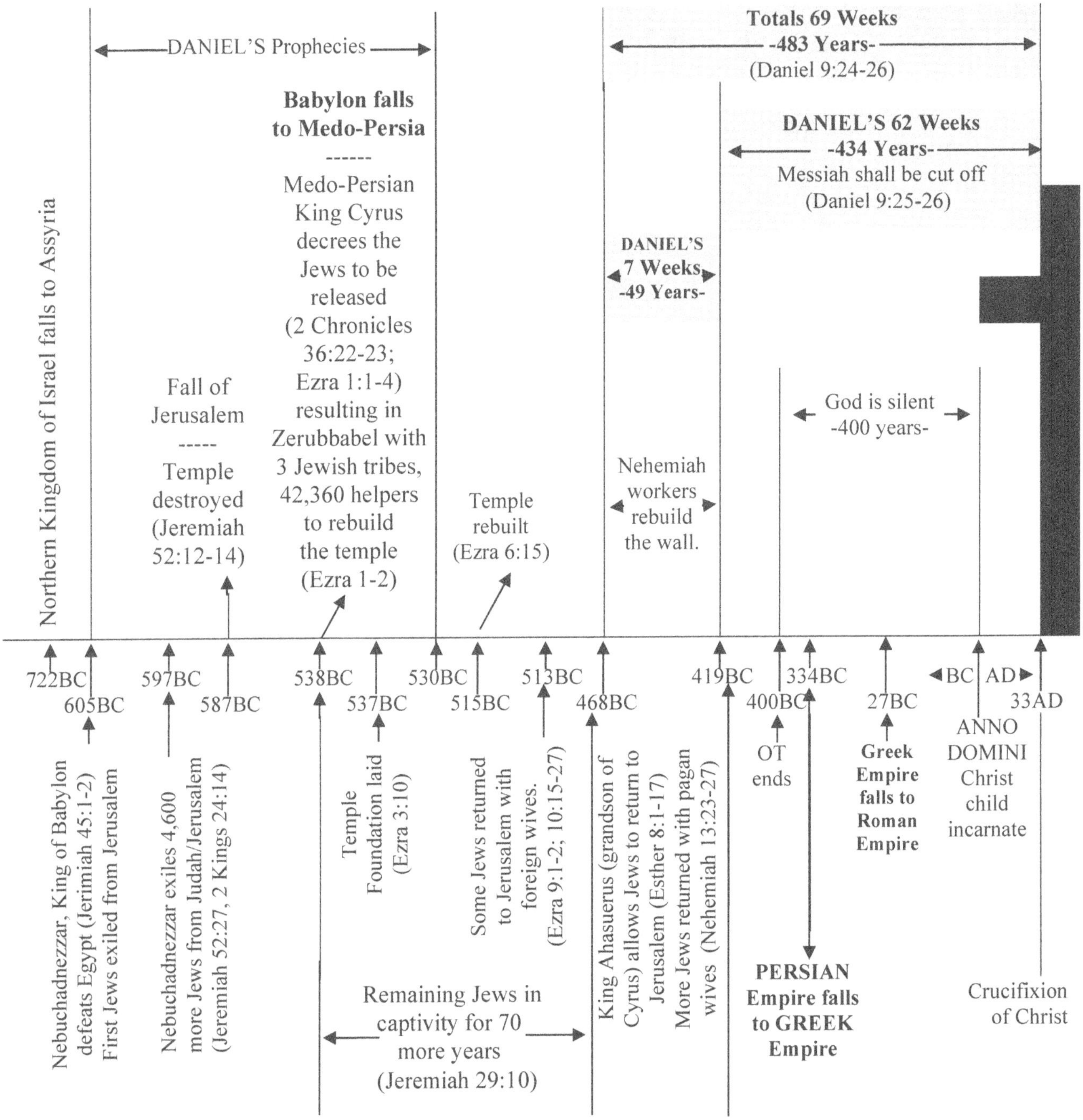

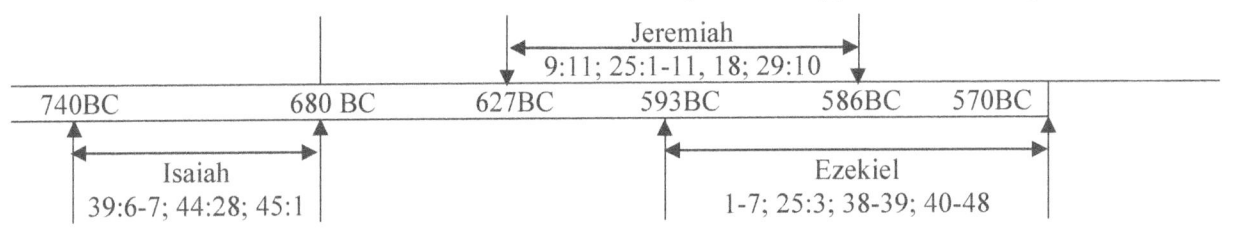

DANIEL'S Prophecies

- Northern Kingdom of Israel falls to Assyria — 722BC
- 605BC — Nebuchadnezzar, King of Babylon defeats Egypt (Jeremiah 45:1-2); First Jews exiled from Jerusalem
- 597BC — Nebuchadnezzar exiles 4,600 more Jews from Judah/Jerusalem (Jeremiah 52:27, 2 Kings 24:14)
- 587BC — Fall of Jerusalem / Temple destroyed (Jeremiah 52:12-14)
- 538BC — **Babylon falls to Medo-Persia** — Medo-Persian King Cyrus decrees the Jews to be released (2 Chronicles 36:22-23; Ezra 1:1-4) resulting in Zerubbabel with 3 Jewish tribes, 42,360 helpers to rebuild the temple (Ezra 1-2)
- 537BC — Temple Foundation laid (Ezra 3:10)
- 530BC
- 515BC — Temple rebuilt (Ezra 6:15)
- 513BC — Some Jews returned to Jerusalem with foreign wives. (Ezra 9:1-2; 10:15-27)
- 468BC — King Ahasuerus (grandson of Cyrus) allows Jews to return to Jerusalem (Esther 8:1-17)
- **DANIEL'S 7 Weeks -49 Years-**
- 419BC — Nehemiah workers rebuild the wall. More Jews returned with pagan wives (Nehemiah 13:23-27)
- 400BC — OT ends
- 334BC — **PERSIAN Empire falls to GREEK Empire**
- God is silent -400 years-
- 27BC — **Greek Empire falls to Roman Empire**
- BC | AD
- 33AD — ANNO DOMINI Christ child incarnate / Crucifixion of Christ

Totals 69 Weeks -483 Years- (Daniel 9:24-26)

DANIEL'S 62 Weeks -434 Years- Messiah shall be cut off (Daniel 9:25-26)

Remaining Jews in captivity for 70 more years (Jeremiah 29:10)

COMPARE TO TIMELINE ABOVE [These are approximate dates!]

740BC — 680 BC — 627BC — 593BC — 586BC — 570BC

Isaiah 39:6-7; 44:28; 45:1

Jeremiah 9:11; 25:1-11, 18; 29:10

Ezekiel 1-7; 25:3; 38-39; 40-48

BIBLE PROPHECY TIMELINE

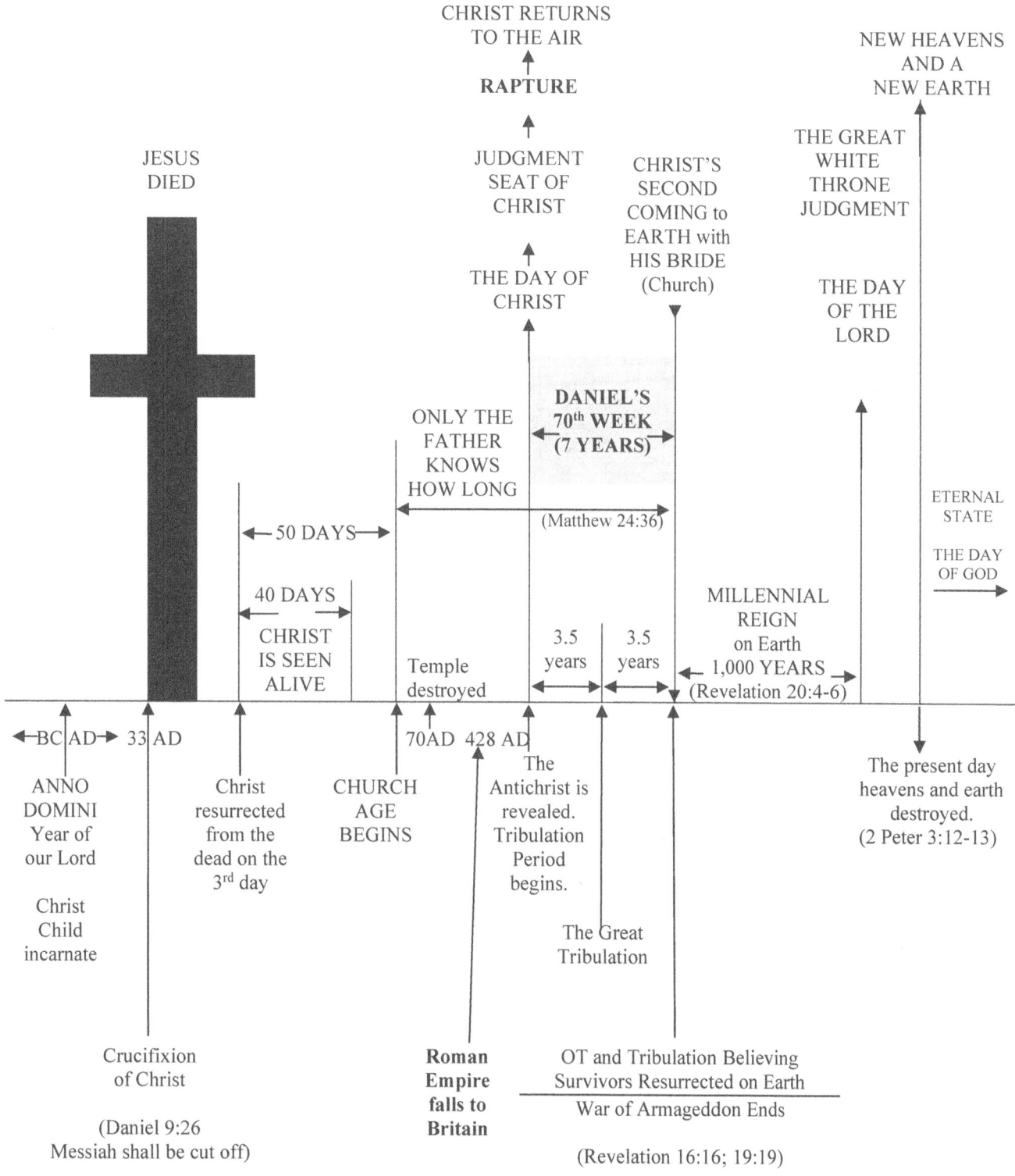

End Times Major Events Time Line

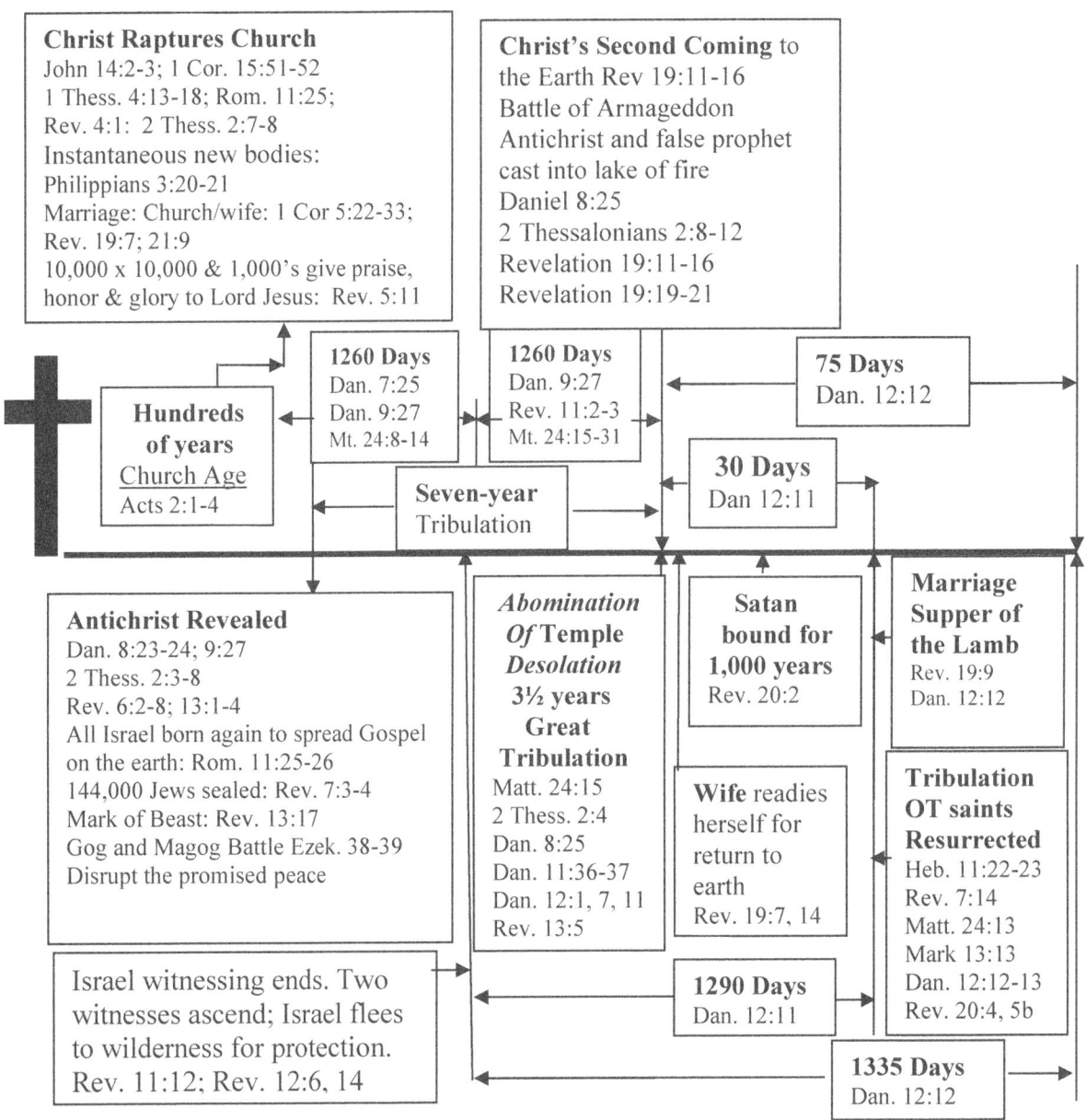

End Times Major Events Time Line

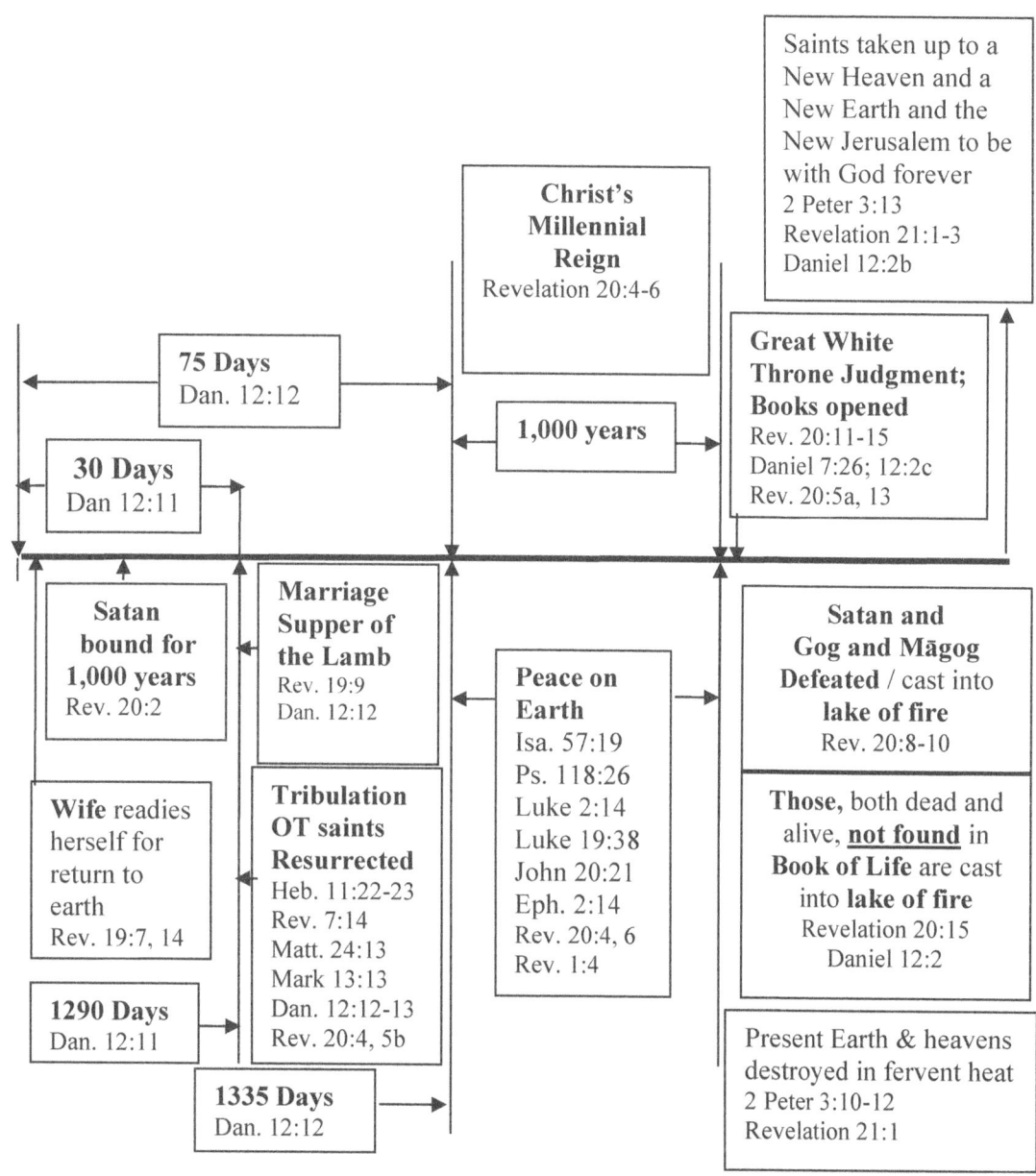

The Beginning of Babylonian Religion

Nimrod of Genesis 10:8-10 was married to a wicked woman named **Semiramis** (Traditional history). Babylon became the beginning of idolatry when Semiramis claimed to be the mother of goddesses on earth. Nimrod and Semiramis had a son named **Tammuz** (Ezekiel 8:14-15). Tammuz became the "*promise*" of the woman's seed. Tammuz acclaimed to be the promised "*deliverer*". Therefore the "*Mystery*" of a "virgin" mother & child was "*solved*".

The image of the queen of heaven (Semiramis) became popular in surrounding nations.
It became the mystery religion of Phoenicia and their people spread it all over the world.
In Phoenicia they named the "mother and child" pair: "Ashtoreth and Tammuz"
In Egypt: Isis and Horus
In Greece: Aphrodite and Eros {also Adonis and Zeus)
In Italy: Venus and Cupid.   And there became many other names in other cultures.

From as long ago as Noah's three generations of descendants: Ham, Cush, and Nimrod—the Babylonian religion became the world's largest religion.

There emerged the doctrine of salvation after death in *purgatory*; forgiveness of sins *by priests*; sprinkling with holy water; burning incense to, and offering round cakes to, the queen of heaven (Jeremiah 44:17-19, 25); women weeping for Tammuz (Ezekiel 8:14) for forty days before the great festival if Istar (pronounced *Easter*), who was said to have received her son back from the dead, for it was taught that Tammuz was killed by a wild boar and afterward brought back to life. To Tammuz, the egg was sacred, depicting the mystery of his resurrection. And the evergreen (for *everlasting*) was his chosen symbol; it was set up in honor of his birth at the winter solstice—about December 21. The sign of the cross, like the letter "t" was sacred to Tammuz, symbolizing the first letter of his name. (Therefore it did not originate with Christianity.)

Cānaan was also a son of Ham. And since, along with his brothers, Ham had received the blessing from God (Genesis 9:1); Noah placed a curse on Cānaan. This curse resulted in Bāal, the lord of the Cānaanite religion. Bāal was worshiped as the god who provided fertility. Bāal was just simply a man-made *statue* that was looked upon by the Phoenicians, Israelites, and Judeans as their supreme god. It was the Cānaanite form of Babylonian religion. Bāal was the sun god, the life-giving one, identical with Tammuz. Imagine what it must have been like for the apostles to take the Gospel message to the ends of the earth!

Nimrod
Genesis 10:8, 10   Cush begot Nimrod; he became a mighty one on the earth. ... And the beginning of his kingdom was Bābel [Greek translation: Babylon],
Jeremiah 51:7   Babylon *was* a golden cup in the LORD'S hand, that made all the earth drunk. The nations drank her wine; therefore the nations are deranged.

Notes taken from *Revelation: An Ironside Expository Commentary*, by H.A. Ironside, Originally published in 1920, Reprinted in 2004 by Kregel Publications, a division of Kregel, Inc., Lecture 18, *Babylon: Its Character and Doom: Revelation 17*, pp. 167-168.

Other Books by Michael Copple

VASTNESS OF PACE – the color edition – Fiction
Paperback ISBN 978-1-777 8325-9-9
eBook ISBN 978-1-738 9735-0-7

VASTNESS OF PACE – the black/white edition
Paperback ISBN 978-1-738 9735-2-1
eBook ISBN 978-1-738 9735-3-8

SOLVING THE SPIRITUAL DILEMMA – Non-Fiction
Paperback ISBN 978-1-7778325-2-0
eBook ISBN 978-1-7778325-3-7

CONSIDERING WISDOM –Non-Fiction
Paperback ISBN 978-1-9736-9622-3
Hardcover ISBN 978-1-9736-9623-0
eBook ISBN 978-1-9736-9621-6

CALLING FROM THE SKY – A Novel inspired by True Events
Paperback ISBN 978-1-7778325-7-5
eBook ISBN 978-1-7778325-8-2

Connect with the Author:

Website/Blog: https://michaelcopple.com
Email: mike@michaelcopple.com

www.ingramcontent.com/pod-product-compliance
Lightning Source LLC
Chambersburg PA
CBHW081152070526
44583CB00021B/2804